THE CIA BOOK CLUB

THE CIA
BOOK CLUB

The Best-Kept Secret of the Cold War

Charlie English

WILLIAM
COLLINS

William Collins
An imprint of HarperCollins*Publishers*
1 London Bridge Street
London SE1 9GF

WilliamCollinsBooks.com

HarperCollins*Publishers*
Macken House
39/40 Mayor Street Upper
Dublin 1
D01 C9W8, Ireland

First published in Great Britain in 2025 by William Collins

2

A catalogue record for this book is available from the British Library

ISBN 978-0-00-849512-1 (hardback)
ISBN 978-0-00-849513-8 (trade paperback)

Typeset in 11.75/15pt Minion Pro by Jouve (UK), Milton Keynes

Printed and bound in Great Britain by CPI Group (UK) Ltd, Croydon

MIX
Paper | Supporting
responsible forestry
FSC
www.fsc.org   FSC™ C007454

This book contains FSC™ certified paper and other controlled sources to ensure responsible forest management.

For more information visit: www.harpercollins.co.uk/green

For Lucy

It was books that were victorious in the fight. We should build a monument to books.

Adam Michnik, editor-in-chief, *Election Gazette*

There is nothing to hide any more. On the contrary, we need to tell it like it was. Not to boast, but so that people don't create a legend.

Jerzy Kulczycki, publisher and owner, Orbis Books

Contents

Maps

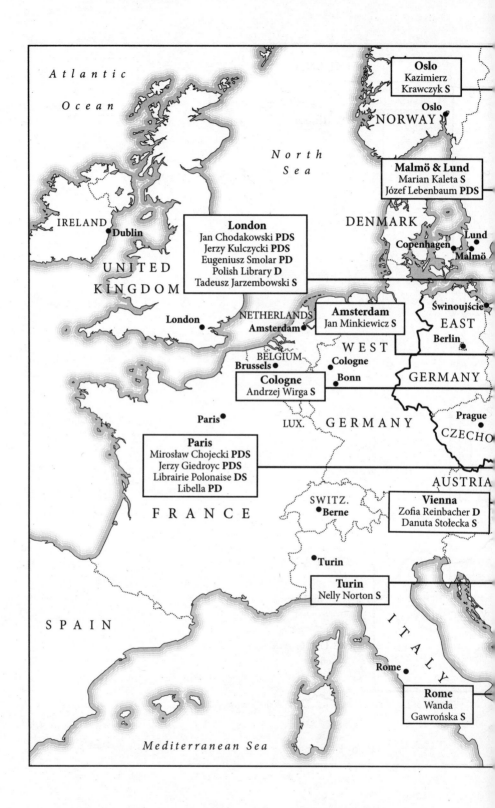

Atlantic
Ocean

*North
Sea*

Oslo
Kazimierz
Krawczyk **S**

Oslo
NORWAY

Malmö & Lund
Marian Kaleta **S**
Józef Lebenbaum **PDS**

DENMARK

IRELAND
Dublin

London
Jan Chodakowski **PDS**
Jerzy Kulczycki **PDS**
Eugeniusz Smolar **PD**
Polish Library **D**
Tadeusz Jarzembowski **S**

Lund
Copenhagen
Malmö

UNITED
KINGDOM

London

NETHERLANDS
Amsterdam

Amsterdam
Jan Minkiewicz **S**

Świnoujście

EAST
Berlin

WEST

BELGIUM
Brussels

Cologne

Bonn

GERMANY

Cologne
Andrzej Wirga **S**

Paris

LUX.

GERMANY

Prague
CZECHO

Paris
Mirosław Chojecki **PDS**
Jerzy Giedroyc **PDS**
Librairie Polonaise **DS**
Libella **PD**

FRANCE

AUSTRIA

SWITZ.
Berne

Vienna
Zofia Reinbacher **D**
Danuta Stołecka **S**

Turin

Turin
Nelly Norton **S**

SPAIN

ITALY

Rome

Rome
Wanda
Gawrońska **S**

Mediterranean Sea

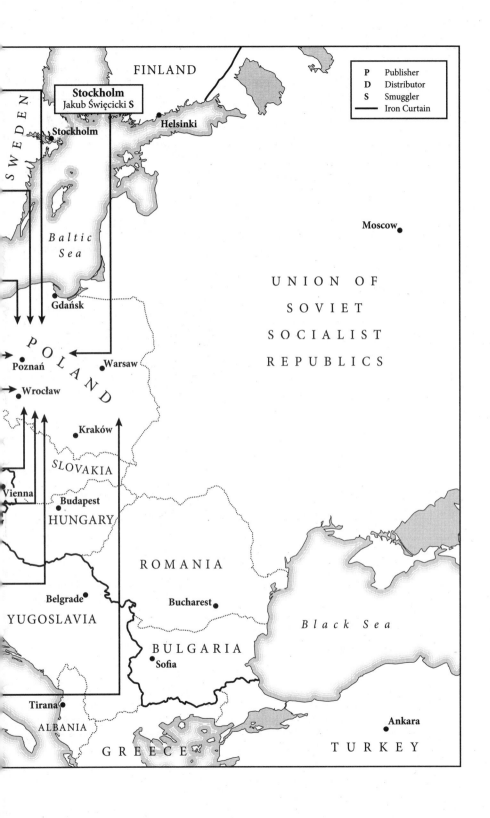

FINLAND

Stockholm
Jakub Święcicki **S**

P	Publisher
D	Distributor
S	Smuggler
—	Iron Curtain

Helsinki

Moscow

SWEDEN

Stockholm

*Baltic
Sea*

UNION OF

SOVIET

SOCIALIST

REPUBLICS

Gdańsk

POLAND

Poznań

Warsaw

Wrocław

Kraków

SLOVAKIA

Vienna

Budapest

HUNGARY

ROMANIA

Belgrade

Bucharest

Black Sea

YUGOSLAVIA

BULGARIA

Sofia

Tirana

ALBANIA

Ankara

GREECE

TURKEY

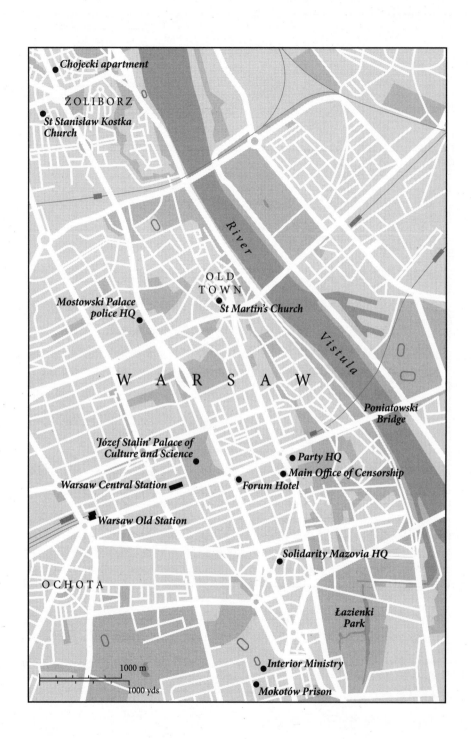

Chojecki apartment

ŻOLIBORZ

St Stanisław Kostka
Church

River

OLD
TOWN

Mostowski Palace
police HQ

St Martin's Church

Vistula

W A R S A W

Poniatowski
Bridge

'Józef Stalin' Palace of
Culture and Science

Party HQ

Main Office of Censorship

Warsaw Central Station

Forum Hotel

Warsaw Old Station

Solidarity Mazovia HQ

O C H O T A

Łazienki
Park

1000 m

1000 yds

Interior Ministry

Mokotów Prison

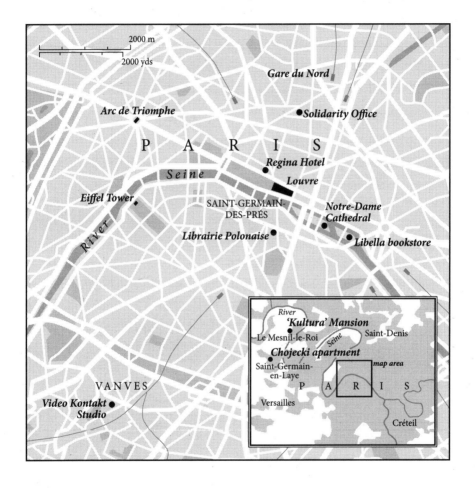

2000 m

2000 yds

Gare du Nord

●Solidarity Office

Arc de Triomphe
◆

P   A   R   I   S

Regina Hotel
●

Seine

Louvre

Eiffel Tower
◆

SAINT-GERMAIN-
DES-PRÉS

Notre-Dame
Cathedral
●

River

Librairie Polonaise ●

Libella bookstore
●

River

'Kultura' Mansion

Le Mesnil-le-Roi   Saint-Denis
Seine

Chojecki apartment

Saint-Germain-
en-Laye

map area

P   A   R   I   S

VANVES

Versailles

Video Kontakt ●
Studio

Créteil

Principal Characters

Mirosław Chojecki
Solidarity minister for smuggling

Helena Łuczywo
Editor, *Mazovia Weekly*

George Caputineanu Minden
Head of the CIA book programme

Jerzy Giedroyc
Publisher, Literary Institute

Grzegorz Boguta
Publisher, NOWa

Marian Kaleta and Józef Lebenbaum
Sweden-based book distributors and smugglers

Joanna Szczęsna
Deputy editor, *Mazovia Weekly*

Author's Note

The quotations at the start of each chapter are drawn from works by authors who were promoted, in one way or another, by the CIA. This doesn't imply that these people or their publishers were all working with US intelligence, or knew the Agency was sponsoring their work, although some were, and some did.

Prologue

Teresa's Flying Library

Words can be like X-rays if you use them properly – they'll
go through anything. You read and you're pierced.
                              Aldous Huxley, *Brave New World*

To begin with, a book. A very special book, which lives these
days in the library of the social sciences department of Warsaw
University, a literary treasure trove heavy with the scent of dust and
old paper, and so jammed with shelves that in places the only way
to move around is sideways. The volume is slim, about the size of a
mass-market paperback, and comes wrapped in a glossy dust jacket
depicting a 1970s computer room, where high priests of the information age, in kipper ties and flared trousers, tap instructions into
the terminals of some ancient mainframe. The only words on the
front are 'Master Operating Station', 'Subsidiary Operating Station'
and 'Free Standing Display', while the back is filled with lists of
codes and technobabble from a bygone era. Is any publication less
appetizing than an out-of-date technical manual?

Turn inside, however, and the book reveals a secret. The pages
here are yellowed, brittle, ragged-edged, and although the spine
has been reglued and the cover boards carefully replaced, the
leaves still threaten to tumble to the floor: this isn't a 1970s publication at all, nor a technical manual. The front papers reveal that
it was first printed in Paris in 1953, and the title page proclaims
the book's name and that of its author: *1984*, by George Orwell. It

is a Polish-language edition of the British socialist's famous anti-totalitarian novel, which was banned for decades by communist censors in the Eastern Bloc. How did it arrive here, and why? To answer those questions, I turned to the woman who owned the book for much of its life.

Teresa Bogucka lives with two cats in the Warsaw suburb of Solec, in an apartment crowded with books and artwork. She has a view to the north over a park, where the trees on this wet autumn day seem to drip liquid gold, and to the south an open window admits the clamour of songbirds wanting to be fed. On the ground floor of the block is a library named for Jan Nowak, the war hero, writer and long-serving head of Radio Free Europe's Polish service, who lived out his retirement in this building. Invisible beyond the east wall is the River Vistula, Poland's defining feature, which oozes north across the flat land towards Gdańsk and the Baltic.

It was Teresa's father, the art critic Janusz Bogucki, who brought the book to Poland. In 1957, during a short window of liberalization that opened after Stalin's death, Janusz was allowed to visit the West for the first time, and he chose to see Paris. He picked up the Orwell translation from a Polish distributor there, probably Libella, a small bookshop on a quiet backstreet on the Île Saint-Louis, not far from Notre-Dame. He took several other titles, too, including a collection of poems by the future Nobel Prize-winner Czesław Miłosz, and several copies of the Polish émigré journal *Kultura*. Although all of these were banned in Poland at the time, Janusz smuggled them back through the border in his luggage and brought them to the rural town where he and his family had moved to escape the Stalinist purges. He gave *1984* to his daughter.

Teresa was ten or eleven years old then, but she was a precocious reader, and Orwell's story struck her like a thunderbolt. 'I was absolutely traumatized by it,' she said.

Even at a young age, she recognized the ways in which communist Poland mirrored Oceania, Orwell's fictional dystopian state. The language her teachers used at school was highly codified, designed to promote communist ideology and prevent dissenting thoughts. Every lesson adopted propaganda points put out by the Party, which assumed Poland was threatened by Western imperialism, that German fascists wanted to invade again and that the Americans planned to drop the Colorado beetle on Polish potato crops to starve the population. This was very different from the way her parents spoke at home, but her mother and father couldn't tell her the school was lying in case word got back to the Party. To live in communist Poland required what Orwell called 'doublethink', which meant the ability to hold 'two contradictory beliefs in one's mind simultaneously' and accept they were both true.

In the mid-1960s, Bogucka won a place at Warsaw University, where she joined a circle of bright young people who wanted to question everything. She took her books with her, including *1984*, and loaned them out. Some of her friends had never seen uncensored material before and were scared: if they were caught with the books they could be thrown off the course and blackmailed by the secret police. But those who did dare to read were bound together by their shared, illegal act. They entered a conspiracy.

Bogucka and her fellow students had all been brought up in the communist system, trained to see the world through Marxist-Leninist philosophy, but they were also confident in their own intelligence. 'Everywhere around us they would be talking about the Marxist dialectic,' she said, 'whereas we believed we were young revisionists. We wanted to understand what it was really all about.' They devoured as many books on economics and sociology as they could, because they wanted to know, was Marx right? Their reputation as radical thinkers led a professor to dub Bogucka and her group 'the Commandos'. In time, the Commandos reached the heretical conclusion that would define their adult lives: Marx was wrong.

Some years later, in 1976, when the country was rocked by strikes and unrest, Bogucka joined the emerging opposition movement. She had the idea then of creating an uncensored library, to give people access to history they weren't meant to know and literature they weren't supposed to read. She told her friends she wanted their books, and donated her own collection, including *1984*. The SB

security service, Poland's KGB, kept continual watch on her, eavesdropping on her conversations, arresting her and searching her
apartment, so she asked neighbours to store the books. Much of the
time, though, they would be circulating among the readers, since
this would be a 'Flying Library', which rarely touched the ground.
The system of covert lending ran through a network of coordinators,
each of whom was responsible for their own tight group of readers. Bogucka sorted the books into categories – politics, economics,
history, literature – and divided them into packages of ten, before
allocating each coordinator a particular day to pick up their parcel,
which they took away in a rucksack. The coordinator would drop
the books back the following month at a different address, before
picking up a new set.

The demand for Bogucka's books was such that soon she needed
to find more. They could only come from the West. Activist friends
smuggled word out to London, where émigré publishers arranged
to send in shipments of thirty or forty volumes at a time. They
would take them to the Gare du Nord in Paris, the western terminus
of the transcontinental sleeper service that shuttled back and forth
across mainland Europe. A courier would board the train there
with a suitcase of books and head to a toilet compartment, where
they would unscrew a ceiling panel and push the case into the roof
space. After leaving the train, they would pass on the number of the
carriage to Warsaw via a coded telephone call. In Poznań, the first
train stop in Poland, another passenger would board, unscrew the
panel and remove the case, bringing the books to Bogucka.

By 1978, Teresa Bogucka's Flying Library had a stock of 500
prohibited titles. She opened sub-branches in other Polish cities,
and when she moved over to other opposition activities she passed
the library to another activist, who continued to loan out the books
through the 1980s. After 1989, when the Berlin Wall had fallen,
the library came here, to the social sciences department at Warsaw
University.

How many people read this copy of Orwell's book in those crucial
Cold War years? Hundreds, probably thousands. And this was just

one of millions of titles that arrived illegally in Poland, which in turn was just one country in the wider Soviet Bloc of nations, every one of which received great quantities of banned publications. Books arrived by every possible means: smuggled in trucks, aboard yachts, sent by balloon, in the post or in travellers' luggage. Mini-editions were hidden in the sheet music of touring musicians, packed into food tins or Tampax boxes. In one instance, a copy of Aleksandr Solzhenitsyn's *The Gulag Archipelago* was carried on a flight to Warsaw hidden in a baby's nappy. From the late 1970s, banned books and pamphlets were also reproduced in huge quantities by underground printers in Poland, on presses smuggled in from the West, amplifying the literature's effect. Increasingly the underground would publish homegrown titles, too, and by the mid-1980s the so-called 'second circulation' of illicit literature in Poland grew so large that the system of communist censorship began to break down.

The impact of this literary tide was huge. Poland was the most crucial of Eastern Bloc nations: when communism collapsed in 1989, this was the first domino to fall, and it was literature that won the war here, as the Polish dissident Adam Michnik maintained. 'We should build a monument to books,' he told me. 'I am convinced it was books that were victorious in the fight. A book is like a reservoir of freedom, of independent thought, a reservoir of human dignity. A book was like fresh air. They allowed us to survive and not go mad.'

What some suspected, but very few knew for sure, was that the uncensored literature flooding the country wasn't reaching Poles by chance. It was sent as part of a decades-long US intelligence operation known in Washington as the 'CIA book program', and part of the programme's strategy was to build up circulating libraries of illicit books on the far side of the Iron Curtain. Bogucka's copy of *1984* is an early example of works the programme sponsored. It was published, along with the Miłosz poems and the issues of *Kultura*, by a US intelligence asset in France known to the CIA as QRBERETTA, and the Libella bookstore where Janusz picked it up was a long-running distributor for the CIA scheme. If Bogucka's book had spent thirty years quietly undermining Soviet communism from within, that was precisely the job it was designed to do.

Almost four decades after the end of the Cold War, influencing campaigns are everywhere. Intelligence agencies, activists and terrorist organizations now have a near-infinite number of ways to launch political-psychological operations and sway opinion, and the propaganda space is in some ways more important than the battles fought on the ground. Disinformation threatens Western liberal democracy as never before, while censorship and book bans are once again turning schools and libraries into ideological battlegrounds. Viewed from today's vantage point, the CIA literary programmes appear almost quaint. They had political goals, but these were not achieved through lies and indoctrination. This was an 'offensive of free, honest thinking', according to the programme's leader, George Minden, which they believed would work because 'truth is contagious', and if they could only deliver it to the oppressed peoples of the Soviet Bloc, it was certain to have an effect.

The result must rank among the most highbrow intelligence operations ever undertaken. As well as glossy lifestyle magazines such as *Marie Claire* and *Cosmopolitan*, the CIA sent copies of the *New York Review of Books* and *Manchester Guardian Weekly*, works by the Nobel-winners Boris Pasternak, Czesław Miłosz and Joseph Brodsky; philosophical texts by Hannah Arendt, Albert Camus and Bertrand Russell; literary fiction from Philip Roth and Kurt Vonnegut; writing advice from Virginia Woolf; the plays of Václav Havel and Bertolt Brecht; and the spy thrillers of John le Carré, to name a few. Where some early titles have a whiff of cultural imperialism and aim to promote American art, say, or the American way of life, in later years the most popular works were often by Soviet or East European writers, chosen and edited by people who lived in the bloc, or by émigrés.

Almost all files relating to the CIA books programme remain classified, as do those documenting the Agency's wider operation in support of the Polish opposition, QRHELPFUL. What follows is based largely on other sources, including Minden's field reports and interviews with many of his contacts. In Poland, the subject of CIA support for Solidarity, the key Polish opposition movement in the 1980s, remains taboo. Some veterans accuse the Americans of trying to steal credit for a Polish victory, or fear being cast as stooges who simply did the CIA's bidding. Neither of these is true: the Agency supported the dissidents more than it directed them. But there is no question that the Americans played a significant role in defeating communism in Poland, and few Poles who knowingly benefited from covert US support had bad words to say about it. They were caught up in a conflict between two superpowers, after all, and were desperate to liberate Poland from Soviet oppression. In such a situation, as one dissident put it, 'I'd almost take money from the devil himself.'

Teresa Bogucka didn't know for sure who was paying for the literature she received from the West, but she was aware of the propaganda line pushed by the Polish regime that American intelligence supported émigré publishers, and the idea didn't concern her at all.

'I thought, wow, a secret service supporting books,' she said. 'That's fantastic.'

PART ONE

HOPE

1980–1981

1

A Snaggle-Toothed Thought Machine

And so they burst into our poor, hushed apartments as though raiding bandits' lairs or secret laboratories in which masked carbonari were making dynamite and preparing armed resistance.

Nadezhda Mandelstam, *Hope Against Hope*

One Tuesday evening in March 1980, they came to arrest the publisher Mirosław Chojecki for the forty-third time.

Aleksandr Solzhenitsyn called it the 'night-time ring', the moment state security agents show up at your door after dark, trailing their insolent, unwiped boots across your floor, and announce that they have orders to take you in. They are experts in arrest science, and they know from millions of cases such as yours that the evening, at home, is the time and place of least resistance. The best response most can bleat is 'Me? What for?' But the agents do not give answers. So you race with trembling hands to grab some things for the unknowable journey ahead, and within a few short minutes you are walking out to the transport that stands idling in the street, wondering how you haven't found time even to say goodbye.

'Each of us is a centre of the universe,' Solzhenitsyn wrote in *The Gulag Archipelago*. 'And that universe is shattered when they hiss at you, "You are under arrest."'

Chojecki, pronounced *hoy-yet-ski*, was thirty years old that night – a tall man, with a mane of red-brown hair and a penetrating, blue-eyed gaze. One Polish author described him as Christlike, 'only somehow bolder', with the same patriotic zeal to fight evil shown by his war-hero parents. He lived with his young family in a third-floor apartment in Żoliborz, a vibrant suburb of northern Warsaw, and was cooking dinner for his young son and talking to his father-in-law, Jacek, when they heard the door. There were three men outside, a local cop in the jackboots and grey tunic of the Citizens' Militia, and two plainclothes agents of the SB security service. They flashed their badges and told him to get his coat. There was no explanation. He had just enough time to calm his crying son, grab a toothbrush and a pack of cigarettes and whisper in Jacek's ear, 'I think it's going to be longer this time.' Then they clapped handcuffs on his wrists and took him to the police Fiat waiting in the road below.

It was 25 March, and the air was still sharp with winter. An iron lid of cloud had stood over the city all day, releasing a light snow-fall that caught in the beams of the Fiat's headlamps as they drove south along Stolichna Street, with its plaintive, tolling trams, past Paris Commune Square, towards the haunted ground of the Nazi-era ghetto. Warsaw, city of cursed heroes, what horror had unfolded in these blood-soaked acres. Here was the Umschlagplatz, the hold-ing yard where the SS assembled Jewish men, women and children before loading them into the boxcars that would carry them to Treblinka. There was the Old Town, rebuilt in facsimile on the dynamited ruins that were all Hitler left. Ahead rose the city's tallest building, whose original name, Józef Stalin Palace of Culture and Science, could still be read in its weathered stonework, and close by it the statue to Feliks Dzerzhinsky, Polish founder of the Soviet secret police, who had murdered and deported hundreds of thou-sands of his compatriots.

A hundred yards before Dzerzhinsky, the Fiat swung into the headquarters of the metropolitan militia, the KSMO. They took Chojecki down to a crowded underground cell, where he passed a sleepless night. In the morning they brought him before the pros-ecutor, Anna Detka.

Detka sat behind a desk, typing. At length she cranked the paper from the machine and gave it to him to sign. He was being detained for three months, the document said, for stealing a state-owned duplicating machine worth around fifty dollars with three co-conspirators. This was an act that was 'highly prejudicial' to the People's Republic of Poland.

He protested. He hadn't stolen any duplicator and had never met two of the men whose names Detka had listed. What was the evidence against him?

'I'm the one who asks the questions,' snapped the prosecutor. Did he have anything to say to clarify this matter or not?

He did not.

Harassment, assault, imprisonment: this had been the publisher's lot for the past half-decade. Sometimes the agents the SB sent against him were violent. A gang had once dragged him off the street, laying into him with fists and boots. Another time, professional thugs ambushed him in a courthouse, headbutting him and pushing him down a staircase. His face was black with bruises for weeks afterwards. They had targeted his family, trying to expel his kids

from nursery, and his livelihood too: he had been sacked from his job at the Institute of Nuclear Research and put on an employment blacklist. They kept a round-the-clock watch on his apartment and hauled in his friends and contacts to try to turn them into informers. They eavesdropped on his conversations and sent spies to win his trust. Their most time-consuming tactic was arrest. They had the power to hold you for forty-eight hours without a warrant, so that's what they did, over and over again. They would release him from one detention, watch him cross the street, then pick him up again on the far side. On average, he reckoned he spent a day a week in the police cells.

Now he was heading to Mokotów jail, a house of terror to rival the KGB's Lubyanka headquarters in Moscow. A fortress of high walls topped with barbed wire, Mokotów prison was one of the few structures to have survived the levelling of Warsaw in 1944. The Red Army had captured it intact, and the communists straightaway put it to use. It stood now as another symbol of Russian oppression, a place where Polish freedom fighters had been brought down the decades, for interrogation and torture in the tested Soviet manner.

Chojecki entered through the main gate, beneath a guard tower. He was made to change and check in his clothes and belongings, before being issued with a bowl, a spoon and a fork. He was then led down a vaulted brick corridor into the dark interior, which rang to the tune of slamming doors and jangling keys and reeked of testosterone, fear and rotting brick. Each block was an open-plan rookery of cells reaching up to the roof, with steel staircases linking the landings, and suicide netting to stop the 'jumpers'. In future decades, researchers would find hundreds of skeletons buried in the prison grounds. Some had been killed in the efficient manner of the NKVD, forerunner of the KGB, with a single bullet to the back of the head; others had been hanged, either outdoors in the yard or – in special cases – in a basement cell, where the execution was hidden from other inmates. The priest who took the condemned prisoners' last confessions was working for the security service. Many of the human remains showed signs of torture. Popular methods used by the Polish secret police included slowly tearing out fingernails, applying 'temple screws' that steadily crushed a victim's skull, and putting on 'American handcuffs', which constricted the flow of blood in a prisoner's hands until the skin burst. They would place lovers or married couples in adjacent cells, so that the strangled cries of one would encourage the other to confess.

Chojecki was brought to Block III, a wing that had been reserved for political prisoners and 'swallowers'. It was common for inmates in Polish jails to force bucket handles, welding rods or anything else that would show up on X-ray down their throats to get transferred out to hospital, but the authorities had grown wise to this and decreed that such prisoners should be held in the jail until the foreign object showed signs of piercing their internal organs. He had been in Block III before, once for 'vilifying the Polish People's Republic' and again for 'organizing a criminal group with the aim of distributing illegal publications' – at least then he had known the real reason for his detention. They put him in Cell 13 on level two, a bare room with four child-sized bunk beds, a basin and a barred and frosted window. There were two men in here already, both around forty years old, who had been sharing this small space for months.

Chojecki dumped himself on a spare steel bed. As the days dripped by, he and his cellmates talked politics and played chess with a set made from heavy black prison bread, and he tried to secure his release.

He wasn't allowed a lawyer. He hadn't even been given a copy of the charge sheet, so he asked the prison supervisor how he could challenge the indictment. The supervisor told him to look it up in the library. When he mentioned this to his cellmates they laughed out loud: the library had been shut for months. How then could he get hold of legal textbooks? A guard told him to speak with the supervisor. The Kafkaesque circle of Polish justice closed.

At Easter, when he had been locked up for ten days without being summoned to court or allowed to contact his family, he decided to take the only option left, the one chosen by powerless prisoners everywhere: he would go on hunger strike. He wrote to the prosecutor to announce that he would refuse food until she either explained the charges against him or set him free. The next day he was brought before the supervisor. This time there was another man waiting in the office, too: the prison warden.

'What are you fooling around at, Chojecki?' the warden jeered. 'I advise you to stop this childish game. It will not change your situation. The authorities have handed you over to us, commended you to our special care. Therefore I am ordering you to stop your hunger strike!'

'I will not.'

'Then I will have to punish you.'

'So be it.'

'For resisting your superiors and breaking the order of the detention centre, for behaving contrary to the regulations, I am giving you fourteen days of solitary confinement.'

'Thank you.'

Solitary in Mokotów usually meant a punishment cell called the *kabaryna*, or 'hard bed'. He had been in there before, and he knew how tough it was. The room was 3 feet wide and just a few inches longer than the wooden cot, where the prisoner would lie on bare boards. The bedding consisted of a thin blanket, which was only allowed at night and was far from sufficient to keep out the Warsaw winter. Whatever time it was, the prisoner found it impossible to sleep, and the cell was so small there was barely room to stand, let alone exercise. They would shut people in here for up to two weeks at a time. He had never heard of a hunger striker being put in the *kabaryna*.

For now, though, they returned him to his shared cell, where he continued to starve and await his fate. Each day he was allowed thirty minutes to walk around a small outdoor cage with his cellmates. He would gaze up at the patch of open sky between the high concrete walls and feel his life force ebbing away. There was still no word of his case from the prosecutor's office.

On the eighth day of his strike, Chojecki was brought to the doctor. At best, medics in Soviet-era prisons had compromised their Hippocratic oath; at worst, they actively assisted in the torture. As Solzhenitsyn had written:

> The beaten prisoner would come to on the floor only to hear the doctor's voice: 'You can continue, the pulse is normal.' After a prisoner's five days and nights in a punishment cell the doctor inspects the frozen, naked body and says: 'You can continue.' If a prisoner is beaten to death, he signs the death certificate: 'Cirrhosis of the liver' or 'Coronary occlusion' . . . whoever behaves differently is not kept on in the prison.

Chojecki had lost seventeen pounds, the doctor found. Did he intend to continue the hunger strike? He did. Then they would start to force-feed him.

They transferred him that afternoon, not to the *kabaryna* but to another cell, identical to the last, where he was held in solitary in the day, and at night was given a chaperone in case he tried to kill himself. They searched him again, taking his few remaining belongings, including his precious cigarettes. All he had was the Party propaganda sheet, the *People's Tribune*, which they brought each evening, and a pen and some paper. Although he could barely stand, he decided he had to write, to force himself to think. At first he wrote to friends and family, but when he realized his letters wouldn't get past the prison censor he began a diary in tiny, cramped handwriting, on scraps of paper he hoped one day to smuggle out.

'In order not to become completely dull,' he began, 'in order to force my mind to work, I start to write this text without knowing how it will develop, without having any sketch, plan, without having any idea apart from describing what I am experiencing here and will continue to experience.' Writing, he found, staved off the loneliness, the hunger and the exhaustion of waiting for the cell door to open and a guard to say he was being set free.

'When they take you, you never know if it will be for two days or two years,' his friend Jacek Kuroń had once said. That was their power.

Around noon the following day, day nine of his strike, the door did open, and the doctor entered with a nurse, flanked by prison guards. They carried a length of half-inch rubber pipe with a funnel at one end, and a pot filled with two pints of sweet, fatty mush. He was told to sit on a stool and open his mouth.

He had imagined this moment at the start of his ordeal and had believed then that it would be possible to resist. For years he had stood up to his oppressors. Each time they had beaten him, he had dusted himself off and told himself it was proof he was doing the right thing. Now he felt broken. His body was weak, but he sensed it most keenly in his head. Never in his life would he feel worse than at that moment. He realized he didn't have the mental strength to say no. He couldn't even raise his hand in protest.

He opened his mouth.

The doctor inserted the hose, pushing it deeper and deeper. It scratched his oesophagus and made him gag. Then the nurse began to pour in the sickly mixture, which slid from the funnel down into his complaining stomach. He felt his eyes prick for the first time in fifteen or twenty years. Tears ran down his face, of helplessness, rage, revulsion. When the food was gone, the doctor

whipped out the tube with a smooth movement, and he and the nurse left without a word. Chojecki stumbled to the toilet bucket and vomited. He fell on the bed and lay there for some time.

He had not yet recovered when the guards returned and forced him to climb three landings up to an interrogation room, where an intelligence officer was waiting. It was Lieutenant Chernyshevsky, an old sparring partner from the KSMO.

How was he feeling? Chernyshevsky asked.

'Bad.'

Eyeing the weakened creature before him, even the policeman registered a flicker of concern.

'Do you know that there is a printing house on Reymonta Street?'

Chojecki didn't answer.

'Do you have Jan Nowak's book *Courier from Warsaw*? If so, where, when and how did you come into possession of it and what is your relationship with the author?'

There were six or seven questions in this vein, all about the underground press. Chojecki gave the same response to each: as long as he didn't know what the evidence was against him, as long as he hadn't received a full justification of the charge, they had nothing to discuss.

Realizing the interrogation was pointless, Chernyshevsky brought it to an end. He offered the prisoner a cigarette, which Chojecki accepted. Then the guards took him back to his cell.

Of course he knew all about Nowak's outlawed text. His publishing house had just printed it. It was, he said later, one of the best books they had ever produced.

He hadn't set out to become a publisher. He was a nuclear physicist by training, and compared with some of his student friends he wasn't even especially well read. But publishing turned out to be the best way to resist, and resistance was in many ways the Chojecki family business.

His mother, Maria, was a Polish war hero. Although only twelve when the Germans invaded in 1939, she had adopted the codename 'Kama' after a literary heroine with a never-say-die attitude and joined the Home Army partisans. While still a teenager, she had enlisted with the Parasols unit, which carried out death sentences passed on Nazi officers by the Polish underground court. She was trained to handle guns and explosives and perform reconnaissance missions. One February morning in 1944, her team struck the resistance's heaviest blow, gunning down the murderous SS police chief

Franz Kutschera in broad daylight. The Germans shot hundreds in reprisals, but Kutschera's death radically cut the number of Poles being executed at random. That August, Maria joined the Warsaw Uprising, the doomed attempt to expel the Germans and establish independence before the Red Army arrived. She carried messages and led groups of wounded to safety through the city's sewage system, as machine guns rattled in the streets above.

Few countries have suffered as much as Poland did then. The number of defenceless people massacred by the Germans was as large as the population of Switzerland: one in five Poles were killed, including 90 per cent of the country's 3.3 million Jews. When Stalin's troops liberated Warsaw there was no let-up, as another Soviet army followed on their heels, made up of NKVD secret police. They imposed the dictator's rule through torture and murder, and installed a puppet communist government. As Warsovians emerged, shell-shocked, from the ruins the Germans had left them, they discovered they had simply swapped one totalitarian occupation for another.

Maria married a fellow Home Army veteran, Jerzy Chojecki, after the war. Mirosław was the elder of their two children, born on 1 September 1949, the tenth anniversary of Hitler's invasion. When Mirek was three, the family home was demolished to make way for Stalin's 'gift' to the Poles, the Palace of Culture and Science, which would squat over Warsaw like a toad. This huge building, designed in the Soviet social realist style, quickly became the city's most hated structure, and the butt of Polish jokes:

Why does the Palace of Culture have the best views in Warsaw?
Because it's the only place you can't see the Palace of Culture.

When he was young, Mirek couldn't talk about his parents' wartime experience, it was too dangerous. Communist propaganda portrayed the Home Army as the spawn of the capitalist West, a 'spit-spattered dwarf of reactionary forces', as one slogan put it, and an 'enemy of the state'. Even as family friends were being dragged away to have their limbs broken in the Stalinist prison system, teachers at Mirek's school, where portraits of 'Uncle Joe' hung on the walls, instructed their pupils that the Soviets were Poland's saviours and protectors. Perhaps this was why he found himself in trouble so often. He was expelled twice, once for annoying his Russian teacher, the head of the Party organization in the school, by turning up late for a lesson. When she asked him how to contact his parents to complain, he gave her their number and said she must ask for a 'Mr Kazimierz in the fish department'. His father was not called Kazimierz and did not work in a fish department.

In the mid-1960s, Mirek arrived at Warsaw High School Number Seven, a liberal institution by Polish standards, where he met some of the people who would later join the struggle against the communists. One of them was his form teacher, Krystyna Starczewska, who would later be dismissed from the profession for the obscure religious offence of 'raising young people in the spirit of fideism'. Somehow, illicit Polish-language editions of banned books were arriving regularly in Warsaw from the West, including works by George Orwell and Hannah Arendt, as well as the famous Polish literary journal *Kultura*, produced by a group of émigrés in Paris. Starczewska introduced Chojecki to this illegal material, setting him on the first step towards his future in underground publishing.

'She got me interested,' he remembered. 'She got me reading.'

Starczewska couldn't physically show her students these books at school: the risks of being caught crossing the authorities were extreme. The secret police once threatened to have her daughter gang-raped if she didn't sign a document agreeing to cooperate. But she did tell her pupils about uncensored literature and encouraged them to seek it out. This wasn't hard for Mirek since his parents were already plugged into the dissident intellectual circles where these books were passed around, often disguised in sheets from Party newspapers. He was never allowed much time with each publication as they had to be given to other readers. But the fragments he read, often overnight, were enough to sow the seeds of dissent. 'They showed you there was somewhere out there in the world where culture is free,' he remembered.

'WAR IS PEACE. FREEDOM IS SLAVERY. IGNORANCE IS STRENGTH.' These three 'doublethink' slogans are inscribed on the towering Ministry of Truth in Orwell's novel *1984*. The ministry is ironically named: its purpose is not to safeguard the truth but to destroy it, to edit history to fit the present needs of the Party and its leader, Big Brother, since 'Who controls the past controls the future: who controls the present controls the past.' Orwell's hero Winston Smith comes here each day, to work at falsifying the public record, redrafting reports of speeches given and production forecasts made, and airbrushing out politicians who have fallen from favour. After applying his changes, he covers his tracks by throwing his instructions in an incinerator chute known as the 'memory hole'.

Every country in the Eastern Bloc had its equivalent of the Ministry of Truth, modelled on the Moscow template, the Main Directorate on Literature and Publishing Affairs, and in Poland the system of ideological manipulation was one of the most complex in the world. The Main Office for the Control of Presentations and Public Performances occupied the better part of a city block on Mysia Street, opposite the Party headquarters in downtown Warsaw. Here, state censors, supervised by the Politburo, worked to align the thoughts of the people with the aims and edicts of the Party. The Main Office reached into all aspects of Polish life. It had sub-branches in every city and region, and employees in every television and radio station, every film and theatre studio and every publishing house. Every typewriter in Poland had to be registered, access to every photocopier was restricted, and a permit was needed even to buy a ream of paper. If you wanted to create a business card, a rubber stamp, a piece of sheet music or a theatre programme, you needed approval from the censor. More than merely prohibiting and cutting inconvenient facts and opinions, the Main Office also instructed the media on which subjects to cover and how to handle them.

Unlike the Nazis, who burned books as a public ritual, in the Soviet system the destruction of literature that didn't fit the Party's ideas was designed to be invisible. The lists of banned titles sent round to libraries and bookstores every year were secret, works were pulped covertly, and when censors made pre-publication changes, they wanted the reader to think the adulterated text was what the writer believed. Authors who kicked up a fuss were suppressed. The existence of censorship was itself censored: instructions to Main Office employees were sent around the country in code, and kept under lock and key until such time as they were to be used. Allusions to censorship were not allowed.

In the Stalinist 'terror' years of the late 1940s and early 1950s, entire genres of pre-war literature were destroyed in a bid to erase the pre-communist past. A list of prohibited publications from 1951 details 2,482 items, including 238 works of 'outdated' socio-political literature and 562 books for children. Mostly these were proscribed for ideological reasons, such as showing the Soviet ally in a poor light, or referencing figures who had suffered the Orwellian fate of being 'vaporized'. Works by or about the pre-war nationalist leader Józef Piłsudski were destroyed, as were many books with Jewish themes. Western books, such as *Gone with the Wind* by Margaret Mitchell and the works of Agatha Christie, were restricted even if they had no overt political message, since the depiction of life outside the communist system was deemed propaganda enough. Some of the censor's rulings made little sense even within the bizarre logic of the Party: an anthology of Grimms' fairy tales could be published by one house but not by another; a book about growing carrots was destroyed for implying that vegetables could sprout in individuals' gardens as well as in those run by collectives.

Polish culture came in for particular scrutiny. Since Moscow was intent on Sovietizing the country, anyone who wrote about a distinct Polish identity, as the poet Czesław Miłosz did, was rendered invisible, along with any information that revealed the Soviet Union for the aggressor it had been. It was forbidden, for instance, to refer to the Secret Protocol to the Molotov–Ribbentrop

Pact of 1939, in which Stalin and Hitler had carved up Poland
between them, or to Stalin's deportation of more than a million
Polish women and men – almost the entire professional class – to
Siberia, where half of them would die. Perhaps the most totemic
cover-up in Polish history was of the Katyń massacres, a series of
executions in 1940 in which the NKVD murdered 22,000 Polish
prisoners of war, mostly military officers, policemen and intellectuals. No Soviet crime would preoccupy the Polish psyche more
than this. With so many important gaps, Polish history under
communism had come to resemble Kurt Vonnegut's description of the totalitarian mind in *Mother Night*, 'a system of gears
where teeth have been filed off at random. Such a snaggle-toothed
thought machine . . . whirls with the jerky, noisy, gaudy pointless-
ness of a cuckoo clock in Hell.'

Few areas of society were so damaged by censorship as the news
media. Knowing certain subjects were off-limits, Polish journalists
simply stopped addressing them, which meant areas of great public
concern were missing entirely from national dialogue. Important
information and ideas were pushed down the Orwellian 'memory

hole', and in their stead the Party created what Miłosz described as a 'logocracy' – a government of words, which bore little relation to reality. In the logocracy, language was manipulated to promote Marxist-Leninist thinking and reinforce communist propaganda, just as 'Newspeak' aimed to reinforce the Party's ideology in *1984*. It was assumed, in this parallel world, that the Warsaw Pact protected Poland from attack by 'revisionist' German neo-Nazis and 'Western imperialists', even though the main imperialist threat came from the East.

Orwell was inevitably on the censorship lists for pointing these things out, but when his stories did reach Poland they had an extraordinary power, even among Party members. *1984* was 'difficult to obtain and dangerous to possess', Miłosz wrote, soon after his defection to the West in 1951:

> . . . it is known only to certain members of the Inner Party. Orwell fascinates them through his insight into details they know well, and through his use of Swiftian satire. Such a form of writing is forbidden by the New Faith [communism] because allegory, by nature manifold in meaning, would trespass beyond the prescriptions of social realism and the demands of the censor.

What amazed people most about Orwell, Miłosz continued, was that a writer who had never lived in Russia should have such a keen perception of its society. This idea, of Orwell as the Cassandra of totalitarian communism, held true all over the Eastern Bloc. As Zofia Reinbacher, an émigrée bookseller who read smuggled literature in Poland as a young woman, recalled: 'We were living in Orwell's world. Everybody was afraid of everybody else. The circumstances were different, but that was how people behaved. What Orwell wrote came true. He was really a genius.' The British academic Timothy Garton Ash, an inveterate traveller in the East, found that 'All over communist-ruled Europe, people would show me their dog-eared copies of *Animal Farm* or *1984* and ask, "How did he know?"'

Exploring the publications and authors his teacher recommended, the teenage Chojecki was struck most by the language: the writers of these books were not bound by the logocracy. The articles he read in *Kultura*, in particular, seemed to describe a new and completely different universe, in which the West was not always Poland's enemy, and Moscow wasn't always its friend. More and more, he understood that there was a deliberate policy of excluding Poles from their own history.

Soon after leaving school, he was shocked to meet a dissident journalist who told him that as Poles they had a duty to fight for independence. Moscow's control of Poland in the late 1960s was more subtle than it had been in the 1950s. No one saw much of the hundred thousand Soviet troops stationed in Poland, and Polish TV even sometimes screened Western movies, or shows that gently poked fun at daily life under communism. But as he spent more time with well-thumbed copies of Orwell, Miłosz and *Kultura*, Chojecki's independent spirit began to awaken. The only nudge he needed was a political crisis or two, and in Poland political crises were never far away.

In 1968, the 'Year of Revolutions', street battles broke out around the world between protesters and security forces as a new, countercultural generation rose up against the authorities. In the US, demonstrations were sparked by the Vietnam war and racism; in Czechoslovakia, people rose up against authoritarianism; in France, it was the war in Algeria. Poles that year took to the streets over censorship. In January, the Party cancelled a National Theatre production of *Forefathers' Eve*, a 150-year-old play by Adam Mickiewicz, Poland's equivalent of Shakespeare or Mark Twain, for being anti-Soviet. Students at the University of Warsaw protested and were brutally attacked by the security services. Chojecki, who was then studying at the Polytechnic, helped organize a march in sympathy. The demonstrators were met by a barricade of riot police, armed with shields, helmets and truncheons, who basically beat them up, he said later. Any lingering doubts he might have harboured about the nature of the Polish state or its independence from Moscow evaporated.

The Party sought to divert attention from the unrest by blaming it on the Jews. There weren't very many left in Poland after the war, but tens of thousands were still forced into exile. The protest leaders who remained in Poland were harassed and jailed. Chojecki was arrested and thrown off his course at the Polytechnic, but he used his connections to enrol at the university the following year. He graduated with a master's degree in 1974, and found a job at the Institute of Nuclear Research. But it wasn't long before a new crisis pitched him back into conflict with the state.

In June 1976, tens of thousands of workers went on strike after the government announced drastic increases in the state-controlled prices of food. The Party responded as it always had, with violence, deploying tanks and helicopters, and a brutal anti-riot militia called the Zomo, whose training involved beating human-sized rubber dummies with their clubs while chants of 'Gestapo!' blared at them over loudspeakers. Several protesters were killed and hundreds injured, and more than a thousand workers were sacked. Chojecki dropped everything to help the victims and their families – 'It was simply a moral decision,' he said later, 'people being beaten by the police for a cause that was my cause.' This brought him into a circle of Warsaw intellectuals who had begun to support the strikers with food, money, medical care and legal aid. They called themselves the Workers' Defence Committee and were known by the Polish acronym KOR.

The epicentre of the violence was the steel town of Radom, 60 miles south of Warsaw. Zomo units here used rubber clubs 2½ feet long, wrapped with barbed wire, to lash out at anyone who came within range. The worst violence took place in the police stations, where protesters were chained to radiators and attacked by groups of drunken officers, who would beat them unconscious. One victim said he had been assaulted for five days; another recalled waking up from a beating with a broken nose and no teeth; a third remembered seeing men beat a pregnant woman. One police 'game' involved forcing prisoners to walk the 'path of health', a 40-yard stretch between two lines of officers, each of whom would compete with their colleagues to do the most damage with their club, their fists or their boots. Chojecki, who led KOR's relief effort in Radom, was an obvious target for the regime thugs. He was regularly arrested, abused and assaulted. As brutal as the police were, he drew strength from the knowledge of what his parents' generation had suffered. 'The fact that I was *only* being treated this way, and not worse, I thought that I was lucky,' he said.

The 1976 events turned a group of bookish young graduates into hardened opposition activists, and it didn't take them long to realize they needed a public voice. All news in Poland was manipulated by the Main Office, but what if they bypassed the censor? The first publications were leaflets, typed out by a network of sympathizers: whenever anyone shared a sheet of KOR information, they told the recipient to copy it out and pass both copies on. This dissident pyramid scheme helped create a wide network of engaged distributors, but it was slow and primitive. At the start of 1977 Chojecki got hold of a spirit duplicator, the sort of machine schools and colleges used in the West to produce blurry, purple lesson handouts. Working secretly in a friend's apartment, he found they could print 500 copies of a small booklet in one sitting.

That spring, Chojecki left Radom to focus on publishing. He wasn't the only pioneer of illicit printing techniques, but the operation he led, the Independent Publishing House NOWa, grew to be the biggest and most successful in the underground.

The mission of NOWa – pronounced *nov-a* – was 'to lift society out of the state of apathy into which it had been dragged by the omnipresence of the Communist Party and its monopoly on power'. Chojecki put together a group of printers, suppliers and distributors, with an editorial board led by a fellow graduate of Warsaw High School Number Seven, Adam Michnik. Sometimes they produced books and publications on the handful of illegal presses that existed in Poland; at other times they persuaded employees in state print shops or collaborators abroad to do the job. The challenges of underground publishing were immense, as they faced the vast resources of the police state. Presses and materials were seized, printers arrested and beaten, but Chojecki was a conspiratorial genius, and somehow the NOWa presses continued to roll. He became a folk hero, celebrated by Poles everywhere for his apparently impossible feats. As one Polish émigré put it, 'In a country that was so tightly, hermetically closed, you hear that someone is still printing and that every copy is legible. It's unbelievable! An absolute phenomenon. How did he do that?'

From the start, NOWa aimed to serve what the historian Jan Józef Lipski called the 'constantly persecuted Polish culture', and by Christmas 1977 it had published short runs of half a dozen uncensored books by blacklisted writers in Poland. It also reprinted titles that had first appeared in the West – Polish editions of *Animal Farm* and *1984*; volumes of poetry by Miłosz; Solzhenitsyn's *One Day in the Life of Ivan Denisovich*; and *The Soviet Bloc: Unity and Conflict*, by the US national security advisor Zbigniew Brzezinski. NOWa took the text from the many copies that were smuggled in from the West. By 1980, it had published around a hundred volumes, from editions of the literary quarterlies *Zapis* (Record) and *Puls* (Pulse) to great novels and memoirs by future Nobel Prize-winners such as Günter Grass. The underground publisher was so successful that others sprang up in its wake. 'NOWa showed the way', Lipski wrote. All of NOWa's books aimed to undermine totalitarian communism in some way, but the most effective blow against censorship was a haul of documents from the Main Office itself.

In February 1977, a young Polish civil servant reached Sweden with 700 pages of secret material taped in watertight bags to his back and legs. Tomasz Strzyżewski had spent the previous eighteen months smuggling papers out of the Kraków branch of the Main Office, where he worked, in the hope of sharing them with the world. It was the greatest leak of censors' materials in Polish history, and included seventy pages from the propagandists' Bible, the so-called 'Black Book', which contained a list of edicts designed to hide the administration's corruption, brutality and incompetence. These are some of the things Poles were not allowed to know, according to Strzyżewski's documents:

- That chemicals used by industry and agriculture posed a direct threat to human life.
- That a pit disaster in Katowice had killed four miners.
- That the chemicals used to seal the windows of a Gdańsk school were so dangerous classes had to be abandoned.
- That Poland had a huge and growing alcoholism problem.
- That Poland was exporting meat to the USSR in spite of its own terrible shortages.
- That the Soviet ally Idi Amin of Uganda planned to erect a statue to Hitler.

As well as being published in the West, Strzyżewski's documents made their way back to Chojecki in Warsaw, who picked out 'the tastiest parts' and reproduced them. Everyone sensed that the regime lied, especially when it came to the 'economic miracle' its leaders had promised, but the documents revealed a 'truly amazing' level of control, as the Polish émigré Leo Łabędź wrote in *The Times*. No subject seemed too trivial to attract a diktat from the Main Office, which prescribed everything down to the colour of the font – red – that was obligatory for the words that must be used to mark Second World War victory celebrations, 'The 30th Anniversary of the Victory over Fascism'. The traditional function of totalitarian censorship was to 'extol the emperor's non-existing clothes', Łabędź wrote. In Poland, however, the spell had been 'largely broken'.

Chojecki's parents had fought for Polish independence with guns and explosives, at the daily risk of their lives. Mirek, inspired by the uncensored, illegal texts to which he had been exposed as a young man, continued the struggle through literature and publishing. At times, his father Jerzy was sceptical of his son's tactics. 'Do you think, Mirek, that you'll be able to bring down the communist system with your little books?' he would ask. 'Do you think your little words will make a difference?'

Chojecki would answer with a question of his own: 'Would you prefer me to shoot someone?'

2

Our Friends Down South

They had come to a time when no one dared speak his mind, when fierce, growling dogs roamed everywhere, and when you had to watch your comrades torn to pieces after confessing to shocking crimes.

George Orwell, *Animal Farm*

To the hard-liners of East and West the Second World War was a distraction. Now it was over, they could get on with the real war that had started with the Bolshevik Revolution in 1917, and had been running under different flags and disguises ever since.

John le Carré, *The Spy Who Came in from the Cold*

The CIA book programme can be traced back to an August afternoon in 1951, when a convoy of eleven large trucks, two buses, six cars, a radio vehicle and several taxis left the yard of Radio Free Europe's headquarters in Munich and headed out into the Bavarian country-side. A hundred and seventy miles later, the snake of vehicles came to a halt at a predetermined spot outside Tirschenreuth and began to disgorge seventy CIA employees, who rapidly transformed this patch of West German soil into a hive of activity. A group of armed guards fanned out to establish a perimeter. Technicians cranked genera-tors into droning life, flooding the area with light. Transport crews unloaded crates filled with gas cylinders, leaflets and – this being an experiment – two different types of balloons, then began hitching on gauges and hoses, and testing hydrogen nozzles.

They launched the 'pillows' first, giant polyethylene bags – each printed with the word *Svoboda*, meaning 'freedom' in Czech – which were deliberately permeable so they would gradually lose buoyancy and sink slowly back to earth. Each pillow was loaded with a cargo of leaflets, weighed to check that it would fly, and released into the warm German night. Next came the 'goomies', rubber balloons designed to climb high into the atmosphere before exploding in the thin air around 30,000 feet.

The CIA employees had chosen this site, 10 miles from the Iron Curtain, since it was due west of Prague and, if the weather boffins had it right, the wind at 18,000 feet would be blowing eastwards at a steady 50mph. The weather boffins did indeed have it right, and by dawn the sky to the east was a scene from a science-fiction film, filled with 3,000 bobbling gas bags heading across the frontier into Czechoslovakia. Soon leaflets would be raining down on the Eastern Bloc, four million of them in all, each of which carried a message:

TO THE PEOPLE OF CZECHOSLOVAKIA
  A NEW WIND IS BLOWING
  A NEW HOPE IS STIRRING
  Friends of Freedom in other lands have found a new way to reach you.
  They know that you also want freedom.

'Winds of Freedom', as this operation was codenamed, was the brainchild of the Free Europe Committee, a psychological warfare arm of the CIA set up in 1949 to combat what Washington saw as the 'vicious covert activities' of the KGB in trying to spread the virus of communism. The FEC had been established in the aftermath of the war to mobilize the East European political refugees who had fled to the West, and who had a burning desire to liberate their countries but little money and few resources. The committee's great

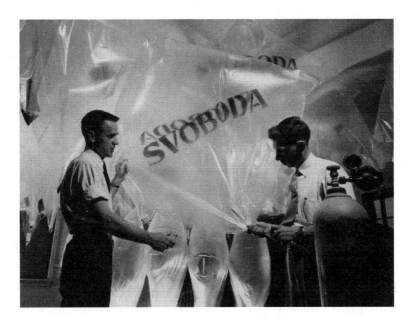

early success was with broadcasting. Radio Free Europe, which first aired in 1950, targeted the so-called 'captive nations' of Bulgaria, Czechoslovakia, Hungary, Poland and Romania, with bulletins and information in those countries' languages; Radio Liberty, founded three years later, focused on Russia and the republics of the Soviet Union itself. The 'radios' – whose CIA subvention was hidden behind the Crusade for Freedom fundraising campaign, fronted by a young Ronald Reagan – were a powerful propaganda tool, but they were susceptible to jamming, so the FEC began experimenting with other ways to deliver its messages. Between 1951 and 1956, it launched more than half a million balloons into the East, dropping 300 million leaflets and posters created by the FEC subsidiary, Free Europe Press. One of their late operations, which ran between February and May 1955, carried 260,000 copies of Orwell's political fable *Animal Farm*, specially printed on lightweight paper.

The balloons infuriated the communists, as they were meant to do. Eastern governments scrambled fighter planes to shoot them down, and sent police to arrest anyone caught with the subversive literature. But the operations were not a success. The delivery was too scattershot, the balloons were a threat to air traffic and the propaganda was too crude, so after five years they were scrapped. By this time, Free Europe Press had devised a new delivery system: direct mail. They would send anti-communist material to names and addresses culled from East European phone books. Although Soviet Bloc countries censored the post, they couldn't catch everything, and some of the material got through. The main problem was that the propaganda was received with no more enthusiasm than the leaflets that fell from the sky. But when the mail programme experimented with books, the response was very different. People wanted to keep the books. Sometimes they sent a letter of thanks or a request for more. There was an opportunity here, and no one saw it more clearly than an ambitious young employee in the FEC's New York office, George Minden.

Minden was an ideal FEC recruit: an East European exile with reason to detest the Soviets. Born in 1920 in Bucharest, to a British father and aristocratic Romanian mother, he had been highly educated, graduating top of his year at law school. In 1938, when he turned eighteen, he inherited vast tracts of land that straddled some of Europe's largest oil reserves, making him one of the richest men in the country overnight. The oilfields were bitterly fought over in the war – twice he found himself on the receiving end of American bombs – and in 1945 Romania lay in Stalin's territory. The communists seized Minden's wealth, and he was forced to flee with his wife Margarete and their two young children, carrying nothing but a few precious items hidden in the shoulder pads of his suit. They arrived in Britain as refugees, and prepared to start life over again, but George and Margarete's marriage would not survive the upheaval, and he soon left for Spain, where he hustled for a living, selling cars and running a language school. In Madrid he met Marilyn Miller from Pittsburgh, who became his second wife, and in 1955 they moved to New York, where George joined the Free Europe Committee. A year later, he was running the FEC's Romania desk. Two years after that, he was promoted to head the Free Europe Press Book Center, which handled the mailing project.

The mail programme had been created to 'reduce the efficiency of the communist administration by weakening the loyalty of the Party and state cadres', according to its founding text, and to 'demonstrate the superior achievements' of the West. Minden disliked this propagandistic tone. As he saw it, the enemy wasn't Eastern inferiority but the intellectual straitjacket imposed by Moscow. The Americans should offer something to fill the vacuum of ideas in the bloc, a sort of literary humanitarian aid, the bookish equivalent of the food packages sent east by CARE. He proposed 'an offensive of free, honest thinking and accurate information' to counteract the Soviet stultification, since 'truth is contagious'. They should target the influencers, academics and literary figures who felt starved of the oxygen of debate. The overarching goal was to reassure the people of the East, to 'give proof of continual Western interest'. Through their gifts of literature, they would try to express 'the feeling of communion in this world, integration into the spiritual life of our age, and the knowledge that they have not been abandoned'.

In 1959, Minden was vetted and security-cleared, category one, and briefed on the true identity of his bosses, the CIA, known in New York as the 'Executive Committee' and 'our friends down south'. Under his supervision, more and more books were sent in the mail. They included overtly political works such as *1984*, Aldous Huxley's *Brave New World* and Albert Camus' essay *The Rebel*, as well as material with no obvious anti-communist message. The Whitney Museum's *Three Hundred Years of American Painting* was an early hit, as were lifestyle magazines such as the French-language *Marie Claire* and the German *Madame*. These publications, Minden understood, had a wholly different meaning in the totalitarian East, where every aspect of life was controlled by the state, from art to music to fashion. As he would write in 1969: 'All book distribution is politically significant because all books – political and literary – accomplish the political task of making the ideological isolation of Eastern Europe difficult and thus frustrate one of the communists' main political objectives. For the communists, too, all Western books, whether political or non-political, are politically significant and feared as such.'

As the programme developed, they began to send catalogues, inviting recipients to take their pick, and hired agents in London and Paris to negotiate special rates with publishers, who often fulfilled the orders themselves, helping to mask the literature's real source and speed it through the mail censors. By 1962, at least 500 organizations were sending books on the CIA's behalf, including some of the most prestigious names in publishing: Doubleday, Barnes & Noble, the Oxford English Dictionary, Encyclopaedia Britannica, Allen and Unwin, Chatto and Windus, Faber and Faber, Macmillan, Gollancz, Bertelsmann and Hachette. No country responded with greater enthusiasm to these gifts than Poland, the largest of the 'captive nations' and the most liberal. Poles sent more replies and requests to Minden's unit than any other nationality.

In the late 1950s, the brief political thaw that followed Stalin's death meant many Poles could visit the West for the first time. Why not try giving them books to take home? The first person-to-person giveaways were run from 1958 by the young Free Europe Press employee Andy Stypułkowski, who began handing out literature to Polish travellers who visited his suburban house in Chiswick, west London. Carrying banned books through the Iron Curtain required courage and chutzpah, but frontier confiscations proved to be rare. The CIA gave Stypułkowski's operation the cover name Polonia Book Fund Ltd, and as word of the giveaways spread in Poland, more and more people showed up at the Stypułkowskis' home. Andy began to expand his distribution to bookstores, churches, libraries and community centres all over Western Europe. Soon, CIA-bought books were being passed out anywhere Poles could be found: in Scottish ports where Polish fishing boats tied up; at French basketball tournaments where Polish teams competed; at concert performances of touring Polish choirs in London. It helped that a black market in uncensored books developed in the East, feeding demand. By 1963, the Polonia Book Fund had given away 101,000 copies of books to 37,000 Polish visitors, at an annual cost to the CIA of £60,000.

That year, Polonia and its person-to-person programme were wrapped into Minden's unit targeting Eastern Europe, now known as the FEC's Press and Special Projects Division. Its tactical aim, Minden wrote at the time, was 'to place as high a number as possible of books containing vital information in all fields of knowledge in the hands of those best suited by their position to a) receive books coming from abroad and b) act as centers of knowledge-spreading with a minimum risk to themselves'. The ultimate goal, however, was broader, to reach 'the news-eager masses' of the East who were starved of the printed word. To this end, he hoped to be able to build up circulating libraries of books behind the Iron Curtain, which would help keep the isolated people of the Soviet Bloc 'in touch with the Free World's thinking'. Only then, he believed, could they 'have the facts that their Russian and national oppressors try to hide from them'.

In the late 1960s, against the backdrop of the Vietnam war, CIA activities were increasingly scrutinized by the media and public officials. In 1971, after its covert funding was revealed, most of the FEC's activities were shut down and the radio networks were brought under Congressional oversight. But the books programme would remain secret. At first it was put under a pre-existing CIA cover, the International Advisory Committee. Then, in 1975, it merged with a parallel books programme set up to target the USSR, Bedford Publications Ltd, and took a new identity: the International Literary Centre (ILC).

From this moment on, Minden controlled covert CIA literary influencing programmes across the Eastern Bloc, from Prague to Vladivostok.

3

The French Connection

In their pockets they carry the constitution, penal codes, the texts of international human rights pacts and the poems of great poets. They read banned books and want to learn as much as possible about the world . . . From unevange-lized, blind hatchlings, lost in a hypocritical reality, grows a resilient and truly ideological cadre of fighters for truth and freedom.

Marian Brandys, *My Adventures with History*

By the third week of his hunger strike, during which time his only nutrition came from the nurse's sickly mix, force-fed to him daily at noon, Chojecki had lost twenty-four pounds. His body was shutting down. His immune system was weak, his muscles shrivelled, and he felt permanently cold. At the start of his time in prison he had walked several miles a day, from one end of his cell to the other, to keep himself in shape, but now he could only manage half of what he had once done in an hour. He spent his time sitting at the small corner table, trying to concentrate. His eyes hurt from writing tiny, barely legible letters on paper scraps under the light of a 40-watt bulb.

On 27 April, the warden came to see him. This was a first in Chojecki's experience: he had never heard of the head of the prison visiting an inmate in their cell before.

'How's the starvation?' the warden asked.

'Very well.'

'Is nobody bothering you?'

'No.'

'Do you intend to starve for a long time?'

'Until I leave prison.'

'That's five years.'

'Less.'

'Four and a half years?'

'A few days, Citizen Warden.'

The warden seemed irritated. He told Chojecki to clean the sink, then left.

He was wrong, as it turned out. Two weeks later, on Saturday 10 May, the order came through that Chojecki was to be released. Guards entered his cell and told him to pack, and an hour later he was stepping through the prison gate on to Rakowiecka Street. He had been arrested in the snow; now the season had turned. As he squinted out from the shadow cast by the prison wall at the sunshine blazing down on the far side of the boulevard, he could pick out green shoots budding on the branches of the trees.

He had no appetite, but he knew he needed to eat. He struggled round the corner to a café, where he bought a small coffee and two doughnuts, and sat at a window table. He ate very slowly, savouring the sweet pastry with absolute delight. People passed by on the other side of the glass, oblivious to his starved, elated state.

'They think they are free,' he thought.

He returned to his Żoliborz apartment, where he sat in an armchair by the window. Word had run round that he was out, and that evening a queue of around seventy visitors came to wish him well. Only then did he begin to realize the scale of the campaign to free him. More than a hundred members of the official Polish Writers' Union had petitioned for his release, asserting in defiance of the regime that NOWa 'fills glaring gaps in our cultural life caused by censorship'. The conference of Polish bishops had released a statement approving of NOWa's attempts to show the young generation 'the unadulterated and full history of the nation, its culture and achievements of the human spirit'. A group of twenty-six activists had even begun their own hunger strike, in a church outside Warsaw. Most embarrassing for the regime was the international interest, as Poland had built up huge debts with Western governments and banks, which did not want to be seen financing repression. NOWa was the only publisher that dared print Günter Grass's *The Tin Drum* in Poland, and Grass, a future Nobel Prize-winner, had appealed to Warsaw to 'grant Polish literature, in the person of Mirosław Chojecki, that freedom which, for publishers and authors, is the condition of their work'. The Swedish PEN club had issued a similar call, as had printers' and publishers' unions in the US. All these proclamations were regularly broadcast by Radio Free Europe.

Among the people who came to visit Chojecki after his release was the Warsaw correspondent of the *New York Times*, which published an extensive interview at the front of its news section under the headline 'Polish Underground Publisher Flouts Censor and Thrives'. Chojecki was 'one of Poland's most influential publishers', it read; he employed 'scores of people willing to type smuggled manuscripts for free' and had 'printing presses stashed away at secret locations throughout the country'. NOWa's publications were the 'backbone of the dissident movement in Poland'.

Despite the international pressure, the regime was determined to prosecute Chojecki and his co-defendants. The trial was set for 12 June. As he prepared for his moment in the dock, it was more important than ever for the dissidents to show that underground publishing operations would not be stopped. Five days before the court date, two young NOWa printers set out on a job that would turn into a cat-and-mouse game with the secret police.

The night before leaving for work, Jan Walc went through his pockets to check for any scraps of paper. In this line of business, you had to assume you would be caught, searched and interrogated, and he couldn't be found with anything that would incriminate him or his friends. Next he packed a few essentials – clothes, a portable stove, headphones, a sponge – and took a long bath, knowing it would be his last for some time.

He knew where to meet his partner, Zenek Pałka; it was always the same café. The only extra piece of information he needed was the time, and Pałka had given him that over the phone. Without saying his name, he had announced that they should get together at 11 a.m. on Monday 9 June. Walc recognized the voice. He also knew what the wiretap sergeant listening in to the phone call didn't: namely, that he had to subtract two from everything, so the rendezvous was set for 9 a.m. on Saturday 7 June. That morning, he said goodbye to his wife and young son and walked out into a humid Warsaw day.

As he left the building, Walc discreetly scanned the street. No one suspicious seemed to be hanging around, which was a relief. As a rule the secret police – known as 'Ubeks', or simply 'Gestapo' – liked to watch your apartment or place of work and follow you from there, so if you didn't pick up a tail right away the prospects of avoiding one were good. All the same, he kept checking behind as he made his way to the meeting point, and he was still alone when he reached the café and ordered a drink. Soon Pałka, a giant of a man with frizzy red hair, was settling into the seat next to him.

'Is the place far away?' Walc asked.

Pałka took a paper serviette and wrote down an address in Rembertów, a sleepy suburb on the far bank of the Vistula, before burning through the words with his cigarette. Poles had been working in the underground against their oppressors for so long that the word for conspiracy, *konspiracja*, had lost any negative connotation it might once have had, and it came with a whole set of procedures, known as 'health and safety' rules, that had been fine-tuned over the generations. One rule was that you didn't say an address out loud, since you didn't know where the SB had planted bugs, and you certainly never left one written down.

'A new place?'

'Yes.'

'Who's the guy?'

'Krystyna's uncle. You know, Paula's friend.'

Walc didn't know Krystyna or Paula.

'What's it like?'

It was another rule that you shared as little information as possible, but since Walc was soon going to find out anyway, Pałka passed on a few more details. 'Uncle' had built the house himself. He lived alone and was writing a book about Józef Piłsudski – a sure indicator of his anti-communist politics. Water came from a well, but they would need a week's worth of food, since Uncle was too poor to supply meals, and they wouldn't take the risk of leaving the job to go shopping. The printing machine they were to use was a mimeograph made by A. B. Dick of Chicago. Mimeographs, which reproduced text written or typed on to a stencil, were favoured by the underground as they were simple to use and relatively easy to repair. The machine had already been delivered to the house, along with a tonne and a half of paper, six full carloads. The job was to print several thousand copies of the KOR newsletter *Information Bulletin*, plus some pages for NOWa's literary journal *Pulse*. They would need to buy ten bottles of turpentine to run and clean the press.

It was the turpentine that gave them the problem. By the time they'd bought and packed all the food they needed – mostly eggs, cheese and soured cream – they had no room for the bottles of solvent, so they decided to stop by at a friend's place to borrow an extra bag. They didn't realize the friend was under surveillance, and when they left his building they spotted a boxy grey Fiat saloon with three men inside which shadowed them as they walked along the road.

Walc suppressed a twinge of nerves. The main thing was not to let on that they'd spotted the car until they had come up with a plan. In the meantime they could try to lose their tail surreptitiously, as if by accident. Reaching a tram stop, they saw the Fiat pull into a side road and park illegally, a sure sign it was the secret police, and when the tram arrived and the printers boarded, two plainclothes agents jumped out of the car and ran across the street, climbing up behind them. All four men now sat in the same streetcar as it rattled towards Zawisza Square, a transport interchange in the west of the city. The Fiat kept pace alongside.

How to get rid of them? They needed to think.

As they reached the Zawisza Square stop, the printers saw the Fiat was boxed in at the traffic lights, and they took their chance, leaving the tram at the last minute. When the lights changed and the unmarked car had to pull away, Walc and Pałka were hurrying in a different direction, towards the commuter rail station. A part of their tail was lost, but the other two agents had been alert and were keeping pace behind them as they ran down the station platform. Here, Pałka made a call. They would use two tricks from their arsenal of 'health and safety' procedures: 'French Connection' followed by 'bypass bridge'.

The agents were close as they boarded a train for Warsaw Central. Walc made a show of placing his bags on the luggage rack and settling into his seat, but as the doors closed Pałka jammed his leg between them and slipped out – this was the 'French Connection', named for the Gene Hackman movie where they'd first seen it. Walc now had the two remaining agents to himself. His job was to drag them around long enough for Pałka to prepare the next move.

The men were behind Walc as he left the train at Warsaw Central and ducked into the warren of passages beneath the station. He knew police radios wouldn't work down here, and he could keep them occupied for a time. He ordered a Coke at a bar, bought some cigarettes, browsed the shops. When twenty minutes had passed he emerged from the tunnels and headed for the taxi rank. He could see one of the men talking into his lapel as he climbed into a cab, but there were other cars in the rank and the Ubeks were behind him as Walc's driver merged on to Jerusalem Avenue, heading east towards the Vistula. Time for phase two.

Warsaw's Poniatowski Bridge is as much a viaduct as a river crossing, carrying Jerusalem Avenue above the city for several hundred yards before it reaches the Vistula – hundreds of yards where the roadway is linked to the streets below by a series of stone staircases. Speeding east, Walc gave the driver his instructions. Midway along the viaduct, the taxi came to a sudden halt, and the printer dived out and ran down the steps to the road below. The chasing agents pulled up behind and raced down the staircase in pursuit, but as they reached the lower level Walc was already climbing into another cab, where Pałka was waiting. The policemen watched as their quarry pulled away. Knowing the Ubeks would now be radioing in the cab's licence plate, after a few hundred yards the printers swapped into another vehicle, their third taxi of the morning. They transferred their bags, left a generous tip and gave the new driver an address on the far side of the city.

It was almost midday. They took some time now to calm their jangling nerves and make sure they had shaken off the police. A few hours later, around 3 p.m., they caught the train to Rembertów.

The rain clouds of the morning had given way to bright sunshine, interrupted only by a few high, pale wisps of cloud, and after lugging their heavy bags from the station to the property their shirts were soaked with sweat. The place looked ideal. It was set back from the street, at the far end of a large garden overgrown with a tangle of bushes and weeds. Dogs barked.

Uncle turned out to be a large man in overalls, younger than they had expected, who spoke Polish with a Lithuanian accent.

'We're Krystyna's friends,' Walc said. This was all the introduction their host seemed to need.

The house consisted of three small rooms plus a large kitchen dominated by a copy of an icon of the Virgin Mary. The space Uncle had set aside was filled with furniture: two old beds, a table, wall hangings, armchairs. They began by shifting out what they could, to create space to work. The printing machine and the paper were hidden in an outhouse, 500 reams stacked almost to the roof. The paper was a little damp, which was far from ideal, but they would have to make it work somehow. It took ten trips through the garden to carry in what they needed, then they covered every surface – floor, walls, windows, the furniture they couldn't shift. Ink always got everywhere.

At 5 p.m. they made themselves a meal of scrambled eggs and fried cheese, Walc noting guiltily that their host ate only margarine, and cubes of stale bread he soaked in his weak tea. As underground printers paid a few dollars a day they had a lot more than he did. After eating they got back to work.

By evening their small room was like any other underground print shop in Poland, filled with the fumes of cigarettes and turpentine, and the sound of the duplicating machine beating out its regular, soporific rhythm, *bad-dum bad-dum bad-dum bad-dum*.

Underground printing was filthy, exhausting work. The duplicators were old and inclined to break down, and the paper was poor. *Bibuła*, the Polish word for uncensored publications, means 'blotting paper', which reflected the stock they had to work with, which was too absorbent and so poorly trimmed it had to be hand-fed into the machine, three pages a second, hour upon hour. A single publication might take half a million or more hand movements, and a small mistake could mean dozens of pages lost as misprints. This meant they worked round the clock, in shifts, for days, until the job was done.

Pałka had brought along a Soviet-made transistor, which they tuned to Polish Radio, switching to Radio Free Europe when the communists' 'indoctrination hour' came on at 11 p.m. RFE maintained a regular commentary on Chojecki's upcoming trial. It seemed that the regime had blundered with its plan to put him in the dock, since it thereby called global attention to Polish censorship and human rights abuses. On Tuesday, two days before the court date, they listened again to the RFE bulletin. Chojecki's case seemed to be everywhere. There was a supportive column in the London *Times*, which described him as a 'heroic freedom fighter' who had made 'a genuine and important breach in the state publishing monopoly', and a long article in the Belgian daily *Le Soir*. American printers and British lawyers were protesting at what they called a show trial. The union of Second World War veterans in London had praised the underground press. KOR had declared it would use all available means to support the publisher. Amnesty International was sending a legal representative.

'A great day is coming,' Walc thought, 'and we are stuck in a printing shop!' If they hurried the job, they might still be able to get to court.

Early on Thursday morning they had twenty reams left to print. By 8 p.m., Pałka was finishing the last stencil and Walc was burning misprints in the garden. Before leaving they had to strip the machine down, wash all the parts and lubricate them. Radio Free Europe had some details of the trial, but all they could ascertain was that Chojecki had pleaded not guilty.

At last they were ready to put the machine back in its box and hide it in the outhouse. They replaced all the furniture, washed quickly and said goodbye to their host. Carrying fifty copies of the *Bulletin*, they found a taxi and gave the driver the address of the apartment where they had been told to report to collect their pay. They arrived around 11 p.m. The apartment was crowded with people, including half the *Bulletin*'s editors, who were surprised to see they had finished the job so early. They congratulated the printers, examined the new issue and relieved them of almost all of their copies. The rest of the edition would be transported from the print shop to different sites to be collated and distributed.

Walc asked about the trial. What courtroom was it in? They still hoped to make the second day. He was astonished to hear it was already over. The sentence had been read an hour ago. One of the editors had just come back from the court.

The interior ministry had packed Warsaw District Court with its own recruits, who applauded when two of the defendants arrived in handcuffs. But a few independent journalists and activists had managed to talk their way into the room, where they saw Chojecki deliver an excoriating indictment of the 'doublethink' imposed by the communist system.

He told the court that his flat had been searched seventeen times in the past four years, on a litany of made-up pretexts: they were looking for a murderer, they had said, or a poisoner or a thief, but all they ever took away for evidence were books, typewriters and manuscripts. He had been held in custody for almost 200 days in

that period, and on only five occasions had he been accused of offences related to the real reason they were harassing him: publishing. They had accused NOWa itself of various crimes including forging money, breaking into private apartments, theft and even trying to poison the population of Warsaw, none of which was true.

'Why are such accusations levelled against people who fight against the destruction of history,' he asked, 'who fight against the pillaging of our culture?'

The answer was that in Poland people were forced to lead double lives, with a double morality. On the one hand was the 'life of appearances', dominated by a 'pretend press' that couldn't report the truth, 'pretend radio and television' that didn't address Poland's many problems, and 'pretend art' that was detached from reality. Beneath the surface of this sham public life lay another Poland, private Poland, where citizens spoke the truth out of earshot of the SB agents who could punish them by refusing them an apartment, a job, a passport, holidays or a place for their children in school. This double standard, instilled in Poles from kindergarten, caused great moral damage, and its effect could be seen in every workplace and in every street across the country.

Nowhere were the public lies and gaps more destructive than in the field of Polish culture, where vital literary works and historical deeds had been eradicated. 'Officially, half of our recent history is erased from textbooks, studies, encyclopaedias,' Chojecki told the court. 'The fate of hundreds of thousands of Poles, scattered across the vast expanses of the Soviet Union, [and] the places where they died in mass murder do not officially belong to Polish history.' It was the same in literature, where the state gave itself a 'monopoly of thought' and a 'monopoly of the word'. The lists of banned authors contained some of world's best writers, he said. That was why he and his colleagues had set up NOWa, to fill the silences and correct the falsification.

Reaching a rousing finale, Chojecki announced that the trial was not about the accused at all, but about 'free speech and thought, about Polish culture, about the dignity of society'.

Of course, none of this would change the verdict. The court duly convicted Chojecki and his co-defendants of theft of state prop-erty. He was sentenced to eighteen months in prison, suspended for three years. But to the opposition, and to everyone gathered in the editors' apartment, this was a tremendous victory. Chojecki was a hero. The day was theirs. 'Everybody around us rejoices,' Walc wrote in his account of that week's events, which would be published in the following month's *Bulletin*.

Someone pressed a cold beer into his hand. It was midnight.

4

An International Spider Web

In connection with Recommendation No. 167, we would like to inform you that a number of substantive objections have been formulated against the *Encyclopaedia for Children*. These concern . . . lack of emphasis on the roles of the Polish Army and Soviet Army in the liberation of Warsaw, inadequate elaboration of the entry 'Polish United Workers' Party' (omission of . . . the names of leading party activists), failure to include an entry concerning the working class, etc.

Information Note 2, Main Office for Control,
February 1977, *The Black Book of Polish Censorship*

In the run-up to Chojecki's trial, a memo had worked its way through the White House from Paul Henze, a former CIA officer, to his boss Zbigniew Brzezinski, President Carter's national security advisor. Henze was livid. He had just come off a phone call with the CIA's comptroller, who had told him the Office of Management and Budget was refusing to provide funds to keep the book programme going through the next year. Minden's entire operation was hanging by a thread, and at a crucial moment in the battle against the Soviets, too. Just six months earlier, on Christmas Eve 1979, Moscow had sent its troops into Afghanistan. This was the first time the USSR had ever invaded a country outside the Eastern Bloc, and it marked a watershed in the Cold War, massively escalating

East–West tensions and unleashing a brutal, decade-long conflict in which a million civilians would die. As Henze told Brzezinski, it was 'appalling that these excellent programs should have fallen into such jeopardy at a time like this'.

What was more, at that moment a certain Polish dissident was demonstrating just how effective the books operations could be. 'You probably noticed the piece in the [*New York Times*] last week on Chojecki,' Henze went on. 'These programs relate to his activity in many ways – and what he is doing in Poland is an example of what others like him may eventually be able to do in other places, including the USSR, if we keep these activities going.' Of course the activity of which Henze wrote so approvingly was Chojecki's underground publishing operation, which was doing a fine job of amplifying the CIA programme's effect by reprinting many of its books in the Eastern Bloc. More than just a dissident with an international profile, Chojecki was being touted in the White House as the prime example of what the literary campaigns could achieve, and a reason to keep the funds flowing.

In truth, Brzezinski had been fighting a rearguard action on the book programme's behalf since his first days in the job, in the face of deep scepticism on all fronts, not least inside the Agency. It was said that CIA officers in the clandestine Directorate of Operations tended to split into two groups. On the one hand were the 'ground-pounders' or 'knuckle-draggers' – paramilitary types who saw themselves as part of an elite combat battalion that ran dirty little wars in the world's trouble hotspots. On the other were the more cerebral political-psychological staff, highly educated country specialists who had a keen interest in the territories they worked on and often spoke several languages. There was palpable tension between these two cultures, but it was the action men who tended to take the top jobs, and they had little time for literature. 'The paramilitary guys thought, "Real men don't sell books," ' the former CIA chief historian Benjamin Fischer recalled. 'Real men recruit spies. Books are not important. You go to one of these guys and say, "Look, I need $100,000 to buy books from the Silver Age of Russian literature," or "I need to buy 500 copies of Vladimir Mayakovsky's poetry," they would look at you like, "Are you a moron? Why would you waste money on stuff like that?" '

It wasn't only the CIA that wanted to pull the plug. The State Department also objected, believing all covert action was sneaky and underhand, no matter how 'soft' it might appear. With such powerful enemies, the programme's survival hinged on a few key players in and around the National Security Council, in particular a coterie of Poles and Polish Americans who'd had contacts in the ILC for years and were well aware of its value – not least because it promoted their own books. Brzezinski, a former Harvard professor who had been born in Warsaw, was one of them: at least four of his works were on ILC purchase and distribution lists. Another favoured Polish author was Brzezinski's friend Jan Nowak, founding head of Radio Free Europe's Polish service. Nowak had moved to Washington on his retirement to act as an unofficial ambassador for the opposition, and Brzezinski had brought him on to the National Security Council as a Polish affairs specialist. The two men went hunting together every Sunday during the season. Nowak's CIA-promoted works included his autobiographical account of working as a liaison with the Polish Home Army during the war, *A Courier from Warsaw* – the same book Chojecki had been grilled about in jail after NOWa reprinted it. NOWa had also republished Brzezinski's *Unity or Conflict*, which explored Soviet totalitarianism and predicted its eventual demise.

Within weeks of Jimmy Carter's inauguration in January 1977, Brzezinski had sought the president's approval to expand the books programme. Carter had agreed, but in January 1979 the head of the CIA, Admiral Stansfield Turner, had blithely accepted the view of the bean counters at the Office of Management and Budget and ruled out planned book-programme expansions costing around $1.5 million a year. At that moment, too, Henze had fumed at the stupidity. Turner had 'probably not actually given this . . . any serious thought', he told Brzezinski, and had failed to realize that 'a program such as this contributes as much to our national defense as any of our weaponry, besides which its costs are chicken feed'. Henze had taken soundings in the CIA and been told that there was no good reason to let the programme plateau off: 'Funds added to it are among the most productive CIA spends for covert action. In fact, this program constitutes a large part of what is left of CIA's covert action program and they constitute most of what we are doing against our highest-priority target – Eastern Europe and the USSR.'

Brzezinski and Henze would continue to fight Minden's corner, instructing the CIA to find the necessary cash for continued expansion of book-programme activity against its 'highest-priority targets for sustained covert action impact'. When he read Henze's memo in June 1980, the national security advisor agreed that the action must continue.

'I will back it strongly,' he wrote at the foot of the document. 'Make a compelling case, factually and budget wise. ZB'.

The questions over the book programme's future, and the wrangling over funding, would be felt at every node of the CIA's book network. That may partly explain why Minden was so cautious with his budgets and such a stickler for financial efficiencies – an obsession that was apparent to anyone who visited the ILC offices in New York.

Number 475 Park Avenue South was a nondescript 1960s-built tower in an unfashionable part of midtown Manhattan. If there was one great advantage in being at this address, it was the proximity of the major New York houses – Doubleday, Simon & Schuster, Random House, Harper & Row – which formed the engine room of the global publishing industry and which had supported the CIA, wittingly or not, in its mission to flood the East with uncensored books. But there were disadvantages too. In 1980, the city was sliding into the worst crime epidemic in its history, with record numbers of murders, burglaries and car-jackings, which would only worsen as the decade progressed. This part of town was not immune. The Belmore Cafeteria, a taxi drivers' hangout 200 yards south down the

avenue, drew drug dealers and sex workers to ply their trade among
the cab ranks. New York had such a bad reputation that certain CIA
officers at the Agency's headquarters in Langley refused to visit the
ILC at all, fearing they'd get mugged as soon as they stepped off the
plane.

For the ILC's mostly East European staff, New York crime was
a fact of life. It was one of Minden's rules that you should never
live more than ten minutes' walk from the office, to save time
commuting, and he shared an apartment nearby with his wife
Marilyn and their two children, strolling into work each morning
through the snorting Manhattan traffic. Reaching number 475, he
would ride the elevator to the fourteenth floor and push through
a door marked 'INTERNATIONAL LITERARY CENTRE LTD'
with a metal sign – the British spelling an added layer of subterfuge. From here, a passageway led around to the right, past a
small mailroom and a store for thousands of Russian-language
books, to the Soviet desk, overseen by Veronica Stein, a cousin
by marriage of Solzhenitsyn. To the left, a door opened on to the
East European section, home to the Czechoslovak, Hungarian,
Romanian, Bulgarian and Polish programmes. Minden's private
office, guarded by his long-serving secretary Rebecca Lief, occupied the north-west corner of the floor, with views over the
avenue. He liked to shut the door – even here, in the nerve centre
of the books operation, he was wary of eavesdroppers – sink into
his Eames chair and begin the daily business of managing his
secret literary smuggling ring.

The atmosphere in the ILC was quiet, serious, a million miles
from the bang-bang world many CIA officers inhabited, but no
less effective for that. Each employee knew how important their
task was, since almost all had suffered directly under the Soviet
system. Ioana 'Nana' Alimanestianu was a mother of four who had
fled Romania to the West in 1947, and began working for the book
programme a decade later, typing out addresses from the Romanian
phone directory. She now ran the Romanian and Bulgarian desks.
Zdena Horák had escaped Czechoslovakia in 1948, dashing 200

yards across the 'death zone' to West Germany, in her panic leaving a shoe behind in no man's land. She ran the Czechoslovakian and Hungarian sections.

The job, they all knew, was to get as many books and periodicals of the right kind through the Iron Curtain as possible, and at this point they were shifting publications at the rate of almost a million a year. Candidate volumes arrived in the East European section continually, where they stood about in teetering stacks on editors' desks. Mainstream titles produced in the US and Western Europe were called in from catalogues, while more specialist books, including those produced by émigré publishers in East European languages, came in direct to the desk editors, who would decide whether to subsidize and distribute them. Minden liked to review books himself, and once they were approved the editor would place a slip inside with a list of suggested target countries, then circulate the volume around the relevant sections, starting with Poland. The number of copies allocated to each country depended partly on population size. So Poland received around a third of all publications sent to Eastern Europe – excluding the USSR – whereas Bulgaria received only around one in twenty.

Paperbacks could be sent in greater quantities than hardbacks, and the most expensive books, such as art books and encyclopaedias, were sent least often.

When the teams had worked out what was to go where, they would decide how to get them there. The mailing programme provided a pinpoint system for reaching known 'targets', and over the years they had built a vast database containing details of every person or institution ever contacted. The files included the names, addresses, occupations, languages and fields of interest of the recipient, as well as a code indicating which books they had received, and copies of any correspondence. There was so much detail, it allowed the ILC editors to have quasi-personal relationships with tens of thousands of people living under communist rule, including celebrated personalities, writers, artists and politicians. So law books, for instance, could be sent to lawyers or law libraries, art books to painters, medical books to doctors. Controversial or political books were sent to recipients who were unlikely to be persecuted for receiving them, such as members of the Party, church officials, journalists, universities and colleges. In October 1978, when Cardinal Karol Wojtyła was elected Pope John Paul II, the CIA told Carter's national security team with pride that the new pontiff had been one of the book programme's correspondents. Its staff had sent him a 'considerable quantity of material in both Polish and English', and Wojtyła, who probably didn't know who was behind the scheme, had responded with a postcard thanking them. Many American publications were sent direct from Manhattan: the ILC mailroom down the street had become so busy that at one point the New York Post Office launched an investigation into its suspicious activity, and the CIA had to step in to explain the scheme to the chief postal inspector in Washington.

Where books were sent from American or European 'sponsors' – third-party publishers and bookstores who discounted or donated books and mailed them on the ILC's behalf – the editors would send over a list of targets and addresses. Any responses from the

Eastern Bloc would be forwarded to Minden's team. Further lists were sent to cover organizations, such as the Polonia Book Fund in London or the Centre International Littéraire (CIL) in Paris, which held thousands of books in their own storerooms. These organizations also acted as hubs for person-to-person distribution, as did a wide range of associated bookstores in Minden's European network where travellers could pick books up. Enterprising distributors used their own initiative: hearing that a Polish dance troupe was coming to perform at the pope's summer palace, say, they would set off for Italy with a case of books to hand over in person, sending the bill to the ILC.

Like other CIA constructions, the system was deliberately opaque. Minden described it as 'a complex organization . . . consisting of bookshops, publishers, libraries, book exporters, and Russian and East European personalities living in London, Paris, Vienna, Munich, Karlsruhe, Copenhagen, Geneva, and Rome'. According to another ILC veteran, the New York office was at the centre of a 'huge international spider web' which encompassed many territories and organizations in the US and Europe. The further away from the centre one went, the more difficult it became to locate and identify it.

The all-important Polish desk was run by one of Minden's most valued confidants, Adam Rudzki, who at seventy-nine was the most venerable staffer at the ILC. Before the war, he had run the port authority in Gdańsk, and escaped the Nazis by fleeing through Latvia, joining the FEC in 1952. His section was by far the largest in the East European room, rivalled in scale only by the Soviet programme. While it was important to target the USSR, Russia had always been hard to penetrate, as it had the most ruthless security service and no great history of free speech and democracy to build on. Poles, by contrast, had been electing kings since the Middle Ages, they had a centuries-long tradition of trying to fight off the Russians and, despite its authoritarianism, the Polish regime was relatively liberal compared with the brutal dictatorships in Romania or East Germany. Poles also felt strongly tied to the

West, where there were large and well-established Polish communities. Millions of émigré Poles lived in France, West Germany and Britain – the government-in-exile had been based in London since the war – and the city with the second largest Polish population in the world, after Warsaw, was Chicago. Little surprise, then, that Poland had responded more eagerly than any other nation to the book programme.

Rudzki oversaw a network of dozens of Polish publishers and book distributors, with contacts in the US, UK, France, Austria, West Germany, Sweden, Italy and beyond, which he supported through commissions, purchases and subsidies. There were many exceptional assets among the ILC's Polish associates, but none would have more influence than the leader of a group based in the western outskirts of Paris, an émigré known to Poles all over the world as the 'prince' or the 'duke', but addressed by Rudzki and others in the book programme simply as 'the Editor'.

His name was Jerzy Giedroyc, and he would soon become Chojecki's chief promoter, ally and mentor.

Even as a young man, Jerzy Giedroyc's face tended to fall into a sceptical droop, with a lugubrious fish-like mouth that turned down even in a smile, and liquid, heavy-lidded eyes. Combined with his love for cravats, this gave him the air of a world-weary Oscar Wilde invention more than Poland's public enemy number one, and yet that in many ways was what he was. Years later, he would be credited with both bringing down communism and keeping Polish literature alive during the long decades of communist darkness. In recognition of his achievements, the United Nations and the Polish parliament would designate 2006, the centenary of his birth, the 'Year of Jerzy Giedroyc'.

By 1980, the 74-year-old had been running his private intelligence campaign against the communists for more than thirty years, for most of that time from a large, ivy-covered villa a short distance west of Paris. Poles knew this place as 'Maisons-Laffitte', after the baroque chateau nearby, although it really fell into the neighbouring district of Mesnil-le-Roi. To many of the impoverished émigrés and travellers who climbed the long, gentle slope from the train station, the house at 91 Avenue de Poissy must have seemed like a chateau. It stood in its own grounds, surrounded by lawns, fir trees and converted outbuildings where visitors could stay. Some came here almost as pilgrims, looking for food and a bed, and to lay their problems and desires before the nation's pre-eminent man of letters. Giedroyc was a generous host, and the household was part kibbutz, part army mess tent. He held private meetings in his small office at the rear of the house, where he worked at a modest desk surrounded by double-banked bookshelves, puffing out clouds of grey-blue fumes from his Kool Filter King menthol cigarettes. He was an enthusiastic smoker, who smoked at the breakfast table and at night with whichever typescript he had taken to bed, leaving burn marks on the bedding and on the floor.

He hadn't always lived in such felicitous surroundings. An editor of political journals before the war, he had been evacuated to Romania in 1939, where he served as a diplomat for the Polish government-in-exile in Bucharest. When Romania allied with Hitler, he escaped with the help of the British, and enlisted with the free Poles, who posted him to North Africa and then the Middle East. On a sweltering August day in 1942, in a military camp in northern Iraq, he met Józef Czapski, head of propaganda for the Polish II Corps, which had been recruited by General Władysław Anders largely from Poles held in Soviet Gulags. Czapski, an artist by profession, was a survivor with a capital 'S'. He was one of the few hundred Polish officers who had escaped the NKVD massacres at Katyń, and one of an even smaller group to survive the labour camps. He ascribed this latter miracle to his passion for Marcel Proust: in the most dehumanizing conditions imaginable, he had found a reason to live by delivering lectures to fellow prisoners about In Search of Lost Time, of which he knew whole sections by heart.

Czapski recruited Giedroyc to his propaganda unit, and the two men served the rest of the war together in the Anders Army, as it fought its way up the Italian peninsula and through the bloody victory at Monte Cassino. In 1945, when Poland's fate in the Eastern Bloc was sealed at the Yalta conference, Giedroyc floated the idea of creating a publishing house to support the cause of Polish independence. It would be a continuation of their wartime mission by other means. 'The situation was clear to me,' Giedroyc said later, 'the Polish cause was lost, and it became essential to maintain contact with the country, to influence things there and to work with the émigrés.' The Literary Institute opened in 1946 in Rome, but as Giedroyc could see the KGB were 'running riot' in Italy, he moved the operation to Paris. Here, far from the reach of the regime's censors, they began to build a first-rate independent Polish press. Early publications included Czapski's memoirs of Katyń and the Gulags. In *Inhuman Land*, Czapski recounted his journey through the Stalin-era Soviet Union, as he tried to find out what had happened to his murdered fellow officers:

At every step I saw the expression of a brutal, unbending will; I saw thousands of human faces that were closed or hostile, and I felt the terrible disproportion in physical strength between us and this empire, which in recent years had killed off more Poles than in the whole of history to date.

In 1947 Giedroyc launched *Kultura*, the publication that would become the most popular Polish-language journal in the world, running to more than 600 editions, distributed in more than fifty countries. Everyone in the Polish democratic opposition knew what *Kultura* was and what it stood for: hope, and the forbidden fruit of free thinking, magically spirited in from the West. Coming across a new edition of *Kultura* in communist Poland was like finding 'fresh bread rolls', one former dissident explained; it gave her the illusion that 'maybe I'm living in a free country'. It wasn't only Poles in Poland who found solace in *Kultura*. A dissident in the West described it as 'a legend that shines throughout all Eastern Europe'.

From the start, Giedroyc struggled for money. *Kultura*'s anti-Soviet editorial line didn't endear him to the intellectual class in post-war France, where the likes of Jean-Paul Sartre and Jean Genet viewed Stalin as a hero and Russia as a guardian of freedom. By 1949 the Editor had reached a crisis point. 'At stake is the future of *Kultura*,' Giedroyc wrote to a friend that March. They only had enough cash to last a few more months and desperately sought $14,000 to keep them afloat for the next two years. 'I think that the only way to get this kind of money is to make an appeal in the United States,' Giedroyc went on, 'even though I realize how difficult and nearly hopeless this might be.'

Czapski would act as his envoy. Giedroyc sent him to America early in 1950, but the artist struggled to make any inroads on their funding target. '[He] is mad at me,' Giedroyc wrote. 'I am mad at him, and we both dream of the dollar manna which somehow does not materialize.' But they refused to give up, and in the summer one of Czapski's contacts invited them to join the Congress for Cultural Freedom, an ambitious US intelligence initiative to win over Europe's intellectuals to the anti-communist perspective, led by the CIA officer Michael Josselson. Hundreds of famous names besides Giedroyc and Czapski became linked to this enterprise, including Bertrand Russell, Stephen Spender and Arthur Koestler. Giedroyc found Josselson to be 'a most interesting individual, exceptionally intelligent and very strong minded', and at one point they discussed the possibility of *Kultura* joining the stable of CIA-funded congress journals, which included *Encounter*, edited by Spender. These conversations never got very far, according to Giedroyc, 'because of our determination to retain absolute editorial independence'. But he and Czapski continued to fish in American waters. In the winter of 1950–1 they travelled to the US together and met with CIA officers who offered to support them to the tune of $10,000 a year, a substantial sum at the time. In return, the Editor was to expand his operations, smuggle more publications to Poland and improve distribution in the West. This was everything they had been looking for and Giedroyc agreed. The CIA assigned him the codename 'QRBERETTA'.

As *Kultura* grew in influence, the Soviet and Polish governments denounced the Maisons-Laffitte group as enemies of the state bent on anti-communist 'diversion'. This was rarely more damaging than in 1969, when Polish agents caught a group of young intellectuals smuggling Literary Institute articles and books from Czechoslovakia into Poland over the Tatra mountains. The so-called 'mountaineers' were tried and handed long prison sentences, but the real target of the case was the absent Giedroyc. Prosecutors described him as an enemy agent bent on defaming the Polish nation and its system. This was partially true; in one declassified document the CIA even claimed 'proprietorship' of *Kultura*. But Giedroyc's relationship with American intelligence was more complicated than that. His exchanges with the ILC show he treated them more as wartime partners than as employers. As one CIA officer retorted, when asked by a superior to 'Go tell BERETTA' to do something, 'You don't tell BERETTA. BERETTA tells you.'

In difficult circumstances, Giedroyc had opted to work with the CIA, but he was vigilant about his independence. 'I had always maintained', he once said, 'that if I had to apply absolute political or moral tests to writers, Polish literature would cease to exist. I therefore considered that we ought to distinguish the author from his work, to let the work stand apart . . . for me it is a general attitude of mind.'

The Agency was evidently content with its investment, as it steadily increased funding for QRBERETTA over the years. By the mid-1960s, Giedroyc's annual stipend ran to between $20,000 and $60,000 annually. In 1977, a lean year for the book programme, when budgets overall were slashed almost in half, to $2.6 million, QRBERETTA received $115,000. That Giedroyc had a good reputation in the CIA is clear from another declassified document, analysing a covert operation to support dissident publishers in Ukraine. 'What bothers me about this project', the analyst wrote in 1973, 'is the fact that it seems to lack the kind of spark that QRBERETTA [has] . . . I would like to be sure that what we are supporting [in the Ukrainian case] is not simply a group of aging émigrés living increasingly in the past.'

Seven years later, in 1980, midway through his eighth decade, Giedroyc still retained his 'spark' and was still running his propaganda war against the communist regime in Poland. Increasingly, too, he was admiring the work of the ambitious young underground publisher Mirosław 'Mirek' Chojecki.

5

They Will Crush Us Like Bugs

> Along that same asphalt ribbon on which Black Marias
> scurry at night, a tribe of youngsters strides by day with
> banners, flowers, and gay, untroubled songs.
> Aleksandr Solzhenitsyn, *The Gulag Archipelago*

According to the theories of Arthur Schlesinger Jr, whose work
was distributed by the CIA, history behaves much like a pendulum. People swing one way, gathering speed and momentum, but
as they hit maximum velocity a reaction starts to grow which will
eventually overpower whatever moved them in the first place. At
its highest point the pendulum stops, then history accelerates back
in the opposite direction. The difficult part for the people is that
they can't know precisely what will happen when the pendulum
reverses. This, more or less, was the situation in Poland in 1980,
when communist power appeared to teeter, and dissidents rallied
around a new political movement embodied by the word Solidarity,
or *Solidarność*.

Late summer found Chojecki at the beach. He had escaped the
stifling Warsaw heat to spend time alone with his children. (He
and his wife, the activist Magda Bocheńska-Chojecka, would soon
divorce.) They went to Dębki, on Poland's northern rim, where a
long strip of white sand separates the Pomeranian pine forests from
the lapping Baltic. As usual when he went away, he left his address
with friends in case a crisis blew up, and on Friday 15 August two

colleagues from NOWa dropped by. Konrad Bieliński and Ewa Milewicz were looking for a couple of Germans who had smuggled a duplicator into Poland in their VW camper van. Mirek couldn't help with the Germans, but he was intrigued by some news the pair brought. On their route north they had driven past the Lenin Shipyard in Gdańsk, where it seemed something big was kicking off.

The Lenin Shipyard occupied a special place in the annals of Polish labour. Seventeen thousand people worked on this sprawling 350-acre site, constructing ships for the navies of the Warsaw Pact. It was the sort of shop-window socialist enterprise Party leaders liked to show to visiting heads of state, but it was also a hotbed of industrial unrest, thanks in large part to the catastrophic events of 1970. In December that year, the regime had sought to plug the holes in the sinking Polish economy by announcing a sudden increase in the state-controlled prices of flour, sugar and meat. Workers from the Lenin yard downed tools and marched on the Party's regional headquarters. The protests turned into riots, which spread along the coast, and soon the regime faced a general mutiny of the working class. Always terrified of 'counter-revolution', the government sent in the militia, and when the violence stopped a thousand people had been wounded and forty-four lay dead. Many had been shot in front of the shipyard gates. Poles had killed Poles, a shocking fact in a country still traumatized by the war, and however much the secret police and the censors worked to suppress it, the Lenin yard would not forget.

Ten years later, on 30 June 1980, the Party again announced drastic increases in the price of meat. Food shortages in Poland were already severe, as the NOWa author Kazimierz Brandys noted in his meticulously observed Warsaw Diary. Queues for meat would start to form outside the capital's butchers' shops by 2 a.m., with people bringing folding chairs and pillows, various types of alcohol and picnics to sustain them during their long wait. One Wednesday in June, Brandys was walking past one of these lines when uproar broke out:

A commotion had suddenly erupted in a long line in front of the meat store. People shouted, squeezed together, pressing up against the door. I saw red faces, open mouths, bulging eyes. I thought something had collapsed or exploded. No. The line had spotted a van pulling up. Meat was being delivered.

With such pressure on food supplies, the price hike sparked wildcat strikes around the country that lasted through July. If the Lenin yard were to come out, there was a chance the protests would gather new momentum.

Chojecki dropped his children with a couple of writers he knew who were staying nearby, then drove the 50 miles to Gdańsk with Milewicz and Bieliński. It was evening when they reached the blue-grey main gate of the yard. They found that a strike was indeed under way, but it wasn't about food prices, at least not directly. The action was organized by a friend of Chojecki's from KOR, Bogdan Borusewicz, who ran a small opposition group called the Free Trade Union of the Coast, centred around the underground news-sheet he edited, the *Coastal Worker*. Borusewicz had tried and failed to arrange a strike when the price rise was first announced, but now he had a new pretext: the sacking of a popular shipyard crane operator, Anna Walentynowicz. The secret police had accused Walentynowicz, a *Coastal Worker* editor, of planning illegally to commemorate the tenth anniversary of the 1970 events. As punishment, she had been dismissed a few months before her retirement fell due. Armed with this new provocation, Borusewicz had printed thousands of leaflets and posters demanding Walentynowicz's reinstatement and a general pay rise:

To the workers of the Gdansk Shipyard . . . We turn to YOU, colleagues of Anna Walentynowicz. She has worked at the shipyard since 1950. Sixteen years as a welder, later as crane operator in W-2 section, awarded bronze, silver and in 1979 Gold Cross of Merit. She has always been a model worker, what is more, one

who reacted to every wrong and injustice . . . We appeal to you,
defend the crane operator Walentynowicz.

The leaflet was signed 'editorial board of the *Coastal Worker*'.

An hour before dawn on Thursday 14 August, as ships' horns
played a lachrymose whalesong through the mist blanketing the Bay
of Hel, three young *Coastal Worker* distributors had slipped past the
yard's dozy security guards and begun putting up posters and distributing flyers. Small groups of workers had started to gather, noisily
discussing details of Walentynowicz's case. By 6 a.m., a number of
them were marching around the yard, between the hulls of the huge,
half-built ships and the cranes that towered over them like iron
giants, calling out to their mates to join in. They soon formed a strike
committee and organized a mass meeting which the yard's director,
a vigorous and not unpopular man named Klemens Gniech, sought
to address. As Gniech stood on a bulldozer to remonstrate with his
workforce, an unemployed electrician who had just slipped into the
yard over its 12-foot perimeter fence climbed up to stand behind him.
He tapped the director on the shoulder and said, 'Remember me?'

This was Lech Wałęsa, a 37-year-old, heavily moustached, 5 foot
7 inches tall collaborator with the *Coastal Worker*. A veteran of
the 1970 events, Wałęsa in the intervening years had been sacked
from a string of jobs around the Gdańsk area for his continued
activism. Chojecki had met him several times at KOR gatherings
in Warsaw and had seen no evidence that he would become the
face of the Polish revolution. He would simply 'sit in the corner
and drink his tea', Chojecki recalled. In fact Borusewicz had very
little choice when it came to selecting a public face for his movement: there was a tiny pool of activists in his Free Trade Union,
and the leader had to be someone from the working class, not an
intellectual like himself. But Borusewicz had spotted something in
the portly electrician with the rasping voice that Chojecki hadn't:
'internal charisma'. He had made an excellent choice, as it turned
out, and Wałęsa would prove an inspired leader. He was a tough
negotiator, and Polish workers felt he was one of them.

Word of the strike rippled through the Gdańsk conurbation known as the TriCity area, and by the time of Chojecki's arrival on Friday night other groups had come out in sympathy, including the Paris Commune Shipyard in Gdynia and the regional train and tram drivers. Chojecki, who was drawn to political tension like a moth to a lightbulb, realized this was where he had to be. Early on Saturday morning he went back to Dębki, fed his children and took them to the beach, then returned to the shipyard that afternoon. He arrived in time to hear Wałęsa announce that all their demands had been met and the strike committee had voted to end the action. Yard director Gniech hurried to relay this news over the works radio, instructing everyone to leave the premises by 6 p.m.

Delegates from the workers who had come out in sympathy were furious. What about *their* demands? Without the mighty shipyard they were nothing. They rounded on Wałęsa. 'If you abandon us we'll be lost,' shouted Henryka Krzywonos, who led the bus and tram drivers. 'Buses can't face tanks! They will crush us like bugs!'

Wałęsa realized the strike committee's mistake, but by this point the management had cut the power to the PA system, and the strikers had begun to drift out of the gates. Chojecki sensed their opportunity slipping away with the workforce. At that moment, Walentynowicz and two other women from the *Coastal Worker* group, the shipyard nurse Alina Pienkowska and the teenage kiosk attendant Ewa Ossowska, tried to stem the ebb. Pienkowska – who had learned of the democratic opposition's existence while visiting her uncle in Manchester, where she read *Kultura* for the first time – grabbed a bullhorn and climbed on a barrel. She loved to wear bright colours, and people in the crowd that day could pick out her candy-pink blouse even at a great distance.

'Close the gates!' Pienkowska shouted at the dwindling crowd. 'We are organizing a solidarity strike!'

Chojecki stood up to support the women, climbing on one of the electric trolleys that carried equipment round the yard. Fewer than 2,000 people remained, but it was a larger audience than he had ever addressed before. He gave it his best shot. He was Mirosław

Chojecki, he told them. He was a member of KOR and he had a lot of experience of dealing with the communists. They should all remain in the yard. The strike must go on!

People seemed to recognize him, and some of them listened. Later, he understood it was the power of radio: when he was sitting in jail, Radio Free Europe and the BBC had regularly broadcast his name.

The activists' pleas stemmed the flow of departing workers. When the gates closed there were just a few hundred left, but the strike had been saved.

That night, Chojecki toured factories in the TriCity area, spreading the news that the shipyard would remain out 'in solidarity' with other workers around the country. That day wasn't the first time the S-word had been used in connection with Polish politics, but Wałęsa would later state that the broad-based opposition movement called Solidarity was born that evening, when the strike evolved from a local success to a protest 'in support of other factories and business enterprises, large and small, in need of our protection'.

Borusewicz, Pienkowska and others on the strike committee drew up a new list of demands overnight, based on ideas KOR had been developing for several years, and the following day, Sunday, Wałęsa announced the creation of the Inter-Enterprise Strike Committee, which claimed to represent 600 Polish factories. They produced a list of twenty-one demands, which they wrote in dark red ships' paint on two plywood boards that they hung at the entrance to the yard. What had begun with a call for the reinstatement of a crane driver was now a national stand-off between the people and the authorities. More than a list of workers' grievances, the demands represented a charter for all of Poland, and a new milestone in the Soviet world.

First, the committee called for the legalization of independent trade unions, with no ties to the Party or to their employers – these had never existed in the Eastern Bloc before. Second, they called for the right to strike. The third demand dealt with censorship. It was too much, Borusewicz believed, to call for its complete abolition. 'You know what happened when they abolished censorship in Czechoslovakia in 1968?' he asked the committee. That year, as every Pole knew, the Soviets had sent tanks in to crush the Prague Spring, leading to hundreds of deaths and the demise of the pro-democracy movement. The result was a watered down demand but still a bold one:

> Respect for the freedom of speech, print and publication guaranteed by the Constitution of the PRL [Polish People's Republic], and therefore no repression of independent publications and access to the mass media for representatives of all denominations.

Further demands called for the release of all political prisoners, full disclosure to the public of 'information on the socio-economic situation', guarantees on maternity leave, pension rights, pay increases and more.

Chojecki would support the Inter-Enterprise Strike Committee in the way he knew best: through publishing. The government had tried to keep the shipyard action secret, cutting phone lines to the north and ordering the media not to report it, so the strikers needed to get word out. Chojecki, Bieliński and Milewicz created the *Solidarity Strike Information Bulletin*, the official organ of the striking Lenin yard, to spread the news. At first they printed on a home-made silkscreen frame; later, when they learned that an activist in the nearby Paris Commune Shipyard had simply broken into the works copy shop to use the professional equipment there, they decided to do the same. The first edition of the *Bulletin* – four smudgy typewritten pages – was published on 23 August. It would appear once or twice a day, in runs of up to 40,000 copies, carrying news of the dispute, letters of support from around the world, strike poems, interviews and reportage.

As negotiations began between the strikers and the regime in the shipyard's Health and Safety Hall, Chojecki shuttled between Warsaw and the coast, arranging distribution and publication of other strike news-sheets and training people to use the presses.

NOWa produced thousands of flyers for the giant tractor factory at Ursus, on the outskirts of Warsaw, and when that plant went on strike too, NOWa printers joined forces with the workers there to produce another strike bulletin. Newspapers weren't the only way to spread the word. KOR had a line to Radio Free Europe, which broadcast news of any industrial action back to Poland from the West, bolstering the strikers and triggering further outbreaks.

As the days passed, more and more of Poland's industrial complexes came out, threatening the stability of the regime. The yard by now had the atmosphere of a Woodstock or Glastonbury, with young people strumming guitars, the Beatles' 'Yellow Submarine' blaring out over the works radio and flowers sprouting from the main gate, along with banners and flags and photographs of Pope John Paul II. Each day, crowds of supporters gathered in the narrow street outside and on nearby waste ground covered with rubble. Inevitably, the secret police were out in force too, following people who left the yard, which made travelling between Gdańsk and Warsaw risky for Chojecki. A week into the strike, they stopped him and asked for his papers. When they realized who they'd caught, the police arrested him, and he was taken once more to Mokotów jail.

On the morning of Sunday 31 August, the eighteenth day of the strike, the talks were reaching their denouement. Almost all the committee's demands had been accepted. A famous victory was at hand. Thousands of well-wishers pressed up against the main gate, and when the government delegation arrived, led by a deputy prime minister, they had to run a gauntlet of demonstrators, then push through the scrum of reporters to reach the Health and Safety Hall. The shipyard had made headlines around the world. All over Poland and across Eastern Europe, in Moscow and in Washington, Paris and London, people waited for news that an agreement had been reached. At 11.40 a.m., the negotiations began again, and the few remaining issues were resolved. Then, at the last minute, Alina Pienkowska stood before the microphone to bring a final issue to the table. Mirosław Chojecki, who had come to help show the workers how to produce their Solidarity newsletter, had been arrested while leaving Gdańsk, she said, in a trembling, determined voice. Since he was working for the Inter-Enterprise Strike Committee he should be immune from prosecution as the others were. 'Could the deputy prime minister speak on this matter?'

Wałęsa weighed in. He was ready to sign the whole protocol, but first the deputy prime minister should talk to Warsaw to find out what was happening with those who had been arrested. He ordered a twenty-minute recess.

Chojecki was sitting in his cell early that afternoon when a prison official called him in.

'Mr Mirosław,' the man told him, 'you are free to go.'

The prisoner was surprised, not least because it was Sunday, when nothing much ever happened in the Polish People's Republic.

'Why?'

Because negotiations in Gdańsk were near their conclusion, the man said, and as part of the deal all political prisoners were being released.

Chojecki was in no rush, he told the officer. He didn't have the keys to his apartment and had no idea where his wife Magda was, so he could be locked out. If they put him out on the street, he wouldn't know where to go.

'Don't worry,' the man said, 'we'll drive you wherever you want.' He held out the telephone. 'Please,' he said, 'speak to the shipyard and tell them you are free.'

'But I'm still sitting here in your office.'

'Make the call! It's a question of the agreement, whether it will be signed or not.'

They drove him home, and somehow he found a way into his apartment. Only then did he phone the shipyard to confirm that he was out.

A few minutes earlier, the negotiators had assembled for the last time on the platform in the Health and Safety Hall. Sitting next to a plaster statue of Lenin, who was clasping a book, presumably his own *State and Revolution*, beneath the giant emblems of the Christian cross and the Polish eagle, they took turns to sign the document that

would be known to history as the Gdańsk Agreement, Wałęsa using a souvenir pen the length of a policeman's truncheon that carried an image of the pope. As well as accepting independent trade unions and the right to strike, the government committed to 'the constitutional guarantee of freedom of speech, the press and publication, including freedom for independent publishers'.

The text of the Gdańsk accords would be published in the thirteenth and final issue of the *Solidarity Strike Information Bulletin*, along with the statute of the new trade union, which was to be formally launched by Wałęsa two weeks later. Solidarity would become far more than the first independent labour organization in the Eastern Bloc: it would be a mass social movement, unique in the Soviet sphere.

There was an irony at the heart of the Gdańsk Agreement. A ruling communist party that justified its existence by claiming to represent the proletariat had succumbed to the demand of that proletariat that a different organization should speak for them, calling into question the Party-state's whole purpose. It was a triumph for human dignity and freedom, and a blow against Soviet power and communist ideologues everywhere. Milovan Djilas, the Yugoslav political analyst whose work was published in the underground, described it as 'the most significant development in Eastern Europe since the Second World War'. Uncensored publishing had played a key role. The free trades union movement in Gdańsk was built around the *Coastal Worker*; its footsoldiers were the paper's editors and distributors. Blotchy flyers and photocopied news-sheets such as the *Solidarity Strike Information Bulletin* had helped spread word of the action around the country: without them, the industrial complexes around Poland would have remained isolated. The very idea of 'solidarity' depended on the workers' ability to pool knowledge.

The following night, 1 September, was Chojecki's thirty-first birthday. He held a party at his apartment in northern Warsaw to celebrate their win. So many people packed into the small space, it was almost impossible to raise a toast.

'I had argued that the masses in Poland were passive and in danger of being Sovietized,' Kazimierz Brandys wrote after the agreement was signed. 'I was mistaken. I underestimated their hidden reserves. We awoke to a new society from one day to the next.'

Poland blossomed over the next fifteen months, living through an exuberant period known as the Carnival of Solidarity. People joined the union in droves, swelling its membership to ten million, a quarter of the population and more than three times the number of Party members. Although the Gdańsk Agreement was never wholly implemented, where before 1980 underground publishers had been harassed, arrested and imprisoned, they now occupied a semi-legal grey zone. It was a time, as the poet Stanisław Barańczak put it, when 'the notion of "illegal" publishing . . . lost all of its nega-tive connotations'.

Chojecki worked to push the new freedoms as far as he could, expanding the publishing capacity of the regional and local Solidarity structures that sprang up across Poland, sharing NOWa's expertise and equipment, organizing training sessions and donating presses. Many NOWa personnel would move into the frontline of the new Solidarity publishing enterprises. By the end of 1980, Solidarity duplicating machines regularly printed some 300 serial titles, many of them union weeklies, published in a few thousand copies, which were read out on the shop floors of the factories. In 1981, this number would quadruple. There was an avalanche of new books too: independent Polish publishers produced around 2,500 titles by the end of 1981, including the Soviet Bloc's first unabridged edition of *The Gulag Archipelago*. At the end of October 1980, NOWa launched its hundredth publication, Brandys's *A Warsaw Diary*, at an open gathering of 200 intellectuals, activists, printers and distributors, where the author signed copies. Soon afterwards, as Chojecki was increasingly distracted by Solidarity business, his friend Grzegorz Boguta took the reins of the publishing house NOWa.

Since starting their activities in 1976, Chojecki and the underground publishers had relied on allies in the West for support. This arrived in the shape of presses, inks, matrices, spare parts and 'master copies' of particular works, smuggled into Poland through a variety of routes, in secret compartments built into cars and vans, hidden in travellers' luggage or in hiding holes on the Moscow–Paris transcontinental sleeper trains that stopped in Warsaw. In June 1979, a Polish optician in Sweden, Marian Kaleta, had spied a Polish yacht in Malmö harbour and invited the skipper for a beer. Between them, Kaleta and Captain 'Edek' Waszkiewicz would establish one of the most effective new routes into Poland, sailing supplies across the Baltic in small boats. Edek would carry bootleg Polish vodka and cigarettes on his outward journey, and take home books and printing presses for NOWa. During the Carnival, when the rules covering banned publications weren't always clear even to the border guards, the Baltic yacht trade took off like never before. Many of the books that reached Poland fed 'Solidarity libraries', collections of uncensored material in factories and workplaces which were protected by the union. At the end of 1981, Chojecki estimated that there were 3,000 such libraries in the country. The effect of all this publishing freedom was that censorship in Poland began to break down. By the spring of 1981, a third of all Poles had access to Solidarity publications. The proportion in the cities was far higher.

But the tectonic shift taking place in Poland did not go unnoticed where it most mattered, in the Kremlin, where General Secretary Leonid Brezhnev led a creaking gerontocracy. Under Brezhnev's foreign policy doctrine, no country could be allowed to escape the family of communist nations for fear that the whole system would collapse. Troops would intervene where necessary, as they had in Hungary in 1956, Czechoslovakia in 1968 and Afghanistan in 1979.

Through the autumn of 1980 and into winter, Western spy satellites picked up armoured Warsaw Pact divisions manoeuvring on Poland's borders, while Poles of all political stripes kept one eye anxiously on Moscow.

Would the pendulum swing again? If so, when?

6

The Deal

As more and more books were published . . . there was one consequence that should not surprise us: in Rome, under Alexander VI, the censor got to work. Power, which has its intuitions, soon recognised its enemy.

J. B. Priestley, *Literature and Western Man*

How difficult it is for totalitarian systems to combat the word, which slips over borders more rapidly and effectively than people on the outside imagine.

Czesław Miłosz, *Native Realm*

In mid-October 1981, Chojecki was speeding west along the potholed Polish highway that led from Warsaw to the Baltic ferry port at Świnoujście, the 27-year-old NOWa designer Iwona Rajpert by his side. The publisher was in high spirits. For the first time, Frankfurt Book Fair, the publishing industry's single truly global event, had invited Solidarity, NOWa and other underground publishers to participate, and Chojecki and Boguta had been picked to lead a delegation. Boguta would fly to the west, but Chojecki had chosen to drive so he could carry plenty of books, and he was taking the long route via Sweden to dodge the notorious East German border. He and Rajpert had packed so much literature into his little Volkswagen Jetta that the vehicle swayed beneath the weight of material jammed into its boot, pushed into its footwells, stacked on the seats and piled up to the roof. As a precaution, he had armed himself with letters of authorization from Solidarity's leadership, including Wałęsa, but when they reached Świnoujście they passed easily through the border. Soon they were making their way south from Sweden.

Frankfurt Book Fair. A giant literary marketplace that traced its roots back five centuries, to the moment Johannes Gutenberg invented the printing press in nearby Mainz and launched an information revolution. Books before then had been copied out by hand, a task so laborious and expensive that only a few thousand volumes existed in all of Europe's libraries. Gutenberg's machine, which transferred ink to paper using movable metal type and a wooden press, could produce 250 pages an hour, and over the next half-century, as copycat devices sprang up across Germany, Italy, France and England, printers turned out books in their millions. Costs plummeted, literacy levels soared and the scientific, cultural and religious ideas of the Renaissance spread around the globe. It was natural, after Gutenberg, for the books trade to meet here in Frankfurt. Nowadays, for one week each October, in the million square feet of the city's concrete exhibition halls, and in the bars, conference centres and suites of the city's grandest hotels, thousands of publishers, editors and agents pitch, read and plot, party long into the night, then drag themselves out of bed in the morning to start all over again. Frankfurt is frantic, exhausting, outrageously expensive – and absolutely vital to the lifeblood of the global publishing business.

In the 1980s, Frankfurt played another role, too, as an arena for the cultural Cold War, the only place where the competing philosophies of East and West went toe to toe. In the red corner were the large, official stands given over to state-approved publishers from the Eastern Bloc, sent to present a rose-tinted account of arts and culture flourishing in the workers' paradise across the frontier. In the anti-red corner were the smaller, cheaper stands of the dissidents, who worked to demonstrate that the opposite was true, that communism was choking the

intellectual and economic life out of them. Both sides were secretly supported by intelligence agencies, which meant spies, informers and agents flocked to Frankfurt too, to observe the enemy at first hand.

Chojecki and the delegates from Poland had a small booth in Halle 5, the international hall, which they shared with leading émigré Polish publishers, including Polonia Book Fund, the Literary Institute and Aneks. A sign above the stand read 'Solidarność. From prison cells to independent publishing: the story of uncensored books in Poland'. In this crucial, Carnival year, the dissidents were the talk of the fair. There might have been new releases from Western heavyweights such as Doris Lessing, Arthur C. Clarke and Frederick Forsyth, but it was the political struggle in Poland that the *New York Times* correspondent picked out as the major theme, along with *The Black Book of Polish Censorship* as one of the hot properties of the year. This 'handbook used by Poland's censors . . . replete with the arcane lore of Eastern Europe's cultural lords' had been snapped up by Random

House, the paper reported. Looking on from the vantage point of the 'Uncensored' stand, a euphoric Marian Kaleta observed that Poland and Solidarity were 'the number one issue in the world'. Their books were celebrated like 'holy relics', and their presence at the fair signified nothing less than the 'greatest success of the free Polish word since 1945'. Such a mob gathered around their little booth that the organizers warned the Poles they were a threat to public safety.

What no one in the milling Frankfurt crowds knew was that many of the publishers at this stand were supported, either wholly or in part, by the CIA. A sign on the back wall listed six publishing houses: Polonia Book Fund, the Literary Institute, the Polish Cultural Foundation, Libella, Aneks and Odnowa. Of these, Polonia Book Fund was a CIA front, the Literary Institute was run by the CIA asset QRBERETTA, and the Polish Cultural Foundation, Libella, Aneks and Odnowa were all part of Minden's ILC network. In fact, the independent publishers' entire presence at Frankfurt had been organized and paid for by the Polonia Book Fund – in other words, by the CIA.

The Polish dissidents would meet regularly at the Frankfurt fair after 1981, and the doyen of these gatherings was Jerzy Giedroyc. Giedroyc liked to book into a three-star hotel in Kronberg, a short distance outside the city, while the other, younger publishers and distributors dossed down in shared rooms in the hostel across the road. Often the young delegates would stay out in the city's many nightclubs and bars until the early hours, but the Editor would summon them to breakfast at 8 a.m. all the same. It was Giedroyc, too, whom the SB agents most liked to spy upon and photograph.

Chojecki had met Giedroyc before, at Czesław Miłosz's Nobel Prize ceremony in Stockholm the previous December, and in some ways they had been working together for years, since NOWa reprinted many Literary Institute titles with the Editor's permission. But it was this meeting in Frankfurt that marked the start of a deep and enduring partnership, where Giedroyc would act as mentor and cheerleader for Chojecki, while Mirek gave the older man access to a new generation of dissidents in the homeland he hadn't set foot in for decades. Chojecki was aware of the rumours about Giedroyc's backers in the United States, as everyone was, but he never saw this as a problem. For him, Poland was caught in a life-or-death struggle between superpowers with opposing social systems, and he knew which side he was on: the side of democracy, freedom and Ronald Reagan, who had succeeded Carter as US president in 1981. Chojecki even sometimes called Reagan 'the boss'. In the context of the Cold War, the idea of working alongside US intelligence assets didn't unsettle him at all. 'If somebody from the CIA was in my circles,' he said later, 'for sure, I wouldn't throw them out.'

Giedroyc had been making plans for the young publisher for months in the run-up to Frankfurt, singing Chojecki's praises to his influential friend Jan Nowak in Washington. He was 'one of the few people in whom I have confidence', Giedroyc wrote, 'a great organizer', and far more effective an opposition figure than Wałęsa. He was especially interested in Chojecki and Boguta's idea to use the new freedoms in Poland to revolutionize the way they all worked. Since there were few barriers now to publishing prohibited titles there, why bother with the expensive business of smuggling them in from the West? It made far more sense to print and sell the books in Poland, where the target audience lived, and where the average monthly wage was just $20–$30, which meant costs would be 'lower than in Hong Kong', as Giedroyc put it. If there was need for a particular title in the West, they could ship a few hundred copies out via Sweden, effectively running the book programme in reverse. Any profits they made from Polish sales could be placed in a *Kultura* fund, which Giedroyc would oversee, to promote the independent press in the East.

The prospect of unmediated access to his audience after so many decades of smuggling hugely excited Giedroyc, and that week in Frankfurt the Literary Institute signed a contract with NOWa in which both entities agreed to represent the other's interests on their side of the Iron Curtain. The new method of working presented opportunities not just for the Literary Institute, but for the whole book programme. It was a 'fundamental breakthrough in the relations between the émigré and national opposition', Giedroyc told Nowak with delight, '[which] increases our influence in the country'. It was vital that they pursue this course now, since no one knew how long the Soviets would let the Solidarity Carnival last: 'In the present situation, independent and uncontrolled publishing houses and organizations are the only guarantee against an increasingly dark future.' Would Nowak arrange an invitation for Chojecki from Congress, which could propose that he come to the US to 'arrange publishing issues, supply of books' or suchlike? They could hardly refuse him a visa then.

Nowak would. At the end of the Frankfurt fair, Chojecki agreed that he should try to get to America. He could raise funds there for the Solidarity press and source paper, but he would also go to Washington to see Nowak and explain in person how the new system of publishing in Poland could work. Giedroyc would pay for Chojecki's flight, and between them Nowak and Brzezinski would sort out his visa. In the interim, Giedroyc would also arrange the young publisher's first direct contact with an important American visitor who was shortly to arrive in France: George Minden.

Minden had landed in Paris in October, on his usual biannual tour of Europe, when he met and debriefed the more important associates of the book programme. While away from Manhattan he would dispense with his usual frugality, wining and dining his distributors and publishers in some of Europe's most famous coffee shops and restaurants. One of his favourite places in Paris was the Regina Hotel, which had been popular with celebrities from Audrey Hepburn to Coco Chanel thanks to its central location, next to the Louvre, and to its breathtaking views over the Seine towards the Eiffel Tower. Minden's principal Paris operation, the Russian-language book distributor Centre Internationale Littéraire – a straight French translation of the ILC's name – was just a few hundred yards away from here on the Rue Saint-Honoré, but for meetings with his Polish contacts he preferred to use a venerable bookshop on the Left Bank.

The words 'Librairie Polonaise' – Polish Bookstore – stood out in large red capital letters above the jostling traffic on the Boulevard Saint-Germain. The shop was small but perfectly sited, since these narrow streets, huddled around the bell tower of the church of Saint-Germain-des-Prés, form the heart of literary life in the capital. Throw a croissant in any of the dozens of cafés and bars that spill out on to the pavements here and you will likely hit a writer, a publisher or a literary tourist. A few doors down from the Librairie Polonaise stands the Deux Magots, where Ernest Hemingway drank sherry with James Joyce, and where, later, Simone de Beauvoir and Jean-Paul Sartre would sit brooding in one corner while Juliette Gréco sang in another. Next door, in the Café de Flore, Guillaume Apollinaire and André Breton developed surrealism.

The Librairie Polonaise, which was the oldest Polish bookshop anywhere in the world, had witnessed these comings and goings from its vantage point at number 123 Boulevard Saint-German for the better part of a century. By 1981, it was a growing hub for CIA book distribution in Paris. Travellers from Poland who arrived at the store were allowed to choose a few titles for free, provided they told a shop assistant they intended to take them home. The assistant would note down the titles and prices, along with a small amount of information about the 'target', such as their profession and the area of Poland where they lived, and every month the bookshop's manager, Elżbieta Rybczyńska, would send the bill along with the details they had gathered to New York. Rybczyńska was a new appointment, and her energetic stewardship meant the business was growing rapidly, in large part thanks to the CIA: by the mid-1980s, the Agency would be responsible for half the store's annual turnover. Her financial dependence on Minden meant Rybczyńska saw him as her guide and boss, and he would use her office for important meetings – including his first encounter with Chojecki and Boguta that November.

Slipping through the glass door from the Boulevard, the Poles entered a dark-walled room crowded with competing dust jackets and filled with the familiar bookshop scent of glue and new paper. Even inside, the shudder and honk of passing traffic felt too close. It receded only as they climbed the winding staircase to Rybczyńska's private office, where they would meet Minden. The ILC president was sixty years old then. Hazel-eyed, with greying hair swept back from a widow's peak, he could have slipped from the pages of a Le Carré novel. He was smart, polyglot, hard-working and attentive to detail. Chojecki didn't know exactly who he represented: Giedroyc had said something about him being a rich philanthropist with a passion for East European publishing, although it's difficult to believe Mirek, the arch-conspirator, couldn't see through this thin cover. For his part, Minden was excited to learn that the famous NOWa publishers had arrived in the West, writing in his diary when he heard the news: 'Boguta and Chojecki live at Maisons Laffitte!' Now, in his usual manner, he pumped them for information while giving little away about himself.

Was NOWa truly independent? he asked. What was its legal position in Poland? Its relationship to Solidarity? Its editorial formula? What were their most popular titles?

The Poles responded candidly. NOWa was semi-legal, Boguta said, and he wanted to bring it fully into the open by moving operations into the Ursus tractor plant outside Warsaw, where printers and presses would be protected by the workforce, the ultimate arbiter in the communist state. They did a lot of work for Solidarity, but this was a productive time for NOWa itself too. They aimed to have half original commissions and half reprints and translations, and he reckoned they would publish a hundred titles that year, and 200 in 1982, with a minimum print run of 6,000 per edition. Their biggest title at that time was *Adventures with History* by Marian Brandys, Kazimierz's brother, an account of the secret police's non-stop harassment of his family and his wife, Halina Mikołajska, a famous Polish actress who had joined KOR.

Minden especially warmed to Chojecki, who at thirty-two

seemed 'mature' and 'careful', qualities the ILC president valued highly. He was alive to the threat from Moscow, but told Minden they couldn't afford to be cowed since that would paralyse them into inaction. He had big plans for a new, independent history of Poland post-1918, of which he hoped to print 100,000 copies – an enormous number for an uncensored book – and agreed that Minden could order a few hundred to be run off at Aneks in London for distribution in the West. They also discussed the growing number of uncensored 'flying libraries' in Poland. It had been Minden's ambition since the 1960s to develop repositories of independent books that would circulate behind the Iron Curtain. Now these were being established in Polish factories and workplaces in huge numbers, under Solidarity's protection, and Minden and his network were busily helping stock them. Even government libraries were requesting unlicensed literature, Chojecki told him.

Boguta made a naked play for CIA business, telling Minden how NOWa could undercut Giedroyc or anyone else in the West because of its cheap labour costs. 'I offered Minden a better deal,' he recalled, 'better results for every dollar invested.' By the end of the meeting, the American had agreed to buy 4,000 copies of NOWa's forthcoming title *Tumult and Spectrum*, a series of conversations with Józef Czapski, which the publisher would distribute in Poland on the ILC's behalf. In return Minden would pay $2,500, with $1,000 up front.

As the Poles walked out through the shop, past a display of NOWa titles Kaleta had recently delivered from Poland, both sides could congratulate themselves on their deal. Two thousand five hundred dollars was an eye-watering sum in Poland, enough to pay eight full-time staff for a whole year. Minden, meanwhile, had established direct contact with a publisher in the Eastern Bloc who would print and distribute material on the CIA's behalf, greatly reducing his costs. Everyone seemed overjoyed with the new printing paradigm, even Giedroyc, who stood to lose out as publishing operations moved east. After the meeting, Boguta spoke with Rudzki in New York, to run through the details, and made a very good impression, as Rudzki told Giedroyc. The ILC man was also looking forward to Chojecki's arrival in New York, where they would discuss ways to build on the new system.

Giedroyc replied that he thought cooperation with the young Poles would prove very fruitful, and that printing in Poland would cost the ILC next to nothing.

In Paris, Chojecki donated his Volkswagen to his friend Boguta, to take back to Poland, but first Grzegorz would drive Mirek out to the airport. What neither of them knew, as they said their goodbyes that day in late November, was that all their publishing plans would come to naught, and that this would be the last time they would see each other for the better part of a decade.

As Boguta said later, 'We had different histories.'

PART TWO

WAR

1981–1985

7

The Night of the General

Pietrek, what sort of man are you?
Tell me, how come
We have to carry you to the ambulance
With a bullet in the head?

Poem for the Wujek miners, Mazovia Weekly

A nation of thirty-six million, in the middle of Europe, was cordoned off from the world, atomized into cell-like blocks, so that each could be terrorized and repressed individually. A regime incapable of feeding its population, incapable of supplying spare parts to keep its factories running, was still able to turn an entire country into an internment camp in a single night.

Józef Lebenbaum, War Against the Nation

Helena Łuczywo was such a workaholic, she and her team of mostly women reporters were dubbed the 'Dark Circles' for the panda rings that perpetually surrounded their sleep-deprived eyes. Small, formidable, razor-sharp, in little more than a year she had built the Solidarity Press Agency she led into one of the most reliable sources of information in the country. She was well aware, in the second week of December 1981, that a new crisis was coming. The Soviets had been conducting combat exercises on Poland's borders, hardliners in the Party were calling for military rule, while an increasingly fractious Solidarity had threatened a general strike. In recent days, the press agency had begun picking up reports of unusual military activity inside Poland. Convoys of tanks, trucks and armoured vehicles had been spotted creeping out of their bases and deploying around the country. Reservists and militia cadets were being called up. Rumours flew. Were these the first signs of the long-awaited crackdown? Was this the Soviet intervention everyone anticipated?

On the evening of Saturday 12 December, Łuczywo went with her husband Witek to the cinema, to see *Shivers*, a coming-of-age story about the Stalinist indoctrination of a young boy: only in Poland, of all the Eastern Bloc nations, were such things possible. They emerged around 10 p.m. on to the broad avenue of Marszałkowska Street. The temperature was dropping, and the light snowfall had started to thicken, blurring the city's hard edges and redoubling the thin, sodium glare of the streetlamps. Helena thought she should stop by the office to check what was going on, so they walked the short distance north and east, past the Church of the Holiest Saviour, with its gun-barrel spires holding heaven at bay, to the union's slab-faced Warsaw headquarters on Mokotowska Street.

For ten years now, the Łuczywos had moved in the same young activist circles as Chojecki. They had been on the same protests, gone to the same house parties, dated people from the same crowd, drunk red wine made from the same Gamza grape and woken up with the same hangovers. Where Helena had found success editing the underground *Worker* newspaper, Witek was a guru of independent printing. His most famous innovation in the early days involved attaching one side of a silkscreen frame to a lampshade with a rubber band, so that it lifted itself when a page had been inked, cutting the number of printers required by a third. He'd tried all sorts of stretchy materials for this job, before plumping for some knicker elastic donated by his friend Barbara Feliszko. Opposition publishing had come a long way since then, and while Helena now ran the union's news agency, Witek ran print production operations in the capital.

When they entered the Solidarity building, a score of employees were still inside. It was a busy night thanks to the National Solidarity Commission meeting taking place at the Lenin Shipyard in Gdańsk: the Warsaw office had been tasked with disseminating decisions made there to the international media. Witek wasn't keen to hang about. They had left their eight-year-old daughter, Łucja, with Helena's parents, and he thought they should be getting back. But Helena was preoccupied, calling friends and contacts.

The military activity seemed to have increased. Troops had been spotted heading towards the capital, and a group of 300 militiamen had raided a cinema. At around 11.30 p.m., a telex machine chattering out an update from Gdańsk cut out halfway through the message. They checked the connections, nothing seemed to be amiss, and tried a second machine, but that wouldn't work either. All the telexes were down. Then the phones went dead, one by one. The last line dropped out at 11.42 p.m.

Two people went downstairs to check that the front doors were locked. The other staff huddled in a room to decide what to do next. Within moments, a roar of engines split the night-time quiet and more than a dozen police wagons appeared, charging towards the building from either end of Mokotowska Street. The trucks belonged to the hated Zomo paramilitaries, and soon they were spilling shock troops dressed in full riot gear, with overalls, shields, truncheons and helmets. The two Solidarity workers at the front of the building raced back upstairs, taking the steps four at a time. 'The Zomos are here!' they shouted.

Helena was scared. She knew they had to get out fast. There were no Zomos yet at the rear of the block. They must seize their chance, she told her colleagues, and escape through the back.

She was amazed when they said they wanted to stay put.

It was ridiculous, totally irrational! Helena pleaded. 'What good will it do to wait? They'll just arrest you. They might beat you! Let's go!'

They wouldn't move.

The building now began to echo with the sound of men attacking the steel and glass front door with fire axes. Realizing they had run out of time, she and Witek raced down to the rear exit. The last words she heard from her colleagues were, 'Helena! Get back. They're coming!'

'Why on earth would I go back?' she thought. 'So stupid!'

They burst out into the night, scanning the dark, tree-lined square. Police trucks were now pulling up here, too. To escape they would have to pass through a gate in a fence, but there was a man standing in front of it.

Ubek, Helena thought. Secret police.

Witek wasn't so sure. Either way, they had little to lose by asking him straight out. No, the man said, he wasn't police, he was the janitor of the residential block next door, and yes, he could hide them.

He took them to an apartment that overlooked the rear of the Solidarity building. They turned out the lights and watched as more militia entered by the door they had just used to escape. In a matter of minutes, the Zomos had control of the whole place. The trade unionists would be loaded on to trucks and taken to the cells at the city police headquarters, then shipped out to specially pre-pared internment camps. Watching through the net curtains, Witek felt they were in the swashbuckling movie *Captain Blood*, spying on the enemy while trying to judge the best time to leave their hiding place.

Police circled their block, but none entered. At around 2.30 a.m., during a lull in the Zomo presence, the Łuczywos slipped back out on to the street.

It wasn't safe to go home – they later found out that police had broken down the door of their apartment and kept coming back to see if the couple had returned. They decided instead to go to Helena's parents, who lived a few streets away, but when they got there they thought it would be too dangerous to approach her mother and father's apartment themselves, so they woke up a friend, Paweł Śpiewak, who lived in the same building. When they told him what had happened he said they should warn the only individual with any official authority outside the Party in Poland, the Catholic primate Józef Glemp. They set out on the long walk across the city to the primate's palace.

It was three or four in the morning now, and after the initial burst of police activity, Helena found Warsaw eerily quiet. When they reached the primate's residence no one answered the door, so they stood looking through the gates, trying to think what to do. It was still snowing, and large flakes fell thickly, almost audibly, on the archbishop's cobbled yard.

They realized at that moment that they had to go into hiding.

Similar scenes were unfolding across Poland, as 80,000 soldiers and 30,000 police, equipped with 1,750 tanks and 1,900 armoured cars, launched a surprise overnight invasion of their own country. Under immense pressure from Moscow to crush Solidarity, the Polish premier, General Wojciech Jaruzelski, had made a desperate offer to stave off intervention: let the Poles crack down on the opposition movement themselves. The Soviets had agreed, and Jaruzelski had spent more than a year making preparations. To hold the general's feet to the fire, the Kremlin had ordered large-scale military exercises in Poland and on its frontiers, and sent massed

delegations of KGB and army top brass, including the supreme commander of Warsaw Pact forces in Europe, Marshal Viktor Kulikov, to oversee the plans. By the autumn of 1981, the Soviets were so impatient they were ready to sack Jaruzelski and continue with the next general down the line. Jaruzelski had to move, and if the Polish military failed to crush resistance themselves, Soviet, Czech and East German divisions were standing by.

The general had issued the final order to go at 1.20 p.m. that Saturday, and the major pieces in the heavily war-gamed battle plan started to roll into position. At 10 p.m., a Soviet transport plane landed in Warsaw carrying Kulikov and forty senior Soviet officers. Half an hour later, 5,000 soldiers and SB officers launched Operation Azalea, which sent armed men into 451 telephone exchanges all over Poland to shut down communications. Broadcasters were seized too: commandos strode into radio and television stations with guns cocked and bayonets fixed, and switched off the power. Announcers at Polish television just had time to say 'Thank you. Good night' after cutting off the evening movie *St Michael Had a Rooster* midway through. Other troops sealed the borders, erected checkpoints on major roads and parked armoured vehicles in strategic positions – including, as one news photographer spotted, in front of a cinema screening *Apocalypse Now*. At midnight, the police launched Operation Fir Tree, and arrest squads armed with crowbars set out with lists of targets, working their way from apartment to apartment in the darkness. At 1 a.m., in the Belweder Palace, on the edge of Warsaw's beautiful Łazienki Park, the country's supreme constitutional body, the Council of State, declared a 'state of war' and passed all power to Jaruzelski's new junta, the Military Council of National Salvation, since this was a coup as well as an invasion.

All that night and over the following days, police and militia officers splintered door frames and led away activists, writers and even the odd Party member deemed insufficiently loyal to Moscow. Some were carted off in their pyjamas. Sometimes both parents were taken, which meant the children were too, to be dumped in special children's detention centres. The mass night-time arrests hit particularly hard in a nation where many remembered the massacres and death camps of the war, and in some cases the security forces deliberately played on those echoes. Prisoners were driven out to quiet spots in the woods and ordered to stand in front of ranks of men with guns. One detainee recalled trying to comfort an eminent philosopher as they were loaded into a wagon. 'Don't worry,' the philosopher said, 'I have already been in a camp, in Auschwitz.'

Jerzy Zieleński was in hospital that night. A 53-year-old journalist and veteran of the Warsaw Uprising, Zieleński had often told friends that he could never again face days like the ones he had lived through in the war. He had recently been appointed launch editor of a new Solidarity newspaper, *Mazovia Weekly*, but he struggled with anxiety and depression – 'Am I up to it?' he would ask colleagues. 'Will I manage to make a good newspaper?' He had spent the past week in a clinic on Hoża Street. When a couple of friends came that night to tell him that Zomos had broken into the Solidarity headquarters and were rounding up activists and intellectuals, he waited till they'd left, then got out of bed, put a coat over his pyjamas and leapt from a high window to his death.

Many of the arrested were taken to Białołęka, a maximum-security detention centre to the north of Warsaw, where a whole floor had been prepared to receive them. Grzegorz Boguta had been out for dinner that evening with his wife, Magda. They had agreed to swap apartments for the night with Magda's parents, who were babysitting the kids, and at midnight were lying in her parents' bed when they heard a knock at the door. Magda flew into a rage: he'd only just returned from the West and already his activist friends were waking them up in the middle of the night! Don't worry, Grzegorz told her, they wouldn't answer it. Fifteen minutes later, a key turned in the lock, and three policemen appeared, followed by Magda's father, who had panicked when the arrest squad arrived at the Bogutas' apartment and brought them straight round. Now it was Grzegorz's turn to be furious: 'Why couldn't you have told them you don't know where we are?'

Boguta would be joined in Białołęka by his friend Adam

Michnik, of NOWa's editorial board. A hush descended over the city centre police station when Michnik was brought in, bruised and bloodied, his arms twisted up behind his back by two Ubek thugs. He had been accosted outside his home soon after midnight and had tried to defend himself, so they had given him a thorough beating. Konrad Bieliński, another of Chojecki's NOWa friends, was also brought to Białołęka. He recalled that the prisoners were made to walk in a group between parallel lines of security men with savage dogs that snarled and leapt at them as they passed. The older detainees among them were terrified. 'They thought they were going to their deaths,' Bieliński said.

Many Solidarity leaders were caught that night in Gdańsk, where they were staying after the National Commission meeting. Between 1.30 a.m. and 2 a.m., Zomos surrounded the three hotels the union had block-booked – the Monopol, the Grand and the Heweliusz – and police went from room to room with lists prepared from the hotel registers. As Wałęsa lived in Gdańsk, he had returned home that evening to the apartment he shared with his wife, Danuta, and their growing family: she was pregnant at the time with their seventh child. At 1.30 a.m., a delegation of regional Party leaders knocked on his door. A 'state of war' had been declared, they said, and they wanted to invite him to Warsaw for a meeting with General Jaruzelski. Wałęsa already knew the police were raiding the hotels and replied that there was nothing to discuss while his friends were under arrest. The officials went away, returning at 3 a.m. with a squad of Zomos. They arrested him and took him on a special flight to the capital, where a government villa had been prepared. He would remain in custody for the next eleven months.

Jacek Kuroń, the 47-year-old co-founder of KOR, was also caught in Gdańsk, in a room at the Novotel where he was sharing a bottle of Johnnie Walker with two women from an American press agency. He was taken in a police van to an isolated building on the outskirts of the city and led into a large, brightly lit basement. The far side of the room was riddled with bullet holes, the floor was strewn with sand, and a line of uniformed men with automatic weapons stood by the door. When an officer barked, 'To the wall!', he understood he was to be shot. There had been so much talk of Soviet intervention, he had been preparing himself for death for some time. 'So this is it,' he thought. 'So soon? What a pity.' He waited, but the hail of bullets never came.

Despite the military's careful planning, several Solidarity leaders slipped through the dragnet. One of them was Zbigniew Bujak, the popular 27-year-old president of the union's Warsaw chapter, who had almost as much authority within the organization as Wałęsa. As a young worker at the Ursus tractor factory, Bujak's first job for the opposition had been to distribute newspapers among his co-workers and collect contributions, and he had established a firm bond with the intellectual wing, reading all the books they suggested. 'Once resistance had meant taking up a gun,' he said of that time. 'Now, people instinctively took up typewriters.' When the Solidarity convention ended in Gdańsk that evening, Bujak had gone to a restaurant with a friend, where they sat drinking brandy into the night. Around 2 a.m., they stumbled towards the station to catch the night train back to Warsaw. Standing on the raised platform, Bujak noticed a swarm of police vehicles descending on a nearby hotel. 'Probably a raid on black marketeers,' he thought. Then a delegate he recognized from the conference told them that all the hotels where the trade unionists were staying were under siege.

Fuelled by brandy, still clasping the Solidarity brochures and stickers they had brought from the convention, Bujak and his friend set off to investigate. When they reached the Monopol, the door was locked, so they hammered on the glass. A young Solidarity press assistant on the other side signalled desperately for them to flee, but in their drunken state they failed to grasp her meaning. At last a porter appeared with keys to open the door. The assistant – in fact it was Joanna Jaraczewska, a granddaughter of Marshal Józef Piłsudski – told them that all the union's officers had been taken away and the police were still in the hotel.

Bujak was outraged. 'Are they completely crazy?' he said. 'Don't they realize they are simply forcing our hand?' They would have no alternative but to call a general strike!

Everyone, Jaraczewska repeated carefully, had been taken. Dozens of police were on every floor, going from room to room, checking documents.

Shouts erupted in the lobby: they had been recognized. At last the penny dropped. Bujak and his friend barged through the doors, raced away from the hotel, ditched their Solidarity literature and split up.

At 6 a.m., after hours of silence, radio sets across Poland crackled back to life. The announcer's voice was calm, unemotional:

This is Polish Radio Warsaw. Today is Sunday 13 December 1981. A special day is beginning in the history of our country and our nation. In a moment, army general Wojciech Jaruzelski will speak before the microphones of Polish Radio.

The national anthem played. Then came the soft, funereal voice of the general, the dictator of Poland.

Citizens of the Polish People's Republic. I address you today as a soldier and as the head of the Polish government. I address you on matters of the utmost importance . . .

Jaruzelski had recorded the speech in the middle of the night, once for radio and again for television, on which he would appear that day at noon. The milky picture would show the uniformed, 58-year-old four-star general, his face framed by large, thick-lensed glasses and a vast spread of forehead, sitting stiffly at a desk in front of the Polish flag, which appeared to be upside down. He read carefully from a piece of paper he held in his pale fingers.

Our homeland is at the edge of an abyss. The Polish house, the work of many generations, rebuilt from the ashes, is collapsing . . .

The economy was in freefall, he said. State structures had stopped functioning, living conditions were weighing more and more heavily on the people, division ran through every workplace and through many Polish homes. An atmosphere of incessant conflict, misunderstanding and hatred was wreaking havoc on the national psyche and damaging Poland's traditions of tolerance. Strikes, acts of terror and violence were multiplying, as were robberies and burglaries.

The nation has reached the limits of its mental endurance. Many people are gripped by despair. A national catastrophe is looming; it is no longer a matter of days, but of hours.

He hinted at some errors the Party had made – *the past months have been a busy time* – but there was no doubting where blame for the crisis lay. The increasing aggression of Solidarity's extremists had revealed their desire to 'completely dismantle' the socialist state. It was time to say 'enough!' before the new round of demonstrations set the country alight.

The self-preservation instinct of the nation must come to the fore. The hands of the troublemakers must be tied before they throw the country into the abyss of fratricidal warfare . . .

For that reason, they had created a Council of National Salvation and declared a state of war throughout the country. They did not seek a military coup or a military dictatorship, but intended to 'restore order and discipline' and save the country from disintegration.

We shall consistently purge Polish life of evil.

With his final words he sought to reassure another audience, the more important one, Poland's 'socialist allies and friends' in Moscow.

We greatly value their trust and constant aid. The Polish–Soviet alliance is, and will remain, the cornerstone of the Polish raison d'état, the guarantee of the inviolability of our borders . . . Poland is, and will remain, a lasting link in the Warsaw Pact, an unfailing member of the socialist community of nations . . .

Compatriots!

To all the Polish people and to the whole world, I want to repeat these immortal words:

Poland is not yet dead, as long as we are alive.

The national anthem struck up again.

The general's speech would be repeated at hourly intervals throughout the day. It was even broadcast inside Białołęka detention centre, via special speakers cast into the concrete above the toilets. By the day's end, the detainees knew almost every word by heart.

As morning broke over Warsaw, the snowfall of the night gave way to a hard, bright sunlight, which danced on the blanket of ice crystals that covered the city. Dressed all in white, the capital looked so immaculate that one journalist who couldn't help herself was heard to remark, 'What a beautiful day – we'll remember it for the rest of our lives.' After their long night spent trudging across town, the Łuczywos had found refuge with a friend of Śpiewak's, not far from the cinema where their evening had begun the day before, and when they set out again on Sunday morning they found the city transformed. There were tanks and armoured cars and checkpoints and roadblocks everywhere. People naturally gravitated to the Solidarity building on Mokotowska Street, where a large crowd had gathered by the time Helena and Witek arrived. During a lull in the police presence, some activists had dashed inside to salvage what they could, and Helena's quick-thinking assistant had recovered a precious IBM typesetting machine with the help of her boyfriend, who had a car. The rescue of this device, which composed pages for the printers, would prove one of the Łuczywos' greatest slices of fortune in an apocalyptic twenty-four hours.

The soundtrack to the next days was of the rumble of heavy military equipment and the roar of the Black Marias as they raced up and down with their captive cargo, overlaid by the martial music and hectoring instructions that spewed from the radio: *All the guilt from before 13 December is forgiven! Everyone has a chance to repent!* Proclamations, which had been printed in the USSR, went up all around the city, along with wanted posters for people the arrest squads had yet to catch. Witek found his own face there, and was glad to have thought to shave off his beard.

The junta was suspending Solidarity, banning all strikes and political gatherings, and introducing a curfew from 10 p.m. to 6 a.m. It was forbidden for anyone over thirteen to leave home without ID papers. Anyone over sixteen and under sixty could be conscripted to work for free for the purposes of national defence. All petrol belonged to the state, so private vehicles were effectively banned. A long list of misdemeanours could be met with a punishment 'up to and including the death penalty'. Military commissars took control of key enterprises and institutions, including the railways, the roads, the media, telecoms, fuel distribution, the ports, energy companies and fire brigades. Employees of these 'militarized' companies were subject to military law, which meant workers who failed to obey orders could be sentenced to death. The working week was extended to six days from the five Solidarity had negotiated, and the junta reserved the right to make it seven. A shift could last twelve hours, and annual leave was cut to twelve days. The mail censors were given new powers, and Polish media was restricted to one television channel, one radio station and two newspapers, namely the Party's own *People's Tribune* and the army's *Soldier of Freedom*. The crackdown particularly targeted the independent press. Censorship was to return to strict, pre-1980 levels. Printing equipment was exclusively to be used by state-run institutions and then only with written permission. Anyone who disseminated news that fitted the broad definition of 'weakening the defence preparedness of the Polish People's Republic' would be subject to a jail term of one to eight years. Anyone who spread news that could cause a public disturbance faced between six months and five years. Anyone who prepared, collected, stored, transported, transferred or transmitted a piece of writing, printed matter, a recording or a film containing any such information would also receive up to five years, and anyone who printed would be jailed for up to ten years.

There was little in fact that citizens of the new Poland *could* do, except work, stand in line for food and consume state propaganda through the media. The newsreaders wore army uniforms now, and the 'entertainment' consisted of bloody films about the Red Army's 'liberation' of Poland from the Nazis, or the crushing of the Hungarian uprising in 1956.

Helena Łuczywo's prime concern that Sunday was her daughter,

whom she still hadn't been able to see. She passed a message through
Śpiewak to her mother, Dorota, suggesting a time and a place for
them to meet. The following day she went to Ujazdowski Park,
the closest open space to her parents' place. She chose a spot on
a small hill next to a stream with stepping stones where she had
come as a child, thinking it safer to talk on the higher ground, so
they could see anyone who approached. While Łucja played, Helena
and Dorota discussed the future. There wasn't all that much to say.
They both knew what had to happen. Helena would work for the
opposition, which meant she could not afford to get caught, and
she could live in hiding only if she left Łucja with her grandparents.
She would feel guilty about this decision even years later, believing she and Witek had never been good parents, since they had to
put their work before family life. But her mother understood, and
Łucja, a smart child, would thrive in her grandmother's care. 'Don't
worry,' Dorota said, 'we'll take care of her.'

The Łuczywos spent the next nights hopping from one apartment
to the next, trying to stay one step ahead of the secret police, keeping their distance from anyone who knew them well. This meant
moving in with a succession of friends of friends, or neighbours of
friends. A pattern began to emerge, where they spent their days out,
trying to meet opposition contacts and pass messages to people who
hadn't been arrested, while continually shifting sleeping quarters: a
couch here, a foam mattress there. It was a difficult, paranoid existence. Wherever they were, they listened out for the sound of boots
on the stairs, or the authoritative knock of the security service at the
door. It was clear to Helena that if an organized opposition were to
survive it would have to operate underground, the way Poles had
always worked when faced with an oppressor.

In the streets, she had started to enlist people she could trust,
including friends and colleagues from the Solidarity Press Agency.
On Tuesday, she arranged their first meeting, at a safe apartment in
Żoliborz.

All seven of Łuczywo's co-conspirators that day were women,
partly because the Solidarity Press Agency's staff had been mostly

female, partly because the security forces had focused on rounding up men. Joanna Szczęsna, thirty-two, was Helena's deputy at the agency, a veteran of the underground press who had already served time in prison. Ewa Kulik, twenty-four, another journalist, was 'a brilliant manager' in Helena's view, who for a time had run a Flying Library of uncensored books in Kraków. Anna Bikont, twenty-three, was the youngest of the group, a postgraduate student at Warsaw University who had worked as a printer for Helena, an unusual job for a woman. The others – Anna Dodziuk, Zofia Bydlińska and Małgorzata Pawlicka – had all worked for the press agency. Young as they were, the women had extensive experience of dodging the secret police and working in conspiracy, and between them they could all call on a wide circle of opposition contacts.

They also all chain-smoked. One veteran remembered the air in their meetings being so thick you could 'hang an axe in it'.

The Damska Grupa Operacyjna, 'Women's Operational Group', began by setting out a number of objectives. Martial law must end; Solidarity's legal status must be restored; the internees must be released. To achieve these aims they would have to negotiate with the junta from a position of strength, which meant Solidarity would have to reassert its voice. Since political gatherings were now outlawed, the best way to assure people that the union hadn't been crushed was to publish a bulletin. It was obvious to Joanna Szczęsna that they had to collect and distribute as much information about the regime's activities as they could. 'That's our ammunition,' she thought. The underground would also require legitimate, elected Solidarity representatives, so they needed to find any who were still at large.

One immediate result of the first meeting was a newsletter, *Solidarity Information*, which appeared the next day. Since they had no printing presses, they made copies on typewriters, using carbon paper. They could only produce eight or ten of these at a time, but they knew people would follow the rule established by KOR and make another copy before passing both on. They hoped that as the network of readers and distributors grew, people would send news in to them. The first edition carried little more than a few scraps, about a police raid on the Polish Academy of Sciences and a strike at the Ursus tractor factory. Szczęsna was embarrassed that almost every story had to carry a caveat that it was unconfirmed, but conventional news reporting was impossible, and the newsletter's main job was just to exist. 'We needed to show people that we're here,' she said. The message was 'We're not dead, we've survived, and we need to keep this channel open.'

As they had hoped, letters, posters, flyers and other publications containing more information started to reach them, so that newsgathering became almost self-sustaining. Part of their task was to create a written record of the crimes and repression meted out by the regime. This would help people to realize they weren't alone, and show the state that it couldn't act with impunity. The spirit of accountability they sought to foster was captured in a Miłosz poem, 'You Who Wronged', which Szczęsna and her colleagues would publish:

> Do not feel safe. The poet remembers.
> You can kill one, but another is born.
> The words are written down, the deed, the date.

Accountability meant getting reports out to the West, to break the news blackout Jaruzelski had imposed and expose the regime's actions to the bright light of the world's media. Helena knew it was still possible to embarrass the Polish leadership, not least because the government still owed vast amounts of money to Western banks. She knew, too, that Radio Free Europe and the BBC would broadcast information back into Poland. This had long been recognized as a method of defending political prisoners: 'If your name is public and read by Radio Free Europe, it was much, much, much more difficult to hurt you, to beat you, to disappear you.' The best way to smuggle news reports out was aboard the trains that shuttled back and forth across the continent, stopping in the Polish capital.

After *Solidarity Information*, the next task on the women's to-do list was 'find the men' – meaning the elected union leaders who had escaped Jaruzelski's dragnet and were still at large. The best known of these was Bujak, the young and charismatic Solidarity official who also happened to be chairman of the branch they worked in, the Mazovia chapter, which covered Warsaw and its surroundings. He would be the most valuable politician they could find. He was also now the most wanted man in Poland.

Poles would come to call those days before Christmas, when the leaderless remnants of the Polish opposition fought ragged, spontaneous battles against the army and police, the 'winter war'. Leaderless groups of workers and students organized stoppages and sit-ins, advertised on handbills and news-sheets turned out on the few presses that hadn't been seized. The regime responded by deploying specialist strike-breaking Zomo units, backed by the army, which moved around the country raiding one Solidarity holdout at a time. They sent in tanks and armoured vehicles first, to punch through the barricades; the militia followed, with truncheons and tear gas, fists and boots.

The most brutal clashes took place in the Silesian coalfields, where hardened communities of miners responded angrily to the arrests. On the night of 12 December, the police had come for the Solidarity chairman of the Wujek coal mine on the outskirts of Katowice. They broke the official's door down with axes, beat him in front of his terrified wife and children, and dragged him from his apartment, leaving the door frame stained with blood. When news reached the nightshift at the mine in the early hours of Sunday morning, the workforce organized a sit-in. The regime assembled a small army of more than 2,000 men, with seven water cannon, forty-four fighting vehicles, twenty-two tanks and several helicopters, to 'pacify' Wujek, and at 11 a.m. on Wednesday 16 December the local commander ordered an assault. The miners fought back with whatever they had – nuts and bolts, shovels and pickaxes, rocks, chains and drill bits – and when the militia started to fall back under the hail of this counter-attack, a platoon of armed

Zomos opened fire. They shot 157 rounds into the crowd, hitting thirty-two people, mostly in their heads, torsos and upper limbs. Nine miners were killed.

The militia fired into a crowd in Gdańsk that day, too. On the first day of martial law they had interned more than 160 people, and the Lenin Shipyard had gone on strike in response. On Wednesday, 30,000 people marched through the city's streets. As they approached the Party headquarters, the security forces opened up with machine guns and rifles. More than 300 were injured, and one young man was killed. By Thursday the strike was broken.

After his narrow escape at the Monopol hotel, Bujak remained in hiding in the city for a week, but Gdańsk wasn't his natural habitat and he wanted to return to Ursus. Someone found him a railway worker's uniform and spectacles he didn't need; he had already shaved off his moustache. Wearing his railwayman's disguise, he caught the train south and made contact with his deputy from Mazovia Solidarity, Wiktor Kulerski, who had also evaded arrest. Helena's team heard through their expanding grapevine that a priest in Ursus might know Bujak's and Kulerski's whereabouts, and Ewa Kulik sent two letters to him via a courier. Receiving no

answer, she decided to visit the church in person. There, she handed the priest a third letter, which contained codes the fugitives would recognize.

'Bujak and Kulerski will know for certain that this message is from me,' she said.

The following week, Kulik returned and found Kulerski waiting for her.

'What do you need?' he asked.

'We need you.'

She told him their plan to bring the two men to Warsaw and keep them under close protection, setting out details of how they would be picked up, where they would hide and the false IDs she would provide to help them get through the checkpoints. She said they must both come as soon as they could.

A short time later, she and a girlfriend dressed up as farm labourers and caught the bus to Ursus. They met Bujak and Kulerski in a field, then paired off, so they appeared like two couples of agricultural workers. Each couple then made their way separately to Warsaw, where the men were hidden in different safe houses.

With Wałęsa in Jaruzelski's hands, it was vital to keep Bujak out of the clutches of the regime. 'He was our living symbol,' Kulik recalled.

8

This Is Big Casino

To hope and to act, these are our duties in misfortune.
                    Boris Pasternak, *Doctor Zhivago*

One more Christmas ends
Soaking stripes and stars
All my Polish friends
Are behind steel bars
                    Joseph Brodsky, 'Martial Law Carol'

Chojecki was six time zones away in Virginia when he heard the news. He had arrived in the US early in the month, the culmination of Giedroyc and Nowak's scheme to get the poster boy of independent Polish publishing in front of Washington's power-brokers, to explain the new opportunities. Nowak had met Mirek at the airport and taken him back to the home he shared with his wife, Greta, in Annandale, where the blazing colours of autumn in Virginia had faded to winter grey. From the outside, the Nowaks' house appeared to Chojecki like every other American home: it was a suburban brick split-level, with a silver Volkswagen Dasher on the drive and a knoll out the back planted with flowers. Inside, however, the house was wholly Polish. If you couldn't have your own country, Greta would say, as she sat in a living room filled with Polish paintings, Polish rugs and cabinets filled with Polish gewgaws and photographs of the Polish pope, you had to make yourself another one. 'This is independent Poland,' she told visitors. 'Here within these four walls.'

It was a sign of the Nowaks' determination that in 1981 they still lived by their Second World War codenames. 'Jan', born Zdzisław Jeziorański, had been a courier back then, running messages through Nazi-occupied Europe from London to the Warsaw underground. 'Greta' – née Jadwiga Wolska – performed a similar role in Poland, smuggling documents between resistance units and print shops, carrying a vial of deadly poison in case she fell into the hands of the Gestapo. They had married late on the thirty-seventh day of the Warsaw Uprising, in a ruined church, crunching their way to the altar across broken glass, and pledged themselves with a pair of copper wedding rings Greta had swapped for a tin of meat. The ceremony lasted just seven minutes, since the Germans were 300 yards away and the priest also had a funeral to get through.

At the end of the war, the Nowaks had escaped to Britain. Six years later, Jan had set up Radio Free Europe's Polish service, a central plank in the CIA's campaign to combat Soviet propaganda, delivering its first broadcast from Munich in 1952. He ran the station for the next twenty-five years, often broadcasting himself, so that his voice became familiar to almost every Pole. Wojtyła, the future pope, would listen to Nowak every morning as he shaved. After Jan's retirement, the Nowaks had moved to the US, where he had joined the circle of well-connected Polish expats in the intelligence establishment, which included Carter's national security advisor Zbigniew Brzezinski, and Richard Pipes, the hawkish Harvard professor Ronald Reagan drafted in as National Security Council lead on East European and Soviet affairs. Nowak himself served as a consultant to the NSC and operated as a kind of unofficial ambassador for the Polish opposition. He and Greta had chosen their Annandale location carefully: it was just twenty minutes' drive from here to the White House, and fifteen minutes to both the State Department in Foggy Bottom and the CIA at Langley.

Chojecki hadn't met the Nowaks before, but they knew his mother from the war, and Greta insisted he call them 'Uncle' and

'Aunt' and that he stay with them whenever he was in town. One of the upsides of being an exiled Pole was that there was always another displaced compatriot to offer hospitality. Jan had squired Chojecki around Washington, introducing him to various contacts. Soon after his arrival, he took Mirek to the State Department, to brief a group of thirty diplomats and politicians on the Polish situation, and on 11 December took him back to Foggy Bottom to meet Pipes. All Chojecki knew, as he was ushered into an office in the Harry S. Truman building, was Pipes's name, which was written on the door. He had no idea his interlocutor had been born and raised in Poland, or that at the age of sixteen he had watched Hitler parade in triumph through Warsaw. He struggled along for fifteen minutes in broken English before Pipes said, 'Let's speak Polish.'

The 32-year-old Chojecki was wide-eyed in DC. Just two months earlier he had been sitting at home in his small apartment in Żoliborz; the previous year he had been coughing up food in Mokotów jail. Now he was walking the marble halls of the world's greatest superpower, briefing foreign policy experts who'd left chairs at Harvard to be there, and giving interviews to the *Washington Post* with what that paper's reporter described as 'a feverish intensity' which reflected 'a man in the middle of great things, caught up in the rising tide'. Chojecki told everyone he met in the run-up to the 'state of war' that communism was on the brink of collapse, and that, whatever the rumours, the 'Reds' wouldn't dare use force against Solidarity, since so many soldiers sympathized with the movement or had sisters, brothers or parents who were members. 'No way will there be martial law,' he had said.

On the evening of Saturday 12 December, he was visiting the house of a friend who worked at the US propaganda network Voice of America. When the friend came home and told him troops were on the streets of Warsaw, Chojecki's first thought was that young Poles serving in the military would revolt rather than attack Solidarity and that this would lead to the regime's downfall. He wanted to get home as soon as possible to attend the funeral of Polish communism. 'What am I doing here?' he thought.

They started dialling Poland right away, picking numbers from Chojecki's contacts book. It quickly became clear that the security service was shutting down the telecoms network and they had to move fast. They tried journalists – the *Newsweek* correspondent Andrzej Nagórski was one – as well as Solidarity people and friends from KOR, and got through only once, to a biochemist Chojecki knew, who confirmed the reports of a crackdown and said all the phones seemed to have been cut off except his. After that, the result was always the same: a voice saying no connection could be made.

Phone lines in Polish households around the world were humming that night, as people tried to call home, found they couldn't reach Poland and dialled friends in the diaspora instead. In Malmö, the port city in southern Sweden, Marian Kaleta had been trying to reach Grzegorz Boguta, to check he'd arrived safely back in Warsaw after the Frankfurt trip. Struggling to get through, he set his phone to auto-dial, but all he ever heard at the other end was a ghostly silence, and at 1 a.m. on Sunday morning his wife told him to stop and go to bed. He did, but not for long. He was woken at 5.30 a.m. by the ringing telephone and stumbled past his slumbering dog to grab the receiver. It was Eugeniusz Smolar in London, a veteran of Minden's network, who ran the Aneks publishing house while also working for the BBC's Polish service. 'Jaruzelski has started a war in Poland!' Smolar exclaimed down the line. Kaleta was instantly awake, soaking in the details his friend poured out. They had begun arresting Solidarity people. They were taking them to camps, no one knew where.

Kaleta was staggered. 'Now the fun is over,' he thought.

He washed, made a cup of very strong coffee and at 7 a.m. began a round of teleconferences that would last all day. First he dialled Józef Lebenbaum, his smuggling partner in nearby Lund, who had already heard the news. Then Radio Free Europe called, asking him to gather any information he could and pass it on. Kaleta agreed, since, as he said later, 'what we as Poles can do at the moment is to announce to the world that another communist crime has been committed in our country'. At 8 a.m., he spoke with Giedroyc, then with members of the Polish government-in-exile in London. No one had much concrete information to pass on. By noon, Kaleta's phone was busy with Swedish and Danish reporters looking for something new. But what? Lebenbaum, an ex-journalist, came up with the idea of launching a hunger strike in Lund Cathedral to fill the media's need for news. 'I just thought I've got to do something straight away,' he said. The strikers demanded that Sweden ask the United Nations to send human rights observers to Poland. Kaleta would join them.

Towards the end of that Sunday, Kaleta spoke with Chojecki. Nurturing this relationship was 'of crucial importance', Kaleta believed, since the publisher was already famous in the West, and that would be invaluable when it came to organizing future political activity.

'I decided that [Chojecki] would be our beacon,' he recalled, 'and that cooperation with him would bring considerable results.'

After putting the phone down to America, he settled into a big armchair and immediately fell asleep.

'Psychologically unbearable' was how Chojecki described the following days and weeks, as terrible news poured in from Poland and his hope that communism was in its death throes crumbled. Oddly, he could watch the full range of East European propaganda channels on American cable TV, but to understand what was really happening to his friends and family he had to call contacts in Paris, Stockholm, London and Vienna. The more he heard, the more he understood the scale and brutality of what was being done. Everything he had fought for, all the achievements of August 1980, were being systematically destroyed, including the publishing infrastructure. All he could do was try to organize a response, travelling back and forth between Washington and Manhattan on the Amtrak, meeting with activists, journalists and allies, speaking out against the crackdown, fundraising and lobbying.

On Tuesday he was in New York, giving a press conference at the office of the human rights organization, Helsinki Watch. The Polish government was treating its people more harshly than the Nazi occupiers had done, he told the media. 'Virtually the whole society is under house arrest.' He feared that the crisis would escalate and Soviet troops would enter Poland to support Jaruzelski, leading to some kind of civil war. With other Poles in New York, he founded a Committee in Support of Solidarity, and gave more interviews. Now the *Washington Post* journalist who had identified a 'feverish intensity' in Chojecki found his voice 'hollow from the news and the sorrow and the uncertainty'. On Thursday, his name appeared in the *New York Times*, which reported that he was on a pre-prepared list of detainees broadcast by Radio Warsaw. At that moment he realized that if he tried to return to Poland he would be thrown back into jail, perhaps for years. Since that would be pointless, he was forced to consider himself an exile.

At the end of that first week he flew to Switzerland for a meeting in Zurich of Solidarity supporters who had been stranded in the West. Messages and documents from Poland, including one of the first mimeographed opposition newsletters, were already reaching them. It was obvious that they should do their utmost to support their friends in the country who were continuing the struggle. They agreed that Seweryn Blumsztajn, a journalist friend of Chojecki who had worked with Helena Łuczywo, would act as the point person for passing information to the Western media. Chojecki, meanwhile, would try to fulfil the requests for print materials they were already receiving.

He returned to the US – Nowak and Brzezinski sorted out his visas, since his Polish passport had long run out – and gave evidence to Congress based on the information he had received. At least 10,000 people were now being held in more than fifty internment camps throughout Poland, he told them. The regime was putting down protests everywhere with great brutality. Around a hundred people had been killed. Army helicopters were dropping gas that caused paralysis and comas, and firing water cannon in temperatures that sometimes hit −20° C (−4° F), which could be lethal. They had threatened to execute anyone who went on strike, and prohibited printing, distributing leaflets, wearing badges and graffiti. Foreign journalists were being censored, and all photography and filming were forbidden. The response of the US and its allies so far had been weak. He called for across-the-board sanctions against the Warsaw Pact and the immediate repayment of Polish debts owed to Western banks.

The Congressional leaders he met listened to Chojecki's case with sympathy, but offered little practical support. 'Everybody was obviously very kind,' he remembered. They felt sorry for him, about what had happened there, that he'd left a wife and children in Poland, but it amounted to very little.

Then, just before Christmas, Nowak organized a new meeting with his contacts in the Washington security establishment. This time, they would convene at the Annandale house for a dinner. Chojecki was to be the guest of honour, but the most powerful individual on the invite list was William J. Casey, director of central intelligence, the head of the CIA.

The US government had been caught in disarray by the Polish crisis. Washington always emptied out at weekends, and when news reached the White House on Saturday evening at 8.10, in the form of a coded message sent via satellite link from the Warsaw embassy, senior figures in the Reagan administration were even more absent than usual. The president, in only his tenth month in office, was at Camp David, and his closest advisor, White House Counsel Ed Meese, was in Hawaii. Secretary of State Al Haig was on a diplomatic trip to Brussels, and Defense Secretary Caspar Weinberger was on a plane somewhere over the Atlantic. The administration also happened to be between national security advisors, so when Pipes was called in for an emergency meeting he found it thinly populated. The most senior figures were Vice President George H. Bush and Chief of Staff James Baker, but these men stayed only briefly. The key question facing them at that moment was whether this counted as Soviet intervention, which would require a military mobilization in response, or whether it was a purely Polish matter, which wouldn't. Pipes was the NSC's East European lead, but he knew almost nothing about what was happening on the ground. Like other Poles in the West, he had spent much of the night calling round in a desperate bid to gather information, but kept coming up against Jaruzelski's wall of silence.

One person he did reach was Chojecki, who reiterated his rose-tinted early-stage view that Solidarity was too powerful for the regime to crush. Pipes would later blame the publisher for the administration's sluggish response, saying he 'was one of the people from Solidarity who misled the government, one of the reasons we were surprised'. This was an odd conclusion given that the CIA had very clear sight of what was about to happen, through its highest-placed spy in the Eastern Bloc, the Polish army officer Colonel Ryszard Kukliński, known by the codename 'Jack Strong'. Kukliński – whose home incidentally boasted a large library filled with illegal publications – had been deeply involved in drawing up plans for martial law from the start and kept the CIA abreast of developments at every stage. In October, for instance, a CIA analyst was able to write in a memo entitled 'Current Status of Preparations for Martial Law in Poland' that 'The Polish Government appears to be prepared to declare martial law in all or part of Poland . . . The element of surprise is most important in order that members of the opposition have no time to call for mass resistance.'

As the day of martial law approached, Kukliński realized his cover had been blown and alerted the CIA, which hatched a plan to spirit him and his family out of the country before the KGB got to them. The colonel, his wife and their two sons met American agents at a prearranged location in Warsaw. They were taken to the US embassy, where they were bundled into the back of a van and sealed into large boxes. The van then drove west, towards East Germany. When they reached the frontier, the Kuklińskis could overhear their driver arguing with the East German border guards. The Agency had failed to register the van's licence number with border control, which meant it was liable to be searched. If they were caught, Kukliński would certainly have been executed. They sat in silence as the guards moved to the rear of the van, but whatever the driver said, the soldiers didn't open the doors, and instead allowed the van to pass through. The family arrived safely in West Berlin.

When the colonel didn't show up at his office the following Monday, a swarm of uniformed and plainclothes security men swooped on his house, but they were too late. Kukliński was sentenced to death *in absentia* for treason, and in the early 1990s his sons would be killed in separate, mysterious accidents.

The colonel's intelligence was invaluable – so much so that the CIA didn't share it with its allies in Solidarity, or even, it seems, with Pipes. It was hardly Chojecki's fault then if the Reagan administration had been caught by surprise on the night of 12/13 December.

That evening in Annandale, the free world's leading intelligence experts gathered around the Nowaks' table to hear what the young Polish publisher had to say. There were ten people in the large ground-floor dining room, too many for Greta to cook for, so she had invited someone in to do the catering. Chojecki recognized only Pipes and Brzezinski, apart from his hosts, and he didn't catch the others' names, since they were 'really quite garbled' when they introduced themselves and he 'couldn't make them out', he said. One of them was a tall, balding 68-year-old, with protruding teeth and thick spectacles, who was famously hard to comprehend even when he was speaking to the president or to committees on Capitol Hill. This was Bill Casey.

Casey was energetic, inspirational and, as at least two US presidents could agree, entirely the wrong man to lead the CIA. Gerald Ford had been 'absolutely surprised' to learn that Reagan had picked him for his spymaster, since he 'was not qualified', Ford said, while even Vice President Bush described the choice as 'inappropriate'. Casey had served in the Office of Strategic Services during the war, the CIA forerunner, which was led by the hard-charging William 'Wild Bill' Donovan, a man who was once so keen to demonstrate the benefits of an OSS innovation, a gun silencer, to President Roosevelt that he smuggled a weapon into the White House and fired ten rounds across a room into a sand bag. In Donovan's time anything went and no holds were barred, and Casey loved it. When Reagan gave him the top job at the CIA he hung a portrait of Wild Bill in his office and launched the Agency on an energetic and often unaccountable series of covert actions, which led to one of his senior staff dubbing him a 'freelance buccaneer'. Casey's tenure at the Agency would be marked by misadventures all around the world, from Cambodia to Chad, Ethiopia to Beirut, but his most disastrous operation was the plot to fund right-wing rebels in Nicaragua with money made by selling weapons to Tehran, in breach of US law. The cover-up of the Iran–Contra affair would implicate Reagan himself and create the biggest scandal to hit Washington since Watergate.

When it came to Poland, however, Casey was uncharacteristically cautious. He was reluctant to add any new CIA covert action in Eastern Europe to the existing book programme, since the anti-communist AFL-CIO labour union had been doing a 'first rate' job of overtly supporting Solidarity during the Carnival, and if the CIA got directly involved it might well 'screw it up'. But martial law had provoked real anger in Washington, not least in the president. In Reagan's Manichaean worldview, communism was evil and Solidarity was made up of heroes, modern-day American revolutionaries, who were fighting for independence from the USSR much as George Washington had fought the British. He saw Jaruzelski's action as a chance to put unprecedented pressure on Moscow, telling an emotional NSC meeting four days before Christmas that this was 'the first time in sixty years that we have had this kind of opportunity'.

'Can we afford not to go all out?' he asked the team he had gathered in the Roosevelt Room of the White House, which included Casey, Secretary of State Haig and Defense Secretary Weinberger.

'I'm talking about a total quarantine on the Soviet Union,' said Reagan. 'No detente! We know – and the world knows – that [the Soviets] are behind this. We have backed away so many times! Can we do less now than tell our Allies, "This is big casino!" There may never be another chance!'

Bush, Weinberger and Casey concurred. Jaruzelski was 'a Russian general in Polish uniform', Weinberger said. The president should show leadership, seize the initiative and 'talk to the world' to raise support for Poland. Casey called for 'across-the-board sanctions'. Martial law represented nothing less than 'an unravelling of the communist economic system', he said. This was the moment to press their advantage.

Haig, who had the tricky job of trying to bring the US's European allies on board, was more circumspect. 'My problem', he said, 'is the timing in a speech tomorrow will bring the spectre of the terror of World War Three on Christmas Eve.'

'When *is* the right time to warn of World War Three?' Weinberger shot back.

They settled on imposing limited sanctions, which they could expand if the situation deteriorated. Reagan would set out the details in personal letters to Brezhnev and Jaruzelski, and in his Christmas speech, delivered from the White House, he clearly pinned the blame on the Soviets. 'The tragic events now occurring in Poland, almost two years to the day after the Soviet invasion of Afghanistan, have been precipitated by public and secret pressure from the Soviet Union', he told Americans. If the 'forces of tyranny in Poland' did not relent, there would be 'serious consequences', he said. He urged people to light a candle on Christmas Eve 'as a personal statement of your commitment to the steps we're taking to support the brave people of Poland in their time of troubles'.

This was the mood in the administration, then, when Casey and the other officials came to meet Nowak's guest of honour that night, to explore the idea of a renewed CIA push. But what form should it take? They asked Chojecki about his experiences with Solidarity and the opposition. How did underground publishing work? How effective was it? What sort of Poles listened to Western radio broadcasts? Who could tune in?

There were 'lots and lots of questions', Chojecki recalled. As they grilled him through hors d'oeuvres and the main course, smoking and refilling each other's glasses, the young man felt out of his depth, unworldly. It reminded him of the many times he had been interrogated in Poland.

He was relieved when the questions ran dry, dessert arrived and the conversation turned to a more general discussion.

After his meeting with Casey, Chojecki returned to New York, staying at the Manhattan apartment of a young Polish-American friend, Agnieszka Kołokowska, whose father Leszek had represented KOR abroad. But Agnieszka left to stay with her family in Chicago for the holidays, and Mirek couldn't face meeting up with anyone else. Miserable and alone, he wandered the city streets. It was the saddest Christmas of his life. Even the tree in front of Rockefeller Center made him morose.

Requests for help from Poland were pouring in, often sent via Nowak. These were usually technical requests for printing parts and materials to support the few remaining underground presses. They would say that 'a roll is broken here' or 'we're missing some gauze', and ask him to send replacements. It wasn't hard to find funding and support in America. Even the financier George Soros had contacted him, to ask what he could do to help. Sitting in Soros's New York office, they had settled on the idea of buying an IBM Selectric typesetter worth $10,000. The price tag didn't seem to matter to Soros. No, the problem of being in the US wasn't money, it was geography. There was no possibility of smuggling material into Poland from here, as flights to the country had been suspended and he was separated from Europe by an ocean. But it was more than just a practical matter. He experienced his exile viscerally. 'I feel terrible in America,' he wrote to a friend. 'The distance is so great that I can no longer bear it.'

Then, just before New Year, two job offers came to him at once, both in organizations linked to the CIA. Uncertain what to do, he turned for advice to one person he knew who had extensive experience of working with American intelligence: Jerzy Giedroyc.

The first offer came from Radio Free Europe, which wanted to hire him as a journalist. He felt unqualified for this, and he turned it down out of hand: 'I can't do that and I don't want to,' he told Giedroyc. The second was more enticing. Andy Stypułkowski, the long-serving head of the Polonia Book Fund, had recently died, and the CIA was looking for someone to fill his shoes. On New Year's Eve, Chojecki met with two English-speaking intelligence officers who gave him the hard sell. It would be a pity to close down the organization, they said, with its heritage stretching back to the 1950s, or to hand it over to someone who wasn't Polish. Whatever happened in the country in the future, the need for the Polonia Book Fund wasn't going to go away. Even if one day Chojecki was able to return home, it could be possible for him to lead the company from there.

Chojecki knew about Polonia's CIA links. 'Of course,' he told Giedroyc, 'it is no secret to me how the Polonia Book Fund is financed.' Although he felt it would be impossible to return to Poland as a CIA employee, the prospect of working for the Agency in itself didn't scare him. His main concern was whether they would try to restrict his publishing activities. Ironically, the independent press in Poland had been free to print anything they wanted. Would it be the same at Polonia?

'What do you think of or know about Andrzej Stypułkowski's connections?' he asked Giedroyc. 'I am not concerned here with formalities, but with the extent to which the publisher is free to develop the editorial line.'

There was no question the role appealed, and he would 'be happy to accept an offer of employment' from Polonia at some point, but he wanted his mentor's advice, since the industry was so different in the West. 'It is one thing to hide from the militia, organize paper and distribution,' he wrote, 'and another to publish books.'

There is no record of Giedroyc's response in Chojecki's file in the Kultura archive. But six days later, the Editor had begun the task of trying to find money for his protégé, noting in his diary, 'Chojecki – stipend', in a spidery scrawl. Three weeks after that, the young publisher was on his way to France. He had decided against the Polonia job and instead was moving to Paris, to the spiritual heart of the diaspora. He would be among friends there, in a large and well-entrenched Polish community, just a few hundred miles from the motherland. Importantly, he would also be close to QRBERETTA.

9

Citizens versus the Secret Police

I often wondered whether it is right to scream, when you are being beaten and trampled underfoot. Isn't it better to face one's tormentors in a stance of satanic pride, answering them with contemptuous silence? I decided that it is better to scream . . . If nothing else is left, one must scream. Silence is the real crime against humanity.

> Nadezhda Mandelstam, *Hope Against Hope*

And tomorrow, you'll not even find a trace
Of the shadow that slid along the wall at my side.

> Natalya Gorbanevskaya, 'And Tomorrow
> You'll Not Even Find a Trace'

Helena Łuczywo wasn't the type to cry often. A natural optimist, disinclined to self-analysis, she claimed not to even know the word 'depressed' in the 1980s. But after a month of living and working in hiding, the tumult of problems thrown up by martial law had started to get to her. One day that winter she left her safe house for a walk, to clear her head. She and Witek were staying in Ochota, a residential district of large, Soviet-style apartment blocks that marched west along the spoke roads that fanned out from central Warsaw. Arctic temperatures continued to grip the country: ever since Jaruzelski's declaration, the Polish weather had mirrored the intense cold of the political climate. She found herself wandering in a small, snow-covered patch of garden by the city's aged water-treatment plant. She stopped to sit on a park bench and felt tears prick her eyes.

Two enormous responsibilities bore down on her. The first was the newspaper. The Women's Operational Group had been horrified to learn of Jerzy Zieleński's suicide on the night of martial law, which was the direct result, they felt, of the junta's actions. They decided the only fitting riposte would be to launch the title he had been working on, *Mazovia Weekly*, in place of the scrappy, typewritten *Solidarity Information*. Creating a new newspaper was a huge undertaking at the best of times, requiring teams of reporters, editors, designers, administrators, print staff and distributors. Launching one in Poland during the state of war, when even moving around the city was dangerous, would be near impossible. There were military vehicles and roadblocks everywhere. Sentries with Kalashnikovs stood around glowing braziers all over Warsaw, fending off the seeping frost by stamping their boots and rubbing their hands over coke embers, which filled the air with an acrid stink. They stopped everyone, demanding their papers and searching their vehicles. The snitches had been reinvigorated too, and they were as hard to spot as ever. They worked on the trams and on the trains, as cloakroom attendants, teachers, taxi drivers, concierges and priests. Some recruits were grandparents; others were children. They would report any hint of suspicious conversation back to their SB bosses. To operate in these circumstances, Łuczywo would need a long list of safe spaces for people to work in, and a raft of fake identity documents so people could get through the checkpoints.

After the newspaper, her second major headache was Bujak and Kulerski. Bujak might be highly popular in the country, but he wasn't from Warsaw, which meant he didn't have a network of friends and relatives to fall back on, and his fame hadn't translated into a line of trusted people prepared to take him in.

'It's impossible,' she thought, as she sat in the cold garden. 'I won't be able to manage all this. What to do?'

What she did was arrange a meeting with her friend Ewa Kulik, asking her to take on the job of looking after the Solidarity officials. From then on, the operation would be split in two: Helena would continue to focus on preparing *Mazovia Weekly*, with Witek overseeing print and distribution; Kulik would act as a second in command, handling security and logistics – 'the jobs no one else wanted to do', as she put it. They would keep in daily contact through liaison officers, but from now on Helena wouldn't always know where Bujak was hidden – it was safer for everyone that way. Kulik meanwhile presided over a growing empire of apartments, dead-drops, liaisons and bodyguards.

For security reasons, Łuczywo wanted everyone and everything to be in perpetual motion. They should shift apartments every two weeks. This idea was drawn from the 'Flying Universities' Poles had first set up under the tsarist occupation, when activists would meet to share forbidden information in an ever-changing series of private homes. The Flying Universities had been revived in the war and again by KOR in the 1970s; uncensored course literature had been supplied by the ILC, which helped feed great Flying Libraries of books that were almost continuously in circulation. A famous Flying Library in Warsaw contained many hundreds of prohibited titles, which were loaned out via liaison officers, who would deliver the books to borrowers and return them every two weeks to a different address. The principle of 'Flying Offices' was the same: no one working for the underground should stick around one location long enough for an informant to tip off the secret police.

In the first months, when property was in short supply, Helena and the other journalists often worked and slept in the same place. But as time passed and the underground grew they needed more room, and the list of safe houses had to grow too. It was a major challenge to find enough apartments and hosts. Łuczywo's friend Anna Bikont was extremely sociable and had an enormous number of friends with flats, but they had all found themselves tapping the remotest contacts. Helena tried one woman she only knew because they had spent time on the same maternity ward. She could remember her name, but had only a vague recollection of where she lived, so she trawled the housing registries to trace her. When she finally made contact, the woman agreed to host them.

Hosting wasn't something people did lightly. Joanna Szczęsna recalled asking a contact if she could provide space for them three days a week. What would it mean? Their typewriters would be clacking away twenty-four seven, Szczęsna explained. They would keep the lights on day and night, and everyone chain-smoked as if their lives depended on it. They couldn't give any security guarantees, although they would find dead-drops nearby so couriers wouldn't come to the door.

The woman was unsure. 'I've got to talk to my husband,' she said.

When Szczęsna returned a few days later, the couple sat her down, offered her tea and told her gravely that they'd thought it through and decided, yes, they could host the editors. Joanna pulled out a grid of dates and places: they would come on 6 March and then again two months later. The woman's expression switched from anxiety to relief. 'But we thought you were going to come every week!' she said.

Eventually the Warsaw Underground would build up a roster of 300 apartments, to be used as post boxes, meeting rooms, storage units and workshops for parts of the print process. Editors and couriers would lug around heavy bundles of keys to open doors to addresses they had learned by heart. After using one address, they liked to let it cool off for a month or two before returning.

Most hosts were extremely generous, despite the disruption and the danger the women brought with them. 'Wherever I went in hiding, people would welcome me,' Szczęsna remembered. 'They'd feed me, ask if I needed anything, what they could do.' One home Szczęsna hid out in had a near-complete set of *Kultura*, which her host stored on behalf of the Warsaw Flying Library. She loved staying there because she could luxuriate in all the back issues. 'I used that house sometimes to have a rest,' she remembered. 'I'd read the books and have the brief feeling that I was living in a free country.'

Occasionally, host and activist formed romantic attachments, as Witek did after he and Helena agreed to split up for security reasons. The Łuczywos' marriage was one of many that would not survive life in the underground.

Keeping mobile was one form of protection the activists used. There were others. Assuming they were followed whenever they were outside, they made up cover stories to go with their false IDs, and when they met they were ready to hide everything at a moment's notice. There was a perpetual risk of eavesdropping: planting bugs was a favourite Ubek tactic. But the women also knew that if they avoided all incriminating exchanges they wouldn't be able to do any work, so they would talk loudly and quickly for the benefit of the hidden microphones while writing sensitive information – addresses, appointments and the like – on scraps of paper which they burned afterwards with a candle. Where possible, they committed facts to memory, and the leaders each had an 'understudy' who went with them, to learn what they had learned, so that if they were arrested the stand-in could supply the missing jigsaw pieces for the group.

Being female was an advantage, the women found, because the security services were generally chauvinist and tended to underestimate them. 'I was a woman, educated, and a well-known oppositionist,' Szczęsna said, 'which meant that the police would treat me better than others who were male or uneducated or not known.' She also knew that her behaviour would be rewarded and supported by society and by her friends when the time came to tell them about it.

'I did not feel alone,' she said. Most importantly, 'I had no doubt that I was right.'

Ewa Kulik's job didn't stop at finding Bujak and Kulerski safe places to live. The Solidarity leaders also had to be able to communicate, issue instructions and go to meetings with other politicians and journalists. To manage these activities without putting their assets at risk, she needed an equivalent of the US Secret Service, a unit of fit, quick-witted young people who could be trusted to deliver the leaders safely to where they needed to go and take evasive action when necessary. The first activist detailed to keep Bujak safe was a young astronomer Helena knew from pre-martial-law days, whom she had bumped into on a Warsaw bus. To avoid arrest after 13 December, Tomasz Chlebowski had taken to sleeping rough at the Nicolaus Copernicus Astronomical Center where he worked, but he was disturbed by the regime's proclamations that even small misdemeanours could lead to execution. 'I can do anything you want,' he told Łuczywo miserably, 'as long as it's not punishable by death.'

The astronomer began with minor tasks – moving a printing press across town in a suitcase, placing a news bulletin on the transcontinental train – and showed himself to be capable and cautious, so Helena sent him to Kulik. He would work for her for the next six weeks, for most of that time as Bujak's security detail – his 'gorilla', as Chlebowski put it. He would rendezvous with her daily at a time and place she nominated, to receive instructions about where Bujak was and where he needed to go. He took his role very seriously: 'If [Bujak] were to lose a hair from his head,' he recalled, 'it would be an enormous loss for Poland. I could not allow that to happen, [not] at any price.'

Chlebowski brought the kind of scientific rigour to the security business that in better times he might have devoted to investigating a new black hole. He eventually became an underground 'health and safety' consultant, running courses in spycraft for anyone who needed it. He built on the tricks used by printers in the 1970s, and developed a whole list of Warsaw locations where a fit young activist might lose their tail by diving down a stairwell or running through a housing estate. When underground couriers began to use vehicles, he put together a range of techniques for shaking off the secret police, such as heading out into the country at night, switching off the headlights and ducking down a side road before doubling back by another route. Driving up a one-way street against the traffic or running a red traffic signal was sure to flush out unmarked cars. Everyone, he maintained, should train themselves to remember every licence plate around them and every face in a crowd: if they saw anyone twice, they would know they were followed.

During Chlebowski's courses he would hand students copies

of *The Little Conspirator*, which became the most popular underground booklet in Poland in the spring of 1982. It was first published by the Warsaw publisher CDN, but it would be reprinted in a dozen editions all over Poland, as well as in the West, by publishers in the CIA network, and smuggled back into the country. Its first section, 'How to Conspire', explained the origins of Poland's 'struggle against the Reds' and advised would-be activists on finance, phone calls, dead-drops, secret compartments, police entrapment techniques, pain, fear and life in prison. Part two, 'The Citizen vs. The Secret Police' reworked a NOWa pamphlet advising activists on how to deal with arrest and interrogation. The final part, 'The Interrogation Game', invited the reader to play the role of a detainee:

> Imagine a situation when you are arrested and interrogated. The prize is information. What kind of questions will you be asked? What sort of pressure will you be put under? What are your reactions likely to be? Do you know what your weak points are? You'd better find out fast because they will be exposed and mercilessly exploited.

Chlebowski's main contribution to the underground apart from security training was the clandestine postal system he set up with the help of other astronomers. As a group, the Polish astrophysics community were a tight-knit bunch whom the SB had failed to penetrate. They were also spread across Poland. Working with friends and contacts of the Copernicus Center, Chlebowski built a system which allowed them to secretly move illegal books, newsletters and messages around the country via 'mailboxes', mostly apartments, which liaison officers visited once or twice a week for deliveries and collections. To keep couriers safe, he designed a special bag with a false bottom to fool the militiamen at the checkpoints. These were so popular with the underground that they became a problem: when a group of three or four conspirators got together, all carrying identical hand-sewn bags, people would look at them quizzically, wondering if this was a new fashion.

An essential part of underground tradecraft was disguise. It was secret police procedure to describe a suspect's physical appearance in their files, so almost all underground activists experimented with dyeing their hair, growing or shaving beards and trying on various uniforms. Some even dressed in the style of the secret police. Kulik was once approached on a Warsaw street by a man wearing the tight clothes and 'stupid little moustache' of a typical Ubek. She thought she was about to be arrested, but the secret police agent turned out to be the Gdańsk Solidarity leader Bogdan Lis, the man she had come to meet.

One day that winter, Kulik told Chlebowski to take Bujak to three addresses in succession. The first apartment was a simple holding point, the bodyguard discovered, where the leader could wait safely while Tomasz checked out the next address. In the second apartment he found a make-up artist, sent by a famous theatre director, who was waiting with a palette of lipsticks, powders and dyes, as well as false moustaches and beards. She would instruct them on various ways to change the shapes of their features. In the third apartment was an optician with a case of spectacles, who would fit Bujak out with a bookish new look.

Witek Łuczywo needed time to prepare production of the new weekly, but most of all he needed a press. He was fortunate to have the typesetting machine they had rescued, but since they had lost their other machines he didn't have anything to print the type-set pages on. This was a problem all over Poland. The military crackdown had succeeded in destroying a huge section of Polish independent publishing, helped by the fact that many printers had moved their presses into the open during the Carnival: fewer than 5 per cent of the uncensored periodicals produced in 1981 would survive to 1982.

It was Ewa Kulik, once again, who solved the problem, during a visit to St Martin's church in Warsaw's Old Town.

Despite or because of communist attempts to convert Poles into a nation of Marxist atheists, the population remained staunchly

Roman Catholic: when John Paul II made papal visits to his home-land in 1979, 1983 and 1987, millions of people turned out to see him and to take part in his open-air masses. Knowing the church's power, the regime devoted a whole section of the security ser-vice, Department IV, to penetrating it, blackmailing its officials and destroying the reputations of pro-Solidarity priests and nuns. Nothing in the state's war on religion seemed to be off-limits. In 1978, the SB sent no fewer than forty-three agents to infiltrate a series of mass pilgrimages to the holy site of the 'Black Madonna' icon. They planted pornography on the participants, and even slipped priests hallucinogenic drugs in a bid to generate comprom-ising material. Many priests nevertheless used the political cover of the pulpit, which wasn't subject to censorship, to speak out against the Party, as Father Jerzy Popiełuszko of Żoliborz famously did. Sometimes, it wasn't the priest but the church building that was renowned for opposition activity, and nowhere had a bigger repu-tation in this regard than St Martin's in Warsaw Old Town. A large, baroque structure on Piwna Street, St Martin's was a distribution hub for aid shipments from the West, and a place people went to contact the underground. The dissidents knew the secret police kept a watch there too, but sometimes they had to take the chance.

It was here that Kulik met Emil Broniarek, one of a trio of brilliant NOWa printers known as the 'Three Musketeers'. Broniarek was on the run, looking for a place to hide, so he went to the church to find someone who could take him in. After bumping into Kulik, he told her he knew the whereabouts of another 'musketeer', Andrzej Górski, who had worked with Chojecki. He also knew that Górski had kept his offset press hidden. It had survived the police raids and was now in a basement in Radość, on the far bank of the Vistula. Since NOWa's whole editorial board had been interned, Broniarek and Górski were casting around for things to print. Kulik passed details of her encounter to Helena, who relayed it to Witek.

By the end of January 1982, the Łuczywos had much of what they needed for *Mazovia Weekly* in place, including an editorial structure and a team of printers. But to publish the newspaper weekly and grow the Solidarity underground they would need so much more: spare parts, inks, printing plates, radios – and money, a lot of money, to pay the printers, buy paper on the black market and feed all the activists who would devote themselves full time to the struggle.

There was only one place where these things could be sourced: the West.

10

Raphael

Our nation's like a
living volcano:
The top is hard and cold, worthless and
dried,
But boiling, fiery lava seethes inside.

Adam Mickiewicz, *Forefathers' Eve*

What was it about the Poles and the French? Their shared Catholic
faith, perhaps, or their Romantic tradition, which instilled a desire
to rise up against tyranny, no matter what the cost? Their love of
family, bread and heavy stew? Their mistrust of the Russians and
admiration for Napoleon? Whatever the root of their connection,
France had been the preferred European destination for Poles fleeing oppression for at least two centuries. Whenever Warsaw tried to
throw off its imperialist neighbours and failed, a wave of poor and
hungry refugees showed up on French doorsteps, and the French by
and large let them in. The cultural ties between these two European
nations ran so deep, it sometimes seemed that as many great Poles
had forged their careers on the banks of the Seine as they had on the
Vistula. Marie Curie, Adam Mickiewicz and Frédéric Chopin had
all produced their best work in Paris. As well as Polish bookshops,
Polish museums and Polish restaurants, the French capital boasted
a large Polish lending library, a Polish historical literary society and a
Polish church where Polish priests delivered a Polish liturgy. During

the Solidarity Carnival, French labour had developed strong links with the trade union, and after Jaruzelski's coup no country had reacted with more indignation than France, where 14 December was declared a national 'Day of Solidarity'. A quarter of a million people marched through the capital from Montparnasse to Les Invalides to protest against the crackdown. For Poles walking shoulder to shoulder with Parisians in the crowd, it felt as if the whole city had turned out to support them.

When Chojecki landed early in February 1982, the city was so thick with his stranded compatriots there was barely a couch to sleep on. Eventually he found space for a mattress on the floor of a boxroom above a Polish bookshop on Rue Dauphine, a narrow street in Saint-Germain-des-Prés. Here he was back on the buzzing Left Bank, five minutes' walk from the Librairie Polonaise, ensconced once again among the shouts of the late-night drunks, the honks of the early-morning *livreurs* and the all-hours fizzing of the *mobylettes*. As the most celebrated dissident of his generation in the West, he slipped easily into the group of Polish activists in Paris, who by this time had set up a Solidarity support committee, led by Seweryn Blumsztajn, the friend Chojecki had recently met in Zurich. The French Democratic Confederation of Labour (CFDT) had offered the new committee office space at their headquarters in Rue Cadet, in the 9th arrondissement, and money and offers of support had flooded in, from trade unions and from collections held in towns and cities all over the country, so that by the time of Chojecki's arrival they had a team of fifty volunteers and a war chest worth close to a million dollars. Blumsztajn had also established channels to his colleagues Helena Łuczywo and Joanna Szczęsna via the trains that shuttled back and forth between Paris and Moscow. Underground couriers would smuggle messages and copies of newsletters aboard the Ost–West Express sleeper service in Warsaw, and members of the committee would go down to the Gare du Nord to search it when it reached Paris. The sleeper train was made up of two parts, one Polish and one Soviet, and although it was impossible to search the Soviet section, the Poles were more than happy for them to rummage around in their carriages, looking through the bins and the toilet compartment. This was such a fruitful source of communications from the East that the committee pinned a duty rota to the office wall of activists who would go to the Gare du Nord each night. News from Poland was vital in the fight to keep Solidarity's story alive, and Blumsztajn would feed this information to Western reporters in a digest he passed to a few thousand subscribers, including contacts in Radio Free Europe, Voice of America and the French media.

Chojecki took up the role of Solidarity 'minister for smuggling' they had discussed in Zurich. He never formally joined the Paris committee since his highly tuned sense of paranoia told him the fewer people who knew about his activities the better, and he didn't want anyone asking questions about what was being sent where and when. The requests from Poland continued to arrive, from colleagues such as Witek Łuczywo, Andrzej Górski and Bujak himself.

'Everybody knew what I did before,' he said, 'so they were all asking for printing equipment.'

But before he could start building a cell of dedicated smugglers, he needed to find a way to sustain himself and the new enterprise – especially since Blumsztajn believed all cash raised by the Paris committee should be spent on Poland, not on stranded émigrés.

Happily, he could rely on the help of one man who had built a career on funds raised in the West for Polish political activities: Jerzy Giedroyc.

Giedroyc's friends on the Polish desk at ILC had been plunged into slow-rolling shock by the violence in Poland. Any deals that had been done in Frankfurt or at the Librairie Polonaise were now consigned to history, as everyone confronted a wholly new landscape on the other side of the Iron Curtain. Rudzki was especially traumatized, writing to the Editor that he was 'extremely depressed'; he blamed the crackdown on the 'over-enthusiasm, optimism and lack of thought' of the Polish opposition, which should have known better than to provoke Moscow in the way it had. Jaruzelski, he said, was a 'pure Soviet agent' and an 'Ubek'. Because no travellers were allowed in or out of the country, martial law had been a disaster for book distribution, which had fallen to a trickle, and most of their orders were stacking up in storage at the Polish Library in London. Rudzki didn't know how long the CIA would find this sustainable. 'Polish publishers in exile should think about how best to adapt to this difficult period when our large purchases ... are reduced,' he warned.

The situation stressed Rudzki so much that he fell ill with heart problems and had to postpone his annual trip to Europe to make future plans with Giedroyc and other Polish publishers.

Giedroyc, by contrast, seemed galvanized by events in the East. As the most famous Polish publisher, and a don among émigrés, it was natural that people came to him for help, and he had launched himself into the fray. As a CIA 'asset', he dispensed significant amounts to favoured projects, and soon he began sending money to the Warsaw Underground. Helena Łuczywo made sure that whatever her team produced was put on the trains to the West, and Giedroyc was clearly impressed by what they had achieved. He would send $1,000 to the group every month, noting in his diary that spring, for instance: '5,000d for Bujak'. Although in CIA terms this was very little, it was a great deal in Poland, especially when exchanged on the country's thriving black market, where a dollar bought four times as many Polish złoty as it would at the official rate. It was 'an incredible, *incredible* amount of money', Łuczywo remembered, 'so much money ... [it] allowed us to function very comfortably'. With $1,000 a month she could pay the full-time salaries of around forty people. She didn't know exactly how Giedroyc got it to them – it would pass through a chain of people before reaching the underground – but it never failed to arrive. She had heard about his CIA connections, of course she had; the regime had been making allegations about him since the 1960s, and she was no fan of the American intelligence agency, which had done 'awful things', especially in Chile, but if it kept *Kultura* afloat then this was a very good thing. Taking CIA money, if that was what it was, didn't bother her at all, nor did it bother others whose opinions she respected. She once told an American human rights activist friend, 'we probably got the money from the CIA', and he had laughed. 'They helped us,' she said.

Giedroyc also funded Marian Kaleta. Kaleta had been a crucial figure in sending illicit supplies to Poland since the late 1970s, and now he would serve as Chojecki's effective deputy in the smuggling business, coming to Paris once a month to talk strategy with Mirek and Giedroyc. He had closed his opticians' practice in Malmö and devoted himself full time to supporting the underground, but his unemployment benefits from the Swedish government would only last so long. 'Mr. Editor, the matter is banally simple,' he told Giedroyc. 'I must get some money to live on, because if I don't, the Swedes will force me to go out to work.' Giedroyc paid him a thousand dollars a month until the end of 1982. Although Kaleta griped that this was too modest – it was 'the lowest salary in the country . . . that's how much a cleaning lady in a hospital in Malmö earned' – it was enough, combined with some fraudulent billing, to keep him smuggling.

When it came to the important case of Chojecki, Giedroyc and his friends cast the net wide. Of course, the books programme was a reliable source of funding, and soon after his arrival in Paris the Editor instructed him to set up a monthly magazine, which the ILC would back. Every generation of exiled Poles had its own publication, Giedroyc told him, which acted as a rallying point for the émigré community, and it was high time the Solidarity exiles had their journal too. At first Chojecki was reluctant. He didn't know how to set up a new publication in the West; he didn't even like to write. This was what made him perfect for the job, Giedroyc said, since he wouldn't be sucked into the egotistical trap of pushing his own material, but would step back and give space to others. Giedroyc wasn't a writer either, which was one reason *Kultura* was thought to be such a success.

Chojecki did as he was told. The result was a monthly news

magazine, *Kontakt*, launched in the spring of 1982. Rudzki agreed
to regular purchases of several hundred copies a month. Although
Chojecki saw it as a sideline to his real job as chief of smuggling
operations, the magazine's publishing company, Kontakt, would
grow into a substantial organization, with its own office and printing facilities, and in time its own audio and video departments. It
would also act as a noisy distraction from his clandestine activity,
giving Polish spies in Paris something to write home about. 'All the
people who were active in Kontakt would be visible to the secret
police,' Chojecki said, 'but the people who were doing the smuggling were a completely different set.'

Kontakt and its CIA stipend provided one source of income for
Chojecki. There were others. In February, Giedroyc sketched out
the idea of a Polish Publishing and Culture Fund in which Chojecki
would play the leading role, as a salaried secretary. The Editor
jotted down a few names on a piece of paper. Czesław Miłosz, the
Nobel laureate, was inked in as president. Beneath Miłosz Giedroyc
wrote his own name, then that of Konstanty Jeleński, an experi-
enced *Kultura* contributor who had worked for many years in the
secretariat of the long-running CIA front, the Congress of Cultural
Freedom, helping edit the congress's house journal *Preuves*,
which Minden's organization distributed. Polish intelligence files
described Jeleński accurately as 'a long-time collaborator of the CIA
and [Radio Free Europe]'. The names of other Congress for Cultural
Freedom alumni appeared on Giedroyc's list, too, including Józef
Czapski and the author Gustaw Herling-Grudziński.

But who would supply money for the new fund? In March, a
veteran Ford Foundation executive, Francis X. Sutton, arrived in
Paris to meet with Jeleński, who was now coordinator of the
newly created Fund for the Continuity of Independent Polish
Literature and Humanities. Sutton listened to the plan, read some
of the books the fund proposed to publish and thought they could
provide financing as soon as May, a remarkably quick turnaround
by ordinary grant-making standards. The Ford Foundation would
pay Chojecki a salary of around $28,000 a year over coming years,

plus hundreds of thousands to support Polish writers, and to translate and publish works by ILC-favoured authors, including Orwell, Michnik, Miłosz, Kurt Vonnegut, Solzhenitsyn and Milan Kundera. Was Ford in this case acting as a channel for CIA money? It had played that role many times before. In the 1950s, the Foundation acted as proxy – or a 'cutout' in the jargon – to channel funds for the Agency so often its president had set up an internal committee to decide whether to say yes to particular requests from Langley. At that stage, according to one observer, it seemed to be 'simply an extension of government in the area of international cultural propaganda'. Whether or not that was still the case in 1982, Giedroyc and the committee were clearly alive to how it would look in Poland: an early document relating to the Polish literature fund stated that it would be important for any author who received a grant to be able to say that he or she 'knows nothing about the economic side of the business'.

Chojecki would draw a salary from the fund until the mid-1980s. After that, CIA funding would reach him through the Postal, Telegraph and Telephone International union (PTTI), whose general secretary, Stefan Nędzyński, opened an account for him at a bank near his offices in the Lignon area of Geneva, Switzerland. Chojecki would go there every three months to withdraw $10,000 in francs. He never had to sign for the cash or provide receipts when he spent it, which was one indication that it was dark money; another was the fact that Nędzyński told him some time later it came from the CIA.

The first regular support Chojecki received in Paris however came from another source with CIA links: the Foundation for European Mutual Intellectual Assistance (FEIF), another offshoot of the Congress for Cultural Freedom, in which Jeleński was again a major player. For the first six months of his time in Paris, the FEIF would provide Chojecki with a mailbox at their office on the Boulevard Beaumarchais, and a monthly stipend of 3,000 French francs, or roughly $700.

As was often the case with CIA funding, cash flowed through

a deliberately complex web of sources designed to obscure the money's true origins, and was mixed with above-board donations to give the recipient a legitimate front. With his financing in place, and under the plausible cover of *Kontakt* magazine, Solidarity's new minister for smuggling embarked on his clandestine mission of supplying the underground in Poland.

As well as by train, requests for help reached Paris through the confidential embassy postal system known as the diplomatic bag, in the regular mail and, as the weeks passed and Poland's borders began to reopen, via journalists, travellers and transport workers. Poles saw Paris as a 'honeypot', according to Kaleta. They flocked there with letters of recommendation from prominent members of the underground, requesting various things, and Chojecki's team spent much of their time trying to source the right material to fulfill these orders. Poland's needs were extensive and eclectic. As well as masses of printing equipment, they wanted hair dyes, fake drivers' licences, chemicals for forging identity cards, spray paint to write anti-communist graffiti and camera equipment to record acts of repression. One militant group in Gdańsk even asked for 'small explosive devices . . . for setting fire to e.g. militia cars'. Tomasz Łabędź, a fluent French-speaker on the Paris committee who became one of Mirek's closest aides, had a particular nightmare getting hold of the replacement 'golf ball' typing heads used by IBM's Selectric typewriters and typesetters. These lightweight plastic parts broke easily, and the model with the Polish character set was hard to find in France. It would take Łabędź two to three weeks to order typewriter golf balls and up to a month for those for the typesetters, which were even rarer.

The smugglers could send in money and small parcels in much the same ways requests came out, via diplomats, reporters and Poles who had decided to go home despite the crackdown. Łabędź was well connected with French journalists at the newspaper *Libération* and the radio network RTL and would ask them to carry things with them when they went into Poland. Even quite large items such as George Soros's $10,000 typesetting machine could fit into an individual's luggage on the train.

Not all such deliveries ran smoothly. One CIA-sponsored organization Chojecki supplied was Radio Solidarity, an underground station set up by Zbigniew Romaszewski and his wife Zofia, who had escaped the police on the night of martial law. Chojecki successfully sent radio parts to the Romaszewskis, and on 12 April they broke on to the airwaves with their first message: 'Solidarity lives!' When their transmitter was captured, Chojecki acquired a powerful replacement, sending it to Poland with a Belgian citizen named Roger Noël. Determined to complete the handover in person, Noël walked into the Romaszewskis' Warsaw apartment with the transmitter in a large bag, only to find the secret police waiting. A disastrous situation was made worse by the fact that Joanna Szczęsna was also in the apartment, having been invited round to celebrate the Romaszewskis' wedding anniversary. The presence of key underground figures in the same place at the same time as an important piece of technology arrived from the West was a major contravention of the 'health and safety' rules. Zbigniew managed to bolt before the police realized what they had stumbled upon, but the others were arrested. Szczęsna would not be released until the following year. Zbigniew was eventually caught, and the Romaszewskis were tried and given long prison sentences, but Radio Solidarity would continue to broadcast intermittently.

The heaviest items, including offset printing presses and large quantities of ILC books, had to be trucked in. Luckily for Chojecki, charities and aid organizations had been raising funds to send humanitarian supplies into Poland even before Jaruzelski's action, and they redoubled their efforts after martial law. Around 1,500 charitable transports set off for Poland from France alone in the spring of 1982. Sometimes a charity would approach a local Solidarity group first, to ask what to send, and the local group would inform Paris. When Chojecki got wind that a transport was leaving, he drove the material to the departure point in his car and handed it to an activist to place on the truck, since it wouldn't help anyone if he was spotted with the driver. Eight times out of ten, the transporters would agree to carry the contraband, hiding it under heaps of bedding, food and medicines. Given his passport problems, Chojecki was restricted at first to using transports leaving from France, but when he discovered a route into Belgium via an unmanned border crossing he added the Benelux countries to his departure territories. In time, a friend would provide him with a Swedish passport – these were known to be easy to tamper with, since they used a simple glued-on photo and a stamp – which allowed him to travel all over Europe. The only place he couldn't go was Sweden itself, since he had only a few words of the language. Wherever he went, he dreaded meeting a Swedish-speaking official.

The hardest part of transporting material with the aid trucks was arranging someone to receive it in Poland. His only real option here was to send a postcard in code to a local group, telling them a shipment was coming, but he didn't have contacts everywhere, and it often felt like he was shooting in the dark, trying to hit targets a thousand miles away he couldn't see. Even when the materials arrived safely, he couldn't tell what happened next. Were they divided up among the groups, as he intended, or had one faction taken it all? Squabbles often broke out, and complaints reached Paris. If he was lucky, he would get confirmation that the goods had arrived in the form of a message printed in a copy of an underground publication which would find him. He was known for these purposes by the codename 'Raphael'. 'We thank Raphael for the present,' the messages would read.

A shopping list that reached Paris from Witek Łuczywo gives a flavour of how the requests worked. To prove his identity, Witek referred to a conversation he'd once had with 'C' (probably Chojecki) explaining 'the intricacies of the customs system in Poland', and sent greetings from 'a nice brunette' who had returned to Poland after visiting Kaleta's house in Malmö. What Witek wanted most was a recipe for ink for the simple type of Rex-Rotary protein duplicator that the underground often used. They also needed supplies for the large offset machines, including blank printing plates, and film for the photographic process of transferring the typeset pages to the plates. The rest of the list was taken up with the kinds of communications equipment they used for security, including radio scanners to eavesdrop on police conversations:

a) Transceiver – ICOM company with power amplifier and automatic antenna adjustment.
b) Radios – indifferent company – 432 MHz bands.
c) VHF transmitters – range 68–73 MHz – 10 channels – power 40W, company YASU.
d) Transmitters on VHF 68–73 MHz band, 10 channels – power 5 watt – YASU company.
e) Quartz stabilized multi-channel listening devices for the 172–175 MHz range, and 420–450 MHz – company indifferent.

Witek emphasized that they wanted the exact models on the list, as in previous shipments they had received 'non-standard' devices which 'cause more trouble than good'.

Chojecki's heart would sink as he read these detailed requests, as they were hard to fulfill. Orders for American technology gave him a particular headache, since US sanctions on the Eastern Bloc meant he could be prosecuted for sending it. What's more, in this instance Witek gave no specific drop-off address. Where exactly was Mirek meant to deliver it?

11

Ideas for Getting Out of a
No-Win Situation

If we are to believe that, as its perpetrators claim, the war was instigated to save the economy, then the operation was successful but the patient died.

Jacek Kuroń, *Mazovia Weekly*

My mate at the warehouse said one day after a drink or two: 'You know what, Kepka. All Poland, from the Baltic to the Tatra mountains, from the Bug to the Oder, is one big concentration camp, and the prisons are like punishment cells in it, see?'

Marek Nowakowski, *Martial Law Report*

The most important thing about the first edition of *Mazovia Weekly* wasn't the lead story. Nor was it the fact that the paper began at issue number two, in tribute to Zieleński, its deceased founder. No, the most important thing, when the paper was dropped off to its clandestine distributors on 11 February 1982, was the logo printed at the top of the two left-hand columns on page one. 'SOLIDARNOŚĆ', it read, Solidarity, in bright red ink. The emblem of the outlawed movement, designed in August 1980 to show a crowd of individuals shuffling beneath the Polish flag in more or less the same direction – in sharp contrast to communist art, which showed people marching in step – sent a powerful message. Poland might be an Orwellian state once more. Ten thousand Solidarity activists might be sitting in internment camps up and down the land. Secret police might be knocking on doors and dragging people off into the night; and a recorded voice might announce 'Warning: this conversation is being controlled' whenever anyone picked up the phone. But there were still people at liberty who were organized enough to create a quality uncensored newspaper with a crimson logo. There was still hope.

It would have been far easier for Witek and the printers to have produced a black and white masthead, but they had gone to great lengths to add colour to the process to show the authorities that they could not be broken. It was the printing equivalent of blowing a raspberry or a Churchillian two-fingered salute. The red logo appeared on the paper's front page next to a quote from Lech Wałęsa, 'Solidarity cannot be divided or destroyed,' and it would taunt the Polish interior ministry and the KGB chiefs in Warsaw for the following six years, almost until the end of the Cold War. Witek and the printers had done such a good job, some readers thought *Mazovia Weekly* was a false-flag operation run by the security service: it was one of their favourite ploys to try to infiltrate and control all sides in a political argument at once. In fact, this first edition, three thin sheets of A4 clasped by a single staple, was the result of a monumental effort by a small team of no more than twenty or thirty conspirators in the Warsaw Underground.

Even producing the main story had stressed the nascent organization to breaking point. The editors wanted to run an interview with Bujak and Kulerski on the front page of their first issue, as further evidence that Solidarity lived on, so Ewa Kulik had arranged a safe house in southern Warsaw where the politicians could get together with a reporter, and passed the address to Bujak's security detail, Tomasz Chlebowski. Chlebowski liked to scout out his ward's destination in advance, to check he wasn't delivering Bujak into a trap, but on this day he didn't have time, and when he and the leader showed up in the designated street he couldn't find the right building, so they went home to consult a map. The result was a ninety-minute delay, during which Kulik went into meltdown. When he finally arrived, she gave Chlebowski such a bawling out that he quit, deciding he would move back to Helena's side of the underground.

Hard as it was, getting the leadership and a reporter together was a cakewalk compared with printing the issue. Their main priority as Witek saw it was to protect Helena and the editors, so they designed a system based on the principle of canal locks to insulate different parts of the network from each other, and prevent one slip-up allowing the SB to roll up the whole operation. This meant every process, from editing to distribution, would take place in its own location, and materials would be transported between sites by couriers. If this weren't complicated enough, the 'lock' apartments were changed every two to three weeks, and each had to have a back-up in case the first choice was compromised by some last-minute issue with the police or the host. Every lock would also need two nearby locations to use as dead-drops. The system required an army of people to act as couriers, but it meant that no one had the full picture of who was doing what or where.

Production began with moving the IBM Selectric machine from safe storage to the apartment set aside for typesetting. Shifting bulky equipment at a time when private vehicles were outlawed took nerves of steel, as someone had to carry a heavy suitcase on public transport or in a taxi, in full view of the security forces. When the machine reached the right apartment and they switched it on, they realized it made a terrible racket which the neighbours were bound to hear, so they constructed a tent of blankets, in which the typist sat. When the pages had been set, they were moved to another site, where the aluminium plates for the offset printer were created. This process involved photographing the made-up pages and turning them into diapositives, something like large photographic slides, each of which was laid on a blank metal plate, known as a matrix, which was coated with a light-sensitive emulsion. When the combined diapositive and matrix were exposed to UV light and developed, the image of the page was engraved in the plate's aluminium surface.

Witek performed this process himself for the first issue, in a basement belonging to the Polish TV director Stanisław Bareja. The finished plates were taken to the house in the sleepy suburb of Radośc where the Three Musketeers had their hidden shop. The engraved aluminium surfaces were loaded in turn into the press, which worked by applying ink to the plate, transferring it to a rubber drum, then 'offsetting' the result on to paper. Offset presses were the fastest, most efficient printing machines the underground possessed and could turn out thousands of sheets an hour, but they were also very loud, which was why printers preferred to work in the basements of isolated houses in far-flung parts of the city.

The printed sheets were collated, stapled and taken to a set of dead-drop apartments where distributors would pick up their allotted number of copies, which they took to sell mostly in Poland's industrial plants and factories. Very little of the cover price ever made it back to the management, but with Giedroyc's money pouring in from Paris that didn't matter. The point of selling it rather than giving the weekly away was that Helena thought people wouldn't value a free paper as much as one they had to pay for.

Witek and the NOWa printers produced around 10,000 copies of the launch issue. The new publication was sober, measured and knew its readership: they were Solidarity sympathizers who didn't need to be brought round with histrionic arguments. Given the state monopoly on paper, space was always tight, and the editors valued information above all, so they boiled everything right down, chopping out any stylistic pretension. A joke would do the rounds

of opposition circles: 'What is a pole?' 'A tree edited by *Mazovia Weekly.*' Even so, a cold, pared-back fury would emerge from the smudgy blocks of sans-serif, exemplified by the front-page editorial in the first edition, which explained why they had picked up the baton Jerzy Zieleński had left:

> Absent from the funeral were those of us who were in prison, those of us who were in hiding. Several hundred people came. An overwhelming silence over the coffin. Jerzy Zieleński, Home Army soldier, participant of the Warsaw Uprising . . . in August 1980 he was in the Lenin Shipyard . . . The tragic death of our friend interrupted his work. Taking over from Jurek, we are starting to publish *Mazovia* from the second issue.

Beneath this tribute, they ran the interview with Bujak and Kulerski, who expressed a rousing commitment to the cause and set out a political strategy for reaching their goals. It was difficult to know whether it would be months or years before they could force concessions from the military junta, but however long it might be, Solidarity was worth fighting for. The way forward was to pressure Jaruzelski to restore Solidarity. To do that, it would be necessary to build a second trade union structure underground, 'to create basic connections, to organize the flow of information, unofficial publications, communications'. This of course was a task Helena, Kulik and the team had already begun.

Mazovia Weekly carried news too, often written from the growing numbers of regional newsletters sent in from around the country, or from Radio Free Europe, with which they enjoyed a symbiotic relationship, as RFE would also broadcast any new information they published. The first edition revealed what factories around the country had done to mark the first month of martial law on 13 January 1982: stopping work, holding Catholic masses for the internees and the dead, laying flowers. The editors would devote large amounts of space to workers' protests and publish calls to join future actions. They would maintain a public record of regime atrocities and acts of repression, as they had done in *Solidarity Information*, publishing the names of people who had been arrested to keep them in the public eye. They worked to establish contact with those in internment, too. This task was led before her arrest by Joanna Szczęsna, with remarkable success. Imprisoned friends of the underground such as Jacek Kuroń and Adam Michnik regularly wrote for the newspaper.

Even four decades later, Michnik did not want to reveal how he had smuggled his articles past the prison guards, but the usual ways visitors foiled searches were by hiding small pieces of paper around their bodies or in their mouths. Despite being in jail for much of the 1980s, Michnik's writing would appear in underground publications all over Poland, as well as in the West. He found jail gave him a lot of time to read. When he needed an uncensored book, he would ask his partner to visit him with a Russian edition disguised in the jacket of a less controversial work: Michnik had learned to read Russian well by struggling through an early copy of Solzhenitsyn's *The Gulag Archipelago*, which he arranged to have brought to him from the West, but most Polish prison officers didn't understand the language. He received a book by the Soviet dissident Nadezhda Mandelstam in this way, disguised as *The Road to Calgary*, the trilogy that had won Aleksey Tolstoy a Stalin Prize. Michnik didn't know it, but Minden was promoting Mandelstam heavily at the time. He also supported Michnik. At one point, Minden promised a Polish émigré publisher that he would buy 'as many copies as possible' of a book of the Polish dissident's essays.

Through the pages of *Mazovia Weekly*, Michnik, Kuroń and other internees were able to maintain their status as guiding lights of opposition thinking.

But the newspaper meant more than the words it contained. It was a living social movement, which brought together the disheartened, rag-tag pro-Solidarity survivors of the martial-law crackdown. It was Kuroń's axiom that activists needed tasks to perform, otherwise their opposition meant little more than having a conversation or a political opinion, and *Mazovia Weekly* gave people something to do. 'You needed thousands of people to keep everything going,' said Helena Łuczywo, 'and people made friends with each other, they got in touch, they got organized.' Bujak would go as far as to date the launch of the Warsaw Underground to the creation of the newspaper. 'I don't mean that there weren't independent groups of activists from the very outbreak of the "war", he said, 'but simply that until they had a network of distributors in the factories, they were nothing more than groups of activists.' When they started to publish *Mazovia Weekly*, the organization had a practical purpose again. People started to meet up, pay their union dues and produce more underground publications.

Thanks to its reputable journalism and high-quality production, *Mazovia Weekly* rapidly became the leading underground paper in Poland, eclipsing other, earlier newsletters that had been put out more rapidly. Witek came up with the idea of doing deals with multiple publishing houses around the country, making print operations more resilient to police raids and spreading distribution out to the regions. They could produce matrices for all types of presses, which were sent out via the underground postal system. This network grew, so that by the mid-1980s the newspaper was being printed at a score of different sites, employing several hundred people. It was hard with such a structure to estimate the peak circulation, but sometimes 24,000 copies were produced for Warsaw alone, and the higher estimates put the nationwide print run at around 80,000. While this was fewer than a comparable Western newspaper, each copy was shared by many more readers, which meant it had a larger impact than those figures implied.

No one worked for *Mazovia Weekly* to get rich and many staff were volunteers, but the editors received the Polish national average wage, around $30 a month, while the printers, skilled people who took on a lot of risk, were given more. Helena and her team also paid typists and other clerical workers, and spent money on transportation costs, petrol, paper and other print supplies available in Poland. Throughout its life, the newspaper's most important source of income was the West. Even in 1987, a message that reached

Giedroyc would describe the money he sent to Warsaw as 'the basis of our existence'.

As with Chojecki, the editors recorded their receipts using initials or codenames in a 'confirmations' column in the newspaper. 'Thank you Jerzy for 1' meant a $1,000 payment had reached them from Giedroyc, and whenever copies of *Mazovia Weekly* arrived in Paris the column was carefully scrutinized to make sure no money was lost en route. In time, Helena would employ a bookkeeper, who sent full accounts of the editorial budget, showing Giedroyc where the money had gone. The Warsaw Underground developed such a trustworthy reputation that Giedroyc also sent money to be passed to other underground organizations, and sometimes couriers would bring in $10,000 at a time. The coded signal for receipt of third-party money in the newspaper's confirmations column was simply 'and', followed by the amount received. 'Giedroyc told us that we were the only organization that properly accounted for all the money every year,' Szczęsna recalled with pride.

There was no doubt Solidarity had lost the first battles of the 'war'. Jaruzelski's assault on Polish society had been well executed and would be cited by academics as a textbook example of how an authoritarian regime could bring its unruly citizens to heel. The result was a kind of occupation, with censorship of correspondence, curfews, mass raids, searches, arrests and justice meted out by military courts. The fear among the liberal opposition in Warsaw, which Helena particularly felt, was that radicals would launch some kind of hopeless, vainglorious attack, which would provoke another bloodbath in a country that already had suffered so much.

That was why she freaked out when an article reached her in February from Kuroń in Białołęka prison, entitled 'Ideas for Getting Out of a No-Win Situation'. Kuroń had spent much of his life preaching the principle of non-violence. Now he seemed to have reversed that position. They were at war, he said. Violence, threats and desperate appeals for calm were the only language the authorities used to talk to society, and society needed to respond in the same way. The only chance for Poles was a 'popular, well-organized resistance' which would 'liquidate' the occupation in a collective, organized uprising. Everything must be done to make the Soviets realize that if they intervened it would be 'the last act of the USSR'. 'At present,' he concluded, 'I consider the preparation for the overthrow of the occupation in a collective action to be the least of the evils.'

The article sparked a huge row among the top *Mazovia Weekly* editors. Łuczywo declared she could not publish the piece under any circumstances. Szczęsna – this was some months before her arrest – said that she couldn't possibly work for a newspaper that refused to run a piece by Kuroń, even if he was wrong. The argument came to a head when Szczęsna said she was done with *Mazovia Weekly* and was going to turn herself in to the police. Łuczywo didn't believe her. So Szczęsna started to put on her coat – at which point Helena's resistance crumbled. *Mazovia Weekly* would run the piece, but the issue continued to divide the opposition. Radicals, especially those in the regions, called for a more aggressive stance against the regime than the one espoused by the newspaper. To counter the hotheads, Łuczywo decided they should convene a national group of underground leaders to run the opposition in Wałęsa's absence and lay down strategy across Poland. This group would be called the Temporary Coordinating Commission (TKK) and was to represent the trade union's leadership until such time as it was able to operate in the open again. Establishing the TKK became Łuczywo's priority that spring, but it would entail a great deal of risk and effort, as they had to bring opposition leaders from across Poland to Warsaw for a secret meeting, creating another giant security headache.

It took a couple of months to make the arrangements. A call went out in February to leaders of the major regional Solidarity groups, asking them to come to the capital for a meeting. Each delegate would need a safe house and a bodyguard cum liaison officer to carry messages to and fro and deliver the delegates to the congress. If a single informant got wind of the gathering, the most important remnants of the opposition could be taken out in one fell swoop.

They met on 22 April. As well as Bujak, Łuczywo, Szczęsna and Kulik, there were regional Solidarity leaders Bogdan Lis of Gdańsk, Władysław Hardek of Kraków and Władysław Frasyniuk of Wrocław. Michnik would put forth eloquent arguments to the conference from prison. The TKK leaders would make two decisions with major implications for the future, and for Chojecki. The first was that they rejected terrorism or an immediate general strike in favour of the 'long march' strategy espoused by Michnik, because, as he had written, 'any confrontation must lead to tragedy, since [the regime] is full of determination and will not back down even if it means shedding rivers of blood'. What Poland needed was not terrorism and conflict, he wrote, but 'widespread underground activity that will reconstruct society'.

Second, they called for activists in the West to set up a foreign Solidarity bureau to coordinate the mushrooming international support groups. Bujak and the Warsaw contingent opposed this idea on security grounds, thinking SB and KGB agents would soon infiltrate it. 'The most dangerous spot in our whole organization would be the point where we had contact with the West,' Kulik said. But Bogdan Lis argued passionately for the new bureau, and Frasyniuk supported him. The proposal was passed.

On 8 May, Lis sent a message to the West, announcing that Jerzy Milewski, a stranded Solidarity leader from Gdańsk, was to lead a new coordination centre. Milewski would open a bureau in Brussels that summer, choosing the Belgian capital because it was also the home of Nato and of important international trade union institutions they relied on for financing. He would stay in regular contact with the TKK, smuggling encrypted letters to Poland every month with reports of the bureau's activities. Solidarity's centre of gravity in the West now moved from France to Belgium, and much of the Paris committee's money and resources were transferred to Brussels. At the same time, the TKK formally appointed Chojecki head of material and technical assistance to the Solidarity underground, rubber-stamping his appointment as minister for smuggling.

The Brussels bureau would act as a liaison for journalists wanting to contact Solidarity activists in Poland and would keep Solidarity in the public eye in the West. Its principal asset would be the money it funnelled to Poland, largely from overt American sources. Its weakness, as Kulik had spotted, was that it presented a giant, obvious target for Eastern spies.

12

HELPFUL

Poland is not bounded by the land where the Vistula flows
Kultura

In politics one can never do more than decide which of two
evils is the lesser, and there are some situations from which
one can only escape by acting like a devil or a lunatic.
George Orwell, 'Writers and Leviathan'

Bill Casey was on the charge. From Afghanistan to Cambodia,
from the Sahara desert to New Caledonia and Suriname, no report
of communist activity, no matter how insignificant, escaped the
notice of the director of central intelligence, or his insistence that
the CIA counter it. The Agency hadn't been engaged on so many
fronts across the globe since the overreach years of the 1950s.
Casey's management style was to push, push, then push some
more. According to Robert Gates, who in 1982 was appointed
deputy director of intelligence, Casey was 'Always restless, always
flying off to visit "his" war zones. Always poking and prodding,
hectoring, demanding. Always frustrated by a [CIA] Directorate of
Operations he found too sluggish, too timid, too business-as-usual.'
It was strange, then, that although Gates recognized at that moment
that 'no corner in foreign affairs took as much time and energy as
the crisis in Poland' and that 'nothing would have such great consequences for the future', this did not seem to translate quickly into a

lavish new plan to support the Solidarity underground. While top Kremlinologists in Washington were urging the CIA to expand its covert operations in Poland that summer, and in particular its support for Giedroyc, others argued that new activity in the Eastern Bloc would be counterproductive. The result was that in the first half of 1982 no clear strategy emerged from the Reagan administration. Richard Pipes, for one, was frustrated, writing in March, 'It seems to me . . . quite imperative . . . that a decision be made on what our long-term policy toward the Communist Bloc is.'

Hampered by a lack of travellers, the Polish books programme had struggled at the start of the year, but by early summer it was showing signs of recovery. Minden toured Europe in June, holding interviews with some fifty employees, publishers and distributors, and although few of the meetings this time around were with Poles, there were some bright spots to report from the Polish programme. The CIA had appointed a new head of the Polonia Book Fund in London, an affable young English architect named Jan Chodakowski. He would prove a creative and popular choice, although Minden felt he sometimes put too much store in 'gimmicky ideas', such as smuggling miniature booklets and magazines in Tampax boxes or Tate & Lyle sugar packets. His appointment would also lead to ruffled feathers at émigré publishers whose budget Chodakowski wanted to cut, who threatened to take their grievance to the 'Foundation', meaning the CIA, or to Brzezinski or even the newspapers if funding wasn't restored. Minden drew this to the attention of an Agency officer in London, 'Dick B', who smoothed it over.

In Paris, Minden learned from two of his major Polish outlets, the Librairie Polonaise and Libella, a small publishing house cum bookstore on the Île Saint-Louis, that visitors from the East were returning. Giedroyc, too, seemed upbeat about the situation, writing in his correspondence with Rudzki that contact with Poland was 'recovering quite quickly'. He was being inundated by Polish visitors and had begun to receive 'a lot of material' from the country, including short stories and poems, some of which he intended to publish. A huge number of journals were already being printed in the underground, many of which were being sent to him: already by April he was receiving around eighty. 'The courage of the humanities community is truly exceptional,' he wrote.

Giedroyc was pressing ahead with his own busy publishing list, including a collection of reportage from 1981, which told the story of Solidarity, a volume of Kazimierz Brandys's memoirs, and essays by Konstanty Jeleński. Rudzki agreed that the ILC would purchase Brandys and Jeleński in bulk, for distribution to Poland, and sent Maisons-Laffitte several copies of Norman Davies's two-part history of Poland, *God's Playground*, which Giedroyc had requested. He also pressed the Editor to increase the number of miniature editions of books and journals published by the Literary Institute. They had spotted that, in the more dangerous political climate, travellers preferred to take these tiny volumes, around 3 inches wide by 4 high,* as they were easier to hide. Giedroyc agreed that they were the best way of getting literature into the country. From now on, he would increase the run of mini *Kulturas*, as well as print a number of works from the Literary Institute's back catalogue in the reduced format.

By late summer, discussions in Washington about the Polish situation were at last starting to produce results. On 6 August, Reagan's new national security advisor, William Clark, wrote to Casey asking for advice on steps they might take 'to provide modest support to the moderate elements of Solidarity'. The idea, Clark said, was 'to pressure the Polish and Soviet governments to end martial law, release political prisoners and re-establish a social contract with the Polish people'. Casey talked it over with other senior officials, including Defense Secretary Weinberger and George Shultz, who had replaced Al Haig at the State Department, and on 1 September he asked Clark to set up a meeting about an enhanced covert action for Poland. Although any expanded activity would require the written approval of the president, Casey supported the idea, especially if it could be done via surrogate cutouts.

The discussions intensified through September, when Pipes

---

* 8cm × 11cm.

joined a national security working group in the White House, arguing that Solidarity must be kept alive. The movement's importance
extended beyond Poland's borders to the whole Eastern Bloc, Pipes
believed: 'Solidarity was the most important development in the
Soviet camp because it directly threatened the Soviet system and
ideology,' he wrote. 'Nothing like it existed.' It wasn't just about
Poland, but about encouraging a rebellion in the Soviet system. 'We
could not let Solidarity disappear.'

It took several weeks more for Reagan to take the final decision.
On 4 November, he convened a top-secret subgroup of the National
Security Committee in the White House Situation Room, the wood-
panelled bunker beneath the presidential complex. Reagan sat at
the top of the table, surrounded by his senior security advisors,
including Pipes, Casey, Clark, Shultz and Haig. After a brief discussion, the president agreed to sign a Memorandum of Notification
authorizing a new CIA covert action in Poland on the basis of US
national security. The operation's remit was narrow. It would supply
money and non-lethal aid to Solidarity and other moderate opposition groups, to help them organize and communicate their message
to the Polish people. The aim was to apply pressure to the regime to
force Jaruzelski to ease his repressive policies.

The new action was given the cryptonym 'QRHELPFUL'. The
two-letter 'QR' prefix, known as a digraph, denoted the country
or geographical region the operation would target. In Polish
operations, digraphs were commonly QR or QT. The rest of the
codename was picked more or less at random, although in some
cases it seemed to derive from an aspect of the person or programme to which it referred. 'HELPFUL' was what the CIA
programme intended to be to Solidarity.

QRHELPFUL would be a modest CIA operation by the standards of the Casey era. No one, least of all the director of central
intelligence, expected it to produce quite the effect that it did.

On the last day of 1982, Jaruzelski suspended martial law and
released thousands of internees under an amnesty. In practice, this

made little difference to the opposition, since the regime simply wrote the wartime powers it had seized into law and formally banned the trade union, which until then had only been suspended. 'The bottom line is that the situation remains grim,' Casey wrote to Clark on 10 January 1983, enclosing a recent briefing. The regime had achieved a 'clear victory' over the Solidarity underground, and there was no indication that the authorities were about to ease their security measures. Up to 4,000 political prisoners remained behind bars, and the government planned to put five leading KOR activists, including Kuroń and Michnik, on trial on trumped-up charges including trying to overthrow the government by force – the very crime the junta had just committed. Chojecki had also been charged, *in absentia*.

On a personal note, Casey added that Warsaw continued to mount a 'vitriolic anti-US campaign', which included 'posters ridiculing President Reagan'.

The better news was that the first funding for QRHELPFUL was almost in place. The Agency's deputy director for operations, John Stein, sent a memo to the CIA comptroller that month asking for a million dollars to be released from the Contingency Reserve Fund, the Agency's rainy-day budget. Deputy Director of Intelligence Gates described the equipment this money was to buy as 'printing materials, communications equipment, and other supplies for waging underground political warfare'. In other words, the Agency was about to scale up massively the supply of the types of material Chojecki, his colleagues and the book programme were doing their best to send.

In all, the CIA allocated close to $2 million to QRHELPFUL for that first year. This was roughly itemized as:

$600,000 for communications equipment
$300,000 for printing material
$100,000 for families of prisoners
More than $500,000 for Solidarity members outside Poland
More than $400,000 for propaganda.

QRHELPFUL would be housed within the CIA's International Activities Division, the action arm of the clandestine Directorate of Operations. The IAD was the part of the Agency responsible for blowing things up, gunrunning, training rebel groups and launching propaganda warfare, and in 1983 Casey would split it into two departments: the paramilitary Special Activities Division and the Political-Psychological Staff. QRHELPFUL would be run out of the latter division, under the leadership of Richard Malzahn, head of the Soviet–East Europe Group. Malzahn perfectly fitted the Political-Psychological type. Born in Milwaukee, he had won a scholarship to Yale and might have become an academic if it hadn't been for the crushing verdict of the British historian Basil Liddell Hart, who told him his research was riddled with errors, and led Malzahn to opt for a CIA career instead. Malzahn served in The Hague, Saigon and Bonn, but didn't take too well to overseas postings, since immersing himself in a foreign language and culture 'just wasn't his thing', a friend recalled. So he returned to headquarters, where he built on his experience in West Germany to become a leading expert on KGB 'active measures', the spectrum of covert operations used by the Soviet spy agency to advance Moscow's interests, which ranged from espionage, propaganda and disinformation to sabotage and assassination.

Early in 1983, Malzahn began putting together a team of officers to manage QRHELPFUL. London and Bonn would be important hubs, but the key was Paris, where QRBERETTA had been operating for so long. Here Malzahn had a problem: no one on his staff had the right combination of French, Polish and English that the job required, so he cast around in other departments, including the Foreign Broadcasting Information Service (FBIS) based at Reston, Virginia, the branch of the CIA set up to monitor international media. Here he found Cecilia 'Celia' Larkin, probably the only Agency officer ever to have stood vigil beneath Stalin's portrait after his death in 1953: it hadn't been her choice, she was in elementary school at the time. Raised in a small community in Mazovia, Larkin lost her father at an early age, and in the 1960s when she was fifteen her mother took the family to the US. They settled in Detroit, where for a time Celia was employed as a reporter for a local Polish-language radio station, before applying to the CIA in 1980. The Agency set her to work monitoring the Polish media at the FBIS. In normal times this job meant reading between the lines of turgid, state-censored news outlets, but, since this was the Carnival, she instead witnessed the extraordinary flowering of the independent press.

Larkin was in her mid-thirties when she met Malzahn. She was smart and tough, and spoke excellent English with a trace of a Polish accent. It took just half an hour for him to decide to recruit her. Malzahn's group were a diverse, eccentric crew, stuffed with characters who could have come from central casting: there was a guy who thought he was 007, a strongman of Mongolian heritage and a French femme fatale. But she didn't stay at headquarters for long. Since she had no operational experience, Malzahn sent her on a quickfire training course, before deploying her to Paris, where she became a lynchpin of QRHELPFUL, recruiting and working with the Poles in France.

The CIA spent almost $1.5 million on QRHELPFUL in fiscal year 1983 – not quite the $2 million requested, but near enough. By the summer Malzahn's team had around twenty assets, referred to within the Agency by such cryptonyms as QRCARROTTOP and QTOCCUR.

It was natural that Malzahn should draw on people from the book programme, who had decades of experience infiltrating material through the Iron Curtain and long-standing associations with a branch of the Agency. One recruit was Wanda Gawrońska, a Polish-Italian Catholic who had been sending shipments of ILC books from Rome to the University in Lublin for several years. Minden noted in 1981 that Gawrońska had 'many social and business contacts who travel to Poland and the Soviet Union and are prepared to take books with them'. Officers from QRHELPFUL would approach such people and say, 'If you had more money, could you do more?' The answer, often, was 'Yes, I can.'

In February, Rudzki wrote to Giedroyc to discuss a forthcoming action. With exemplary timing, the Editor had just published a landmark op-ed in *Kultura* which could have acted as QRHELPFUL's mission statement. The start of 1983 found the Polish opposition at a low ebb, public signs of resistance had declined, Solidarity's underground structures were weak and the regime had no interest in finding a compromise, according to *Kultura*'s editors. This led them to an ominous conclusion, that the regime and its backers in Moscow might attempt a 'final solution' in Poland, which would mean pacifying the country 'in such a way that it stops causing embarrassing problems for the Kremlin'. Facing this scenario, the only hope for Poles lay with the émigrés, who would have to take advantage of their freedom of action and access to information to support the growth of an entire 'underground society' in Poland. As the author explained:

> It is naturally difficult to expect a nation of many millions to go underground on a daily basis. But . . . a nation of many millions can, while living and working within the framework of an 'official country', remain spiritually faithful to the 'real country', whose living embodiment for a year and a half, and indelible sign forever, became 'Solidarity'.

The 'underground society' was by no means a new concept. It was the way the 'real Poland' had always survived under totalitarian rule, by turning in on itself, keeping the flame of independence alive in the private spaces of family homes, living rooms and Poles' own minds. What was more novel was the emphasis on how it should be supported from the West, where émigrés, reinvigorated by the new wave of Solidarity refugees, had to act not merely as political spokespeople and providers of ideas for the underground, but as organizers of practical and moral assistance:

> The 'underground' without the support of the émigrés – both material and conceptual – has no chance of operating really

effectively. Only this deep, undisclosed backing can provide the kind of protection that voters and an independent judiciary give to political institutions in law-abiding countries.

Providing 'deep, undisclosed backing' for the opposition had in many ways been Giedroyc's mission since the 1950s. The most vital form of secret activity, *Kultura* went on, was publishing: 'Of all the forms of non-disclosed activities, the most important today is to inform, educate and stimulate political thinking. For this we need underground publications, newspapers, magazines, tapes and books.' The editorial ended with a pledge to continue supporting the underground press, since the struggle of the Polish people was not yet over.

Rudzki reacted with enthusiasm to the *Kultura* article, which chimed so closely with thinking at the CIA. He told Giedroyc he wanted to develop the editorial's themes into something more practical. In particular he agreed that they needed to supply and fund the underground from the West, and to do that they must expand the 'émigré platform' with newcomers from the Solidarity generation. Did Giedroyc have anyone particular in mind? If so, Rudzki could help them. 'The solutions in this area are to some extent linked to my work,' he wrote. 'The delivery of books and other materials to the country would probably be one of the main components of the whole action.' They had to move quickly, he wrote: 'If something useful is to come about, no time should be wasted.'

There is no record of Giedroyc's response, but he and Rudzki both knew of a central player among the younger generation of Solidarity émigrés who would fit the bill. He was well connected in Polish circles and had already met Minden and Casey. He would go by the CIA cryptonym QRGUIDE and work with Celia Larkin, and Agency officers would come to regard his contribution as 'outstanding'. His name was Mirosław Chojecki.

At first, Malzahn, Larkin and the CIA officers running QRHELPFUL treated the émigré networks with caution. They wanted to know who was getting their millions and how they were spending it, not least because the Agency had been burned in Poland before. In the 1950s, it had run guns and money to the anti-communist Freedom and Independence Association (WiN), without realizing that the group was entirely in the hands of Polish intelligence and the NKVD. This time around, they wanted every detail, including how the money was sent in, who carried it, how it was distributed and what the recipients did with it. The Poles refused to tell them. Sure, they agreed, it was CIA money, but they were running whole different levels of risk. If they or their friends were caught they faced interrogation, jail and even death. They were also highly aware as East Europeans that there were spies and informants everywhere, which meant it was better to share as little as possible. 'This is what a person from Eastern Europe knows in their bones,' said Benjamin Fischer, the former CIA chief histor-ian.* 'Everybody betrays everybody else. Americans are kind of naive about things like that.' What struck Fischer as unusual in this case was that the CIA agreed to the Poles' terms, saying, 'We're going to take it on faith that these people are doing what they are supposed to be doing with the money.' This was pretty much how the book programme had always been run. 'Some of the people who worked in the book programme kept meticulous notes about who got the books, and where they think they ended up,' said Fischer. 'But even there, we took it on faith that these people were doing what they were supposed to be doing. We didn't send auditors out. It didn't work that way.'

Since it was important for everyone involved that the hand of the CIA remained hidden, the Agency used cutouts to channel money to the opposition, along with so-called 'stand-up guys', people who could be relied upon to do the right thing. A stand-up guy might be a multimillionaire who owned a group of shopping malls in New

---

* Fischer is the only person to have been given full access to QRHELPFUL files for his research. He wrote a book and made a documentary about the programme, but both remain classified.

Zealand, Fischer explained. They would be given a brown envelope filled with cash which they were happy to pass on, and if anyone asked them they would say they had donated their own money and the trail would stop there. There were dozens of figures and groups in the Polish diaspora who were content to play this role. The system didn't just disguise the source of funding, it also saved the CIA's blushes if anything went wrong. 'We could always say we didn't know what they were doing,' Fischer said.

Deniability was key. Many people in the opposition knew or suspected that the CIA supported Solidarity, but the Polish tradition of conspiracy ensured no one would admit it, and the Agency's technique of mixing dark money with clean meant even the movement's leaders weren't sure which funds came from where. So what if people guessed at the secret, if there was no direct proof? The communists regularly denounced all the émigrés for working with the CIA, but since they always cried wolf, no one listened.

Weeks after the launch of QRHELPFUL, in the spring of 1983, Giedroyc rang Chojecki and asked him to come out to Maisons-Laffitte. He couldn't say why because the phones were bugged, but something in Giedroyc's tone told Chojecki that this was an order and not a request. Mirek drove out through the western Paris suburbs for the appointed time, parked up on a side street off Avenue de Poissy and walked through the pines to the ivy-covered villa. As usual, the doorbell triggered a cacophony inside the house from the bad-tempered spaniel Giedroyc kept, which was why the building's inhabitants had installed a plaque that read *cave canem*, 'beware of the dog', at the front door. Chojecki waited in the spacious reception hall where he and so many Poles had stood before, surrounded by Czapski's paintings, and gifts and knick-knacks from Poland, including a toy sheep someone had sent, no one knew why until they thought to open its belly and found a microfilm hidden inside. Giedroyc emerged to usher his visitor into the small office, which they entered past another sign in Latin that read *cave hominem*, 'beware of the man' – one of the Editor's wry jokes.

Giedroyc began with his usual fifteen-minute tirade against whatever was happening in Poland, before arriving at the point. Chojecki was surprised to find himself on the receiving end of a dressing-down.

'Mr Mirek, I'm getting a lot of complaints about you,' Giedroyc told him. 'You're sending equipment out to where it hasn't been ordered, which means it only gets to the right place weeks or months later.'

The smuggling minister tried to defend himself, explaining the difficulties involved in using humanitarian transports whose destinations he didn't control. If he found a charity was taking material to location A, but his equipment was targeted at location B, all he could do was try to get a message to the people in B, telling them they had to get to A to pick it up. This meant more risk for the underground, who had to travel back and forth, but what else could he do?

'You don't have your own transport?' Giedroyc asked.

Marian Kaleta did. In the first months after Chojecki's arrival in Paris, the smugglers had persuaded Blumsztajn to part with $5,000 of the committee's cash to buy a vehicle. Kaleta had found an old florist's van in Holland, fitted it out with a secret compartment, recruited a Swedish driver, Sven Järn, and began running contraband into Poland via the Baltic ferries in the guise of humanitarian relief. It had been, and continued to be, a big success, and Chojecki had considered doing the same, but hadn't got round to it. Giedroyc didn't know precisely how Chojecki worked because they liked to keep each other's operations separate, following Polish 'health and safety' rules.

'Then we will buy you a truck,' the Editor announced.

They discussed the price. Chojecki reckoned 60,000 French francs should be enough. Giedroyc agreed. Then he went back to complaining about the news from Poland.

Mirek didn't have to sign any paperwork for this money: in general when Giedroyc paid him it was 'unvouchered', a hallmark of funds that came from the CIA. The truck was intended to carry the same types of materials Chojecki had been shipping for more than a year. These would be purchased partly by the book programme and by QRHELPFUL, with other supplies from more public sources. The aim as ever was to bury CIA covert support under layers of overt assistance.

Chojecki maintained later that even he didn't know exactly which of his funding streams originated with the Agency. One of the names he had been given in Washington was that of Irving Brown, the international representative of the powerful AFL-CIO union, whose president, Lane Kirkland, was an avid cheerleader for Solidarity. Brown had spent decades working as a CIA 'black bag man', moving great sums of money into covert projects in Europe, and was the principal CIA agent in the International Confederation of Free Trade Unions (IFCTU), a global labour federation based in Brussels. As one former covert-action chief put it, 'I don't believe I ever saw Irving with a nickel that didn't belong to the CIA ... He would say it was from the labor unions. It was a good cover.' When the money raised in the first months by the Paris committee began to run out, Brown stepped in. Chojecki would pick up Brown's money at the Solidarity office in Rue Cadet and would regularly meet him or his representatives in anonymous hotel rooms around Paris to give a rough account of what he had been spending it on. There was always a Polish-speaker in the group. 'Were these people from the CIA?' Chojecki wondered later. 'Or AFL-CIO? I just can't judge.'

What was certain was that, as more money came through, the minister for smuggling developed a reputation in Poland for carrying large sums of cash, which he would hand out to anyone who came to him with a credible story. As Grzegorz Boguta remembered: 'We had this picture here in Poland that Mirek would meet someone and say, "Okay, you need some money, have some money," and produce it from his pockets.' A problem in dealing with so much unvouched finance was that it was easy for his enemies to paint him as wasteful or dishonest, Polish agents and rival opposition activists alike.

'People trusted him very much and he deserved to be trusted,' said Boguta. 'But his disorganized attitude was like suicide, because it was easy for people to say, "I got some money, he didn't ask me to write or to sign anything, so how does he remember giving it to me?"'

With funds in hand, Chojecki and Tomasz Łabędź set about sourcing their new smuggling vehicle. They passed the task of locating the right truck to Maciej Górski, a former sailor who lived in the pretty village of Maillebois, on the outskirts of Chartres, an hour and a half's drive west of Paris, giving him various specifications. It shouldn't weigh more than 3½ tonnes, because you needed a special licence to drive anything over that limit. Ideally it would have a refrigerated compartment, which would be easy to turn into a smuggling cache.

Górski found a second-hand Mercedes L306, a type of flat-fronted light commercial van delivery drivers used all over France, and took it for its makeover to a relative who ran a garage. Chojecki and Łabędź went to inspect the work as it progressed. The design was simple enough: the refrigerated part of the cargo bay was a walled-off box at the cab end. All they had to do was fasten a new, secure cover over this box. When that was done, they spotted a minor issue, which was that when you looked at the van from a certain angle you could see the interior was shorter than the exterior. They could have asked for the cache to be reduced, but they wanted it to fit at least five small offset duplicators, of the type made by Roneo-Vickers or A. B. Dick. Chojecki and Kaleta liked these presses because they weighed less than 100 pounds, which meant a single person could shift them if they needed to unload in a hurry. They left the cache as it was – a decision they would come to regret.

With the van progressing, they began casting about for a driver. They needed someone reliable, a cool-head who wasn't a Pole, as a Pole would suffer far more than a Westerner in an East European jail if anything went wrong. The man they landed upon was Jacky Challot, a left-wing Solidarity supporter and member of the CFDT union who craved a more exciting life than pushing paper around the Versailles tax office where he worked. Challot had travelled to Poland several times before and loved it: he felt this was a place where history was being made, and he was privileged to be among the people making it. On the day of martial law he had hurried to Paris to support the pro-Solidarity protests, and six weeks later he was approached by a man named Christophe Apt, who reminded him of the mysterious spymaster known as the 'Professor' in Alfred Hitchcock's *North by Northwest*. Apt had asked Challot if he would drive a charity shipment carrying secret supplies to the underground, and Jacky had said yes. After returning from a successful drop, Challot offered to take unpaid leave from the tax office to drive for Apt full time. Now, a year later, the Poles at last came back with a job offer.

Chojecki wouldn't meet the driver himself, as that would risk leading SB agents straight to him. Instead, Apt managed Challot, whom the Poles came to know as 'Jacky for Special Tasks'. They would pay him the same as others who worked full time for the Paris committee, the French minimum wage of around $185 a month.

By the start of August 1983, the Mercedes vehicle and its driver were ready for their first foray into the Eastern Bloc.

When 'Professor' Apt gave Challot the go-ahead, Jacky went to Maillebois to fetch the van. The French unions had given Chojecki space to store his contraband in the basement of a grubby lock-up in Gentilly, in southern Paris. This was where Challot loaded the presses, radio sets, ink, emulsion, matrices, photography equipment and other goods. But the warehouse was too open a place to reveal the van's secret, so he drove to a more remote location to stow the material in the cache. Łabędź would rendezvous with him there in his little Fiat, which he had packed with CIA-sponsored books supplied by the Literary Institute, Aneks, Polonia and others in the ILC network. Challot would carry around 800 books in each shipment. They would always load the compartment in the same manner: the offset presses, being heaviest, went at the bottom, followed by books and electronic equipment. The lightest material, fabric for silk-screen printing, went on top. To avoid attracting attention, they would regularly change the location where they packed the secret cargo, although they didn't always pick the right spot. Once, they were loading the cache in the Forest of Versailles, the 2,500-acre wood close to Louis XIV's palace, a major French tourist attraction, when gendarmes swooped in squad cars and arrested and handcuffed them. Łabędź had to call a contact in the French secret service to get them released. He was told never to pack the vehicle in the forest again. 'They said we were crazy,' he recalled.

When the cache was full, they sealed it with enough rivets to deter the most scrupulous border guard, Challot keeping the rivet gun hidden in the cab so he could close it again when he'd offloaded the goods in Poland. Then he drove around collecting the humanitarian aid – medicines, clothes, baby food – from wherever Chojecki had managed to source it. It was sometimes harder to get hold of this type of material than the print supplies. Sometimes Mirek went to meet Nicolas Sarkozy, the young mayor of Neuilly-sur-Seine, a wealthy suburb in western Paris. Sarkozy, a Franco-Hungarian who twenty years later would serve as president of France, arranged the donation of a number of old hospital beds. This suited Chojecki perfectly, since 'old beds in France were like new beds in Poland'. He didn't tell Sarkozy their real purpose, which was to cover the truck's secret cargo.

Apt briefed Challot on his destination at a café in central Paris. The first shipment was destined for Wrocław, in western Poland. The Professor gave him the names and addresses of underground contacts there, which Jacky had to learn by heart. He also provided the cover story Chojecki had devised. If he was caught, Challot was to admit he knew that he was carrying forbidden material, but would say he didn't know who had sent it or where the drop point was. This information was to be supplied by a second French citizen, he would say, who was travelling to Poland by plane and would meet him there. They had not met before, but the Frenchman had been shown Jacky's photo so he would be able to recognize him. To support this fiction, Chojecki reserved a plane ticket for 'Bernard

Debut' and made a visa application in the same name at the Polish consulate. Monsieur Debut was real enough, but he would never board the flight to Poland.

Challot set out from Paris on the afternoon of 3 August and chose the most direct route to Wrocław, through East Germany, which still meant a round trip of 1,700 miles. The vehicle was heavy and slow, and since he was alone he had to stop from time to time to rest. East Germany, formally the German Democratic Republic, was one of the strictest police states in the communist bloc. According to the travel writer Jan Morris, crossing into the East through the inner German border was 'like entering a drab and disturbing dream, peopled by all the ogres of totalitarianism, a half-lit world of shabby resentments, where anything could be done to you . . . without anybody ever hearing of it, and your every step was dogged by watchful eyes and mechanisms'. Challot realized he'd made a mistake as soon as he reached the main Helmstedt–Marienborn checkpoint. This part of the Iron Curtain was one of the most heavily guarded frontiers on earth, a 3-mile-wide, 850-mile-long barrier made of electrified barbed wire, anti-vehicle ditches, mine-fields, tripwires, booby traps, double-layered mesh fencing and a floodlit 'death strip', as well as watchtowers, observation bunkers and runs for attack dogs. At Helmstedt–Marienborn, a thousand East German customs officials and border guards conducted rig-orous inspections of all vehicles and passengers entering the GDR, with little thought to the tailbacks that stretched for miles out to the west. When he reached the head of the queue, Challot was ordered to remove all of the truck's cargo for inspection. The guards refused to help, so this took him most of the night – a cold one for August, with driving rain and mist – and all the while he could overhear the German soldiers sneering at the 'bad organization' he brought to the job. He swore that he would never come through East Germany again. If he was ever to go to prison, he would much prefer to be in Poland than in this 'most unpleasant' country.

Despite their reputation for thoroughness, the border troops failed to detect the cache, and Challot passed through. He reached

Wrocław and dropped his humanitarian aid at the Dominican monastery, as indicated on his official documentation, before embarking on the trickier job of approaching the underground. The contact he had been given was a French-speaking academic. As instructed, he told her the passphrase, 'I've come on behalf of Philippe.' She led him on a lengthy tour of Wrocław's public transport system, regularly switching between trams and buses to make sure they weren't followed. The whole journey was steeped in an atmosphere of secrecy and mistrust. At the end she brought him to one of the leaders of the underground, who gave him a drop-off point 30 miles to the south. They were to make their way there separately.

When Jacky reached this address, he found a church property in a small village. They opened the cache there, unloaded the material and hid it in the building, where people would come to collect it little by little. Before leaving, he was given a bundle of underground newspapers and documents. He put these in the compartment, sealed it up with the rivet gun and set out for home, this time opting for the longer, safer route, via the Baltic Sea ferry to Copenhagen.

Chojecki had never met Challot, but he lay awake for much of the night the driver spent crossing into the East, listening in to Polish state radio. He knew that if the Frenchman was caught, this was how the world would first hear about it, via a crowing communist news bulletin. When several hours passed and there was no mention of a French driver or a van filled with uncensored literature and printing presses, he began to relax. Some time later, a coded phone call came through from Poland: 'Auntie has arrived.'

Challot would run supplies into Poland many times after that, travelling via Copenhagen, delivering equipment to Warsaw, Gdańsk and other locations around the country. Combined with loads conveyed by Kaleta's driver Sven Järn, by Polish yachts and by non-stop humanitarian transports, Chojecki reckoned they were moving at least seventy offset presses a year to the underground, along with other essential items of technical support, cash, books and journals. He and his comrades were keeping Solidarity cells in business all over Poland, feeding the so-called 'second circulation' of uncensored literature, which in turn kept alive the underground society and the idea of a free Poland.

He worked hard, conducting his important, secret business mostly in the mornings, in cafés around Paris – the Dejazet, the Thermomètre, the Café d'Italie – where he picked up the French worker's habit of drinking Café Calva, coffee with a shot of apple brandy, which was designed to prepare French workers for a day's hard labour. The Café Sarah Bernhardt was a favourite rendezvous, since it was near the Châtelet Métro station, which was easy for Poles to reach from the airport. He found it was safest to meet people from Poland straight after they had landed since the SB were unlikely to have picked them up. Some of these people were couriers, who carried information on Fizalene, a synthetic lining material you could write on then sew into your clothing, which meant that even if you were frisked the police wouldn't find anything unusual. Occasionally, the SB would let him know they were close by. Once he came back to his small attic room to find someone had fed a sheet of paper into his typewriter and left him a message: 'Stop what you are doing or your children will die.' It didn't affect him much: he'd received this kind of threat many times before in interrogations in Poland. Still, it was an indication of how bold the SB felt in Paris.

In the afternoons, Chojecki would go to the office to put in the hours at his cover job of editing *Kontakt*. Some days he would go out to Maisons-Laffitte to see Giedroyc, or have lunch with an important American visitor, such as Minden. Paris also offered him a vibrant social life. His marriage to Magda had broken down, and in the first months in France he had met and fallen in love with Jolanta Kessler, a journalist with a cherubic smile who had left Poland in 1980 and worked for a time at Radio Free Europe in New York. Kessler had known Chojecki's name since his days at NOWa and had thought him extremely brave. Meeting him in person, she found him serious, attractive and a little foul-mouthed, and soon she had moved into the one-bed apartment he now occupied above the Kontakt office in Rue Saint-Maur. Their bliss was interrupted only by a Polish musician who arrived from Canada to announce that he'd come to find Mr Chojecki and help Poland, and ended up staying six months. Life was like that. The Solidarity cause and the Chojecki name could draw in people from all around the world.

In the evenings, Mirek and Jolanta would go to see the great Polish writers and personalities who came to speak at the Polish Catholic centre near Place des Invalides or at the centre for Polish war veterans. Polish singers performed in Parisian theatres, and Jacek Kaczmarski, the so-called 'Bard of Solidarity', played semi-private gigs a couple of times a week in a friend's basement.

Three weeks after Challot's first triumphant return, on 27 August 1983, Chojecki and Kessler were married at the Church of Saint-Germain-des-Prés. He sported a moustache now, instead of the Christlike beard he had worn in Poland. His hair was a little thinner and his face tired, but he looked sharp in his grey suit, with a cowboy-style necktie and a Solidarity badge. They had chosen this church because it was where the heart of a famous seventeenth-century Polish king was buried, and a Solidarity priest conducted the service. They arrived in Mirek's Volkswagen, a replacement for the vehicle Boguta had taken back to Poland, Jolanta emerging in

a white dress, lacy in the Polish style, with a veil and a beaming smile. Hundreds of people turned out for the event, including writers, musicians and poets from all three waves of Polish refugees: the Second World War veterans, the 1968ers and their own generation, the Solidarity émigrés. They held a reception near the Jardin du Luxembourg, at the Closerie des Lilas brasserie, where the French impressionists used to meet and where F. Scott Fitzgerald once asked Hemingway to read his new novel *The Great Gatsby*.

They had fallen in love with this beautiful city, where the people were welcoming and sympathetic, and they felt privileged to be there. 'It was a moment, when everyone felt united,' Jolanta remembered. 'A very happy day.'

Later, there was dancing.

13

Oh Sh**! Reactionary Propaganda!

So far, you have remained stubbornly silent. I will try to make you talk. I have plenty of time – and time works in my favour. Loneliness, the stress of prison; it slowly undermines your resilience. I have quite a routine: I use politeness and shouting, I know when to shake hands and when to pound the table. Your psychological reactions after coming back from interrogation are well known to me: I am informed about them on a daily basis by a prisoner working for the Security Service.

Advice on dealing with police interrogations,
The Little Conspirator (1983)

Life underground was sometimes fun, often stressful and always exhausting, but the thing Helena Łuczywo hated most was that she couldn't see her daughter. At the start of 1983, after Jaruzelski had ordered an amnesty for political prisoners and released thousands of internees, she took her chance to come out of hiding. She went to hospital and pretended she was ill, and when they admitted her she made a lot of calls to people whose phones she knew were tapped. After ten days the police came to arrest her, taking her to the Mostowski police headquarters. They asked her a bunch of questions which she refused to answer, and since they had nothing to charge her with – in their sexist way, they never believed *Mazovia Weekly* could be edited by a woman – they let her go. She returned to her flat in Sadyba, in southern Warsaw, and began a new life, split between her daughter and work. From Thursday to Saturday she was at home. On Sunday night, friends would move into her apartment to look after Łucja and she would slip out, beginning a procedure known as 'sinking underground'.

First, she went to the house of some friends on the far bank of the river, who took her out for a drive in their car, heading for the prearranged location where they would begin the manoeuvre. The exact place and method of losing a tail changed every week, but it generally meant a variation on such underground classics as the 'French Connection' or the 'Bypass Bridge'. When they reached the prescribed spot, the car would come to an abrupt halt, Łuczywo would leap out, hurry through an obstacle no police vehicle could cross – down a staircase, say, or through a narrow gate or along a path through a housing estate – and jump into a car that had been waiting on the far side of the obstruction, ready to whisk her away.

Confident that she had shaken off any surveillance, she could now operate as she had before, meeting her colleagues wherever the Flying Office was, preparing the next issue of *Mazovia Weekly* and sleeping in a safe house. On Wednesday evening, when the editorial part of the paper was put to bed, she would return home to Łucja. It was still difficult to live like this, but it was far better than it had been, and she could maintain her job running *Mazovia Weekly*, which continued to grow in circulation and stature.

Around the same time as the police found Łuczywo, Grzegorz Boguta was released. He had spent the better part of a year in internment camps, but developed a serious eye condition, so they moved him to a Warsaw hospital. He was allowed visitors there, and began arranging meetings with NOWa contacts. As the doctors knew who he was and what he wanted to do, they stretched his treatment out for far longer than necessary. He discovered the publishing house was in a terrible state, with no money, no publishing programme, very little equipment and only a few activists. To bring it back to life would require a massive effort of reorganization, refinancing and resupply. 'We had a few very good printers,' Boguta remembered, 'but they needed more machines and materials and secret places to be able to print books, more cars and drivers, more people involved in distribution.'

He was discharged and released from internment at the same time, and made contact with Łuczywo and Bujak. He would meet them regularly from now on, and NOWa and *Mazovia Weekly* would share resources, printers and in some cases writers, although their operations remained separate. He would also become a key member of the committee set up to organize the reception of supplies from the West, 'Club B', named for the shared last initial of its three members: Grzegorz Boguta, Konrad Bieliński and Bogdan Borusewicz.

Boguta sent messages to Kaleta and Chojecki, outlining the situation and requesting help. When a shipment was ready, a reply would reach him, written on Fizalene or on a card in invisible ink, with a date, a place and a passphrase with which the contacts should identify themselves. Just before the vehicle arrived, Boguta would send this information to the former Polish Scout leader Władek Król, codenamed 'Corduroy' since he always wore clothing made from the material. He had one of the riskiest roles in the underground supply chain: arranging the shipments' receipt.

The first Corduroy knew about the imminent arrival of a transport from the West was when a young woman arrived at his apartment carrying instructions from Club B. Król didn't know her, nor did he know the names of Chojecki, Kaleta or Kaleta's driver Sven Järn. He didn't want to know, and under 'health and safety' rules Boguta wouldn't have told him anyway. He took a risk in trusting the young woman, as she did trusting him. She said they should meet a driver at the Forum Hotel, a thirty-two-storey slab in a curious shade of milky brown that Warsovians had dubbed the 'chocolate bar'. The Forum had been created to extract foreign currency from business travellers and tourists; its rooms were said to be bugged, and Ubeks and KGB 'honeytrap' agents patrolled the bar, but it was still one of the more inconspicuous places for a foreigner to stay in Warsaw.

Corduroy and the woman were to pretend they were on a date, bump into the driver as if by chance and strike up a conversation.

To make this dumb-show more credible, Corduroy bought flowers on the way to the hotel, which he handed with a flourish to his 'girlfriend'. They identified the blond Swede and made contact. It was hard to communicate with Järn since the driver didn't speak Polish, but they all understood the word 'rondo' for roundabout and were able to work out a basic plan. They would attempt the transfer the following day, at a little-used goods yard behind Warsaw's dilapidated old railway station, now mostly used for freight.

Overnight, Corduroy put a team of ten or twelve associates together, friends and people he had known from his days in the Polish Scouts, instructing them to take up positions at junctions along the route. They had no radios, but had worked out a signalling system so they could warn each other if they thought the vehicle was being followed. In the morning, a half-dozen pairs of eyes were trained on Järn's ageing blue and white Mercedes van as it edged out of the Forum car park and into the Warsaw traffic, heading north and then west around the towering complex of the Palace of Culture and Science, then south to the turn-off to Kolejowa Street, the minor road that led to the back of the station. No one had spotted any suspicious vehicles yet. As Järn approached the goods yard, a man appeared dressed in the beret and thick work jacket worn by labourers across Poland. Järn recognized Corduroy, who waved the vehicle into a bay they had reserved with crates and boxes. On the other side of a loading ramp stood a yellow removal van whose driver – a man known to the reception team only as 'Bolek' – sat smoking at the wheel, wearing an expression of profound boredom. In fact, he was discreetly scanning the yard for the first signs of a police raid.

As the coast seemed clear, they opened up the back of the Mercedes. The cargo bay was empty, but Järn soon revealed the stash behind the rear wall. It was packed in the usual way, with printing machines at the bottom, fragile radio scanners at the top and hundreds of books stuffed in between. There were metal plates for different types of offset presses, and inks, all good-quality items that were impossible to find in Poland. While the 'workmen' shifted the goods to Bolek's van, the Swede sat in his cab, and Corduroy thought he had rarely seen a man so pale. Järn didn't like the fact that they were working in public, but the Pole felt it was better to hide in plain sight, unloading in a place where trucks were being emptied all the time. Of course, this required nerves of steel.

When they had transferred everything from the cache into the removal van, Corduroy climbed into the seat next to Bolek and they drove off, followed by a couple of activists in a tiny Fiat 126p, a highly popular vehicle in Poland that people knew as a 'Toddler'. If Bolek was stopped and Corduroy arrested, the men in the Toddler were to alert Boguta that something had gone seriously wrong. Other activists remained in the yard with instructions to start a fight as a diversion if anyone suspicious approached, giving Corduroy and Bolek time to get away.

Järn drove off with an empty truck, heading west towards the ferry and Sweden, while Bolek and Corduroy went south, to a garage owned by a professor at Warsaw's Institute of Experimental Biology, Gabriela Drabikowska. Drabikowska allowed Corduroy to use her lock-up whenever he wanted it, and would even help the operation by parking her own car in such a way as to block any police vehicles that tried to swoop while they were unloading. The plan in that scenario was for Król to run and Bolek to remain. If the removal-van driver was arrested, he could say he had been hired to shift some things by some people he didn't know, which was almost true.

Bolek and Corduroy moved everything into the garage, covering it with a sheet to make sure no one could see it through the crack in the door, then locked up and left. It had been no more than two hours since Järn had pulled out of the Forum car park, and the most dangerous part of the job was complete. They would let the contraband cool off for a fortnight, with Król passing by now and then to check if anyone suspicious was hanging around. Drabikowska would drop by, too. She acted like an early-warning system for

them, and was taking a huge risk. She never knew what was in the
garage and Król asked her not to look.

Meanwhile Club B, whose members had the bigger picture,
would decide how to divide up the supplies.

Boguta could also communicate with Corduroy via the neigh-
bourhood kindergarten where they sent their children, leaving a
message or a parcel at morning drop-off, which someone else would
collect at pick-up. Two weeks after the delivery, Corduroy received
instructions via the nursery telling him where to take which items,
and he drove to the garage in his girlfriend's Toddler. Despite their
tiny size, the front doors of these cars opened so wide you could fit
a washing machine in the front seat, and an offset printer was far
smaller than that. He dropped the printing machines and supplies
at various safe houses around the city. Magda Boguta took some of
the radio scanners to hide at her own workplace.

The pressure and stress of the initial operation left everyone
exhausted. Bolek was well paid, but he probably didn't work for the
next day or two, since 'his nerves were shattered, and muscles ached
from moving all the equipment', Corduroy said. Everyone was aware
that if they slipped up they faced years in jail. The exact nature of the
punishment would depend on what the police caught you with. The
Kenwood radio scanners, about three times the size of an old telephone, may have been the most dangerous items, as smuggling that
sort of equipment would be considered high treason. But they were
invaluable for anyone who had to transport equipment around,
as they allowed the activists to hear where police roadblocks were
being placed.

'Corduroy' Król was in awe of foreigners like Järn, who had
chosen to help when they didn't have to. 'He had to go through
every stage, with a whole variety of people, that was a huge risk for
him. What a fantastic person.'

It was only years later, when the secret police files were opened,
that Król realized how close he had come to being caught. A
suspicious neighbour had seen him at an apartment where he occasionally picked up materials and had told the police, who asked the

informant if he knew the man's name. He had overheard others calling him 'Corduroy', the man said.

A surveillance photograph had got as far as taking a picture of
Król, but it was from behind, and the police never came to arrest
him. 'We were young and stupid then,' he remembered, 'and I could
run a lot faster than I can today.'

Chojecki knew it was a matter of time before something went badly
wrong. You couldn't run these sorts of risks forever without a slip-
up, a betrayal or a piece of bad luck. He had almost come to expect
it, and late in March 1984 his worst fears finally came to pass.

Challot was on the road again. By now his journeys followed a
well-worked routine, and everything seemed just as it always was.
He caught the overnight ferry from Copenhagen as usual, and at
dawn on 23 March he looked out towards the low-lying smudge
of land that loomed through the drizzle and steeled himself for
the Eastern Bloc. Customs officers had been giving humanitarian trucks special attention of late, and when the vehicles rumbled
out on to the dock at Świnoujście, Challot was ordered to the back
of the line. Still, the young officials seemed in good spirits as he
handed round dollars, coffee, chocolate and Marlboro cigarettes to
smooth his passage through the checks. They looked over his documents and told him to unload everything. One of the bulkier items
Chojecki had sourced this time was an old dentist's chair, and Jacky
was pondering how to get this out when a senior officer appeared
and told him to stop. The man began to inspect the vehicle closely,
walking around it, climbing into the cargo bay and banging on the
bulkhead wall with his fist. He had noticed that the interior wasn't
as long as the exterior: how could the driver explain this?

Challot pretended not to know what he was talking about.

The man left, and Challot waited anxiously, noticing that the
once friendly officials no longer wanted to speak to him. After a few
minutes the officer returned with a team of specialists, and asked
him to open the hidden compartment. When he again played the
role of confused foreigner, they used force, jemmying their way

through one of the cache's thin walls. The officer evidently expected to find black-market jeans, whisky or cartons of American cigarettes, and when he saw printing equipment and books tumbling out, he swore. 'Oh sh**!' he said. 'Reactionary propaganda!'

They immediately placed Challot under guard: they would keep him standing outside for the rest of that extremely cold Polish day. He had plenty of time to think. Had he been betrayed? It seemed unlikely given how long it had taken them to find the cache. Luckily they hadn't searched his bag yet. His bag! He suddenly remembered friends in Copenhagen had given him a package to deliver, and he'd written down a name and address on a piece of paper that was now in his bag. If the police found it they would connect these innocent people to him. He had to get rid of it.

He told his captors he needed to pee, and they marched him to a filthy cubicle, waiting outside while he locked the door, slipped out the paper and dropped it in the excrement-caked bowl. He was horrified to find that the paper wouldn't sink, even when he yanked on the flush. There was only one thing now to do. He fished it out with his fingers, tore it into pieces and swallowed the lot. As the guards escorted him back out into the cold, he could taste the toilet waste on his tongue.

He didn't understand why they still hadn't taken him to jail. At dusk, the answer came, when a TV crew arrived from Szczecin to film the scene. It would appear on Polish television as a propaganda package, showing Challot, the truck and its boxes of 'reactionary' literature. The journalists were followed by two men wearing the distinctive hats and black leather coats of Ubek agents.

'Well,' one of them sneered at him in schoolboy French, 'are you satisfied? Are you going to become a TV star?'

'I'd prefer not to be,' Challot shrugged, 'but it's out of my hands.'

The policeman laughed. 'You have a sense of humour!'

The second agent was quieter, more sinister. He wore a stupid expression and failed to meet Challot's eye. At one point he seemed to want to assault the Frenchman, but his partner persuaded him it was a bad idea.

When they ordered him into the back seat of an old black Volga limousine, scenes from spy films filled Challot's mind. He had wanted adventure, to escape the grey dullness of the tax office, and now he'd found it. But he couldn't stop thinking about the ordeal that lay ahead. How would they treat him? Would they beat him? What about the interrogation? Would he break down?

The Volga purred through the city streets, pulling to a halt outside the headquarters of the militia in Świnoujście. They took his watch, belt and shoelaces, then the questioning began. He pretended again not to understand what they were asking him.

'Don't worry,' the interrogating officer said, 'we have ways of making you remember everything.'

The police gave their investigation into Challot the cryptonym TRAVELLER. They interrogated the prisoner at length, and brought in experts to comb through the truck and its contents. They calculated the printing materials alone had a value of more than $8,000 at the official rate. Officers from the Polish Radio Inspection unit examined the radiotelephones, and found they were Japanese Kenwood TR-2500 VHF walkie-talkies, illegal in the People's Republic of Poland, worth up to $200 each. Of the 800 publications aboard the truck, only ten were judged to be legal. The contents of the rest included 'fake news capable of causing serious damage to the interests of the People's Republic of Poland', according to the prosecutor, and some of them 'disparaged . . . the People's Republic of Poland, its system and its supreme organs'. The cover of *Fight for Truth*, a collection of articles by the exiled socialist Adam Ciołkosz, was picked out for stating that 'The whole system is sick, it cannot be cured, it must be removed in its entirety and its political superstructure destroyed.' There were also works with 'a clear anti-Soviet content, which could be detrimental to Polish–Soviet relations', such as *Fight for the World* by Stefan Kisielewski, in which the author described Marxist-Leninist-Stalinist doctrine as 'socially and economically outdated, or simply wrong' and blamed it for bringing 'much misfortune to the world and to Russia itself'. Equally dangerous were *Literary Notebooks*, a Paris-based émigré journal supported by Minden, the pamphlets *Human Rights, Poland, Economic Policy of the People's Republic of Poland* and a range of others. There were more than a hundred copies of some titles – clear evidence, according to the prosecutor, 'of the intention to further disseminate them in the country'.

Challot faced a jail sentence of several years.

In Paris, Chojecki had the feeling something had gone wrong even before he knew for sure. He had spent another night tossing and turning, and Jolanta had asked him what was going on. She didn't know who Challot was or what he might be doing, but when Mirek told her that he thought one of his transports might have been captured, she realized it meant trouble. Soon the 'happy communists' were broadcasting their triumph over the airwaves, and he knew they had work to do. They had to tell the French foreign ministry, they had to find a lawyer and they had to launch a publicity campaign to pressure the Poles into setting him free, but Chojecki couldn't personally get involved, since that would make everything worse. It was clear that the French government would bring more diplomatic pressure to bear on Warsaw if a French citizen led the 'Free Jacky' campaign, but in their wildest dreams the Paris smugglers couldn't have wished for a better advocate for the captured driver than the one who stepped forward.

Simone Signoret was a *grande dame* of French cinema. Her five-decade movie career encompassed more than sixty films and dozens of awards, including an Oscar for her role in the 1959 adaptation of John Braine's novel *Room at the Top*. She had Polish-Jewish heritage through her father, and although she'd once been a communist sympathizer and had even been banned from working in the US after a visit to Moscow in 1956, she and her actor husband Yves Montand had been staunch supporters of Solidarity since the movement's birth. When the French press reported Challot's arrest, she called a friend, the president of the CFDT union, who put her in touch with Tomasz Łabędź, Chojecki's deputy, who would coordinate the campaign to free Challot.

Signoret was seriously ill with pancreatic cancer in 1984, but she would bring the same combination of stardust, earthiness and energy to the role of freeing Challot that she had given to her performances on screen.

'Thomas, my little Thomas,' she breathed down the phone when she first spoke to Łabędź. 'You're coming here. Come to my house. We'll talk, we'll prepare Jacky's release.'

Łabędź hurried out to the Signoret–Montand mansion in Normandy to talk strategy. He had already begun the process of finding a lawyer, but Signoret put him in touch with Georges Kiejman, a celebrated Parisian barrister who would later become French justice minister. It was typical of the way she operated, pulling famous names out of her contacts book. They needed a publicity campaign, she said. They would buy a full-page advertisement in *Le Monde*, in which she and a few friends would demand Challot's release. The 'few friends' could have filled a celebrity special of *Paris Match*. Among them were Gérard Depardieu, Pierre Boulez, Patrice Chéreau, Michel Foucault, Costa-Gavras, Françoise Giroud, Bernard Kouchner, Françoise Sagan and Bertrand Tavernier. Signoret took the case so seriously that she insisted Łabędź call her at home every day with updates, and visit the Normandy house once a week to go through the details of what was being done and how. She also phoned Jacky's mother every day. Between them, the

campaigners organized petitions, demonstrations and strikes calling for Challot to be set free, turning the young French tax official
into a minor celebrity. Challot was not carrying bombs or propaganda, they argued, but was a mere traveller, committed to the free
movement of people and ideas.

The high-profile campaign infuriated the Polish government,
which protested to the French foreign ministry at the Quai d'Orsay,
where Łabędź was summoned for a meeting. The Challot business
was putting his right to reside in France at risk, the French officials
told him coldly. He had claimed political asylum in the country,
which forbade him from carrying out political activity on their soil.

What could he do? replied Łabędź. He was torn between the
competing demands of a group of movie stars, the labour unions
and the foreign ministry. Signoret in particular was so committed
to the cause that nothing he could say would stop her.

When the meeting was over, he rang a friend in President
Mitterrand's office at the Élysée Palace and told her what had
happened.

'Don't worry,' she said. 'We'll cover you.'

In Poland, Challot played his part well. He allowed the police gradually to uncover the story Chojecki had devised. He had offered
his services to a Polish organization in France, he said, and had
been approached by a man named Serge who had asked him to
drive the vehicle. He knew it carried contraband, he told them, but
he didn't know exactly what that was and had never been shown
the secret compartment. (He was fortunate that it had been cold
when he packed the cache and he had worn gloves, which meant
they couldn't find his fingerprints on the inside.) He said he had
been instructed to rendezvous with a Bernard Debut, whom he
had never met, in the Old Market Square in Kraków on 25 March
at 18.00. Debut was to take the vehicle on to its final destination,
which Jacky didn't know.

The SB seemed to buy this tale, which Challot thought was
'simple but brilliant'. Chojecki and Łabędź knew the Polish authori-

ties would check Debut's name with the consul's office in Paris, where they had registered it, and it would appear that he was telling the truth.

Challot had prevented the police uncovering anyone in the underground, but he was still in serious trouble. The authorities remanded him in a Szczecin jail, where he and other inmates were forced to watch helmeted guards beat a handcuffed young prisoner with truncheons. He also witnessed one of his cellmates slash his wrists with a razor blade, spurting blood all around the room. The guards dragged the man away and ordered Challot to clean up the mess.

On 27 June 1984, the driver was charged with transporting 100,000 PLN ($10,000) worth of printing equipment and illegal publications into the country, and 'acting in a criminal group' that was producing and disseminating 'printed materials containing false information likely to cause serious damage to the interests of the People's Republic of Poland and defaming the chief organs of the Polish state'. The court found him guilty and sentenced him to two years in jail. But the regime was desperate for hard currency, and on 3 July a $10,000 sum was paid in exchange for his release. Some of this had been raised by the campaign, but Challot thought the balance had come from America: 'It is generally known that the funds for Polish emigration activities came from across the Atlantic, but I have no information as to their exact sources.'

The day after he was freed, he flew from Warsaw to Paris, where he was debriefed by a French intelligence officer. At the end of the interview she told him they had organized a press conference, but Challot said he would prefer to leave discreetly. He wanted to speak to his 'employers' first, to work out his story. They arranged a car to take him away into the night.

When Łabędź met Challot again, he told him about Signoret's role and asked that he call her soon, as she was desperate to speak with him. But Jacky was a film buff and a little starstruck, and he kept delaying. When at last he dared pick up the phone Signoret was furious that he hadn't made immediate contact. The squall soon passed, and she invited him with his siblings to the house in Normandy to recount the full story.

By the time they met, Signoret was exhausted by her illness and almost blind behind her large dark glasses. But she greeted him with a hearty kiss, as if she had known him for years.

Yves Montand raised a toast to their guests. 'To your health,' he said. 'Another glass of wine that Jaruzelski will not drink!'

14

This Turbulent Priest

My hands are full of holes.
Falling out of them
Are the first tiny cherries
Of the year.
I don't think I can carry them
To you,
My little son

> Barbara Sadowska [whose son, Grzegorz
> was beaten to death by the police], 'Untitled',
> in *How Sweet It Is to Be a Child of God*

Three years after Jaruzelski's declaration of war, the regime and the underground had fought each other to a standstill. The general maintained a firm hold on power: whenever it came to a clash on the streets, Zomo and army units would move in, beat people and throw the ringleaders into jail. But he couldn't destroy the opposition or stop its most obvious manifestation, the thousands of dissident newsletters, books and journals that kept appearing and that were kept in secret stashes in Polish homes. Nor could he solve the country's huge economic problems. The result was a hokey-cokey sort of national life, as crackdown followed amnesty and Solidarity leaders were moved in and out of jail as the regime saw fit. All the while, inflation and debt skyrocketed, and the purchasing power of the Polish złoty shrank. In such troubled times, Poles turned as they always had to the Catholic church.

Marx had described religion as 'the sigh of the oppressed creature, the heart of a heartless world, the spirit of soulless stagnation, the opium of the people', and called for its eradication. Following his lead, when the communists seized power in Moscow they had launched a vicious campaign against the Russian Orthodox church, seizing its property, desecrating its buildings and massacring large numbers of clergy and believers, sometimes with their families. Bishops were tortured, beaten, shot and drowned. An abbot in the Don region was scalped and beheaded. In Voronezh, seven nuns were said to have been boiled in a cauldron of tar. Besides staying true to Marx's theories, the Russian war on religion aimed to wipe out a competitor and to replace belief in God with faith in communist leaders. In Poland, the calculus was different. Catholicism was too deeply rooted in society to wipe out. So the Christians and the communists struck an uneasy truce, in which the state allowed the Catholic church to exist but secretly tried to undermine it, and the church agreed not to engage in politics but didn't always rein in its priests. Few were more vocal in their criticism of the Soviet system than Father Jerzy Popiełuszko of St Stanisław's church in Żoliborz.

Popiełuszko was in his late thirties in 1984. Slight, sickly, unafraid, he achieved a remarkable reach through his unabashed support for Solidarity and the downtrodden Polish labourer. The coal miners, the steelworkers, the nurses and even the doctors had all made him their patron. On the last Sunday of every month he held a special 'homeland' mass that was so popular his large parish church couldn't contain the congregation. When 3,000 people had filled every pew, 10,000 more would gather in the churchyard and in the surrounding streets, where his low, rumbling voice was carried to the crowd through loudspeakers. Worshippers came from the countryside in buses to see him, and secret police and regime provocateurs were discouraged by a security detail of hulking steelmen, overseen by a man-mountain known as 'the Mole'.

'O God, who, for so many centuries / Has granted to Poland the splendour of might and glory,' the ranks of worshippers would sing, using the old words to hymns the church had rewritten so as not to offend the communists, 'Return to us, O Lord, a free homeland.'

Popiełuszko knew he was in danger. The SB bugged him, sent death threats, threw bricks and even explosives through his windows, and put electronic trackers on his car. When a group of students gave him a little black puppy, he named it Tajniak – Polish for 'secret agent' – because it followed him everywhere. In the spring of 1983, when regime thugs beat to death Grzegorz Przemyk, the eighteen-year-old son of the dissident poet Barbara Sadowska, the priest was heard to remark, 'I believe I'm next!' But he continued to tell the truth as he saw it. In August 1984, in a sermon marking the anniversary of Solidarity's founding, which could not have been delivered anywhere else in the bloc, he condemned the Party and openly called for the trade union's return. 'One cannot murder hopes,' he told the adoring congregation.

> Today you can see and feel this even more clearly as we marvel at the faith of our brothers returned from prison. We see and feel more clearly that the hopes of 1980 are alive and are bearing fruit . . . That which is in the heart, that which is deeply tied to man, cannot be liquidated with this or that regulation or statute . . . We have a duty to demand that the hopes of the nation begin, at last, to be realized.

Such naked support for the opposition, which was reported in the underground press and international media and broadcast on Radio Free Europe and the BBC's Polish service, was an open sore for the regime in Poland, and a source of great embarrassment when it came to relations with the Soviets. The priest had to be stopped.

On 19 October 1984, Popiełuszko travelled to the industrial town of Bydgoszcz, 120 miles from Warsaw, to deliver a sermon on the theme of 'overcoming evil with good' at an evening service. He was driven there by his regular chauffeur and bodyguard, a former paratrooper named Waldemar Chrostowski. It was dark by the time the two men set off in the priest's Volkswagen Golf for the four-hour journey back to the capital. An eyewitness later told *Mazovia Weekly* that they saw a car that had sat with its lights on and its engine running pull out behind them as they left. There were reports, too, that a person in a militia uniform had been spotted hanging around the church.

Around 10 p.m., Chrostowski and Popiełuszko were passing through a forest near the village of Górsk when a uniformed traffic cop flagged them down. It would later transpire that this man and the two others with him were from SB Department IV, the section devoted to controlling the church.

'Don't drive through,' Popiełuszko told Chrostowski, 'or we could be in trouble.'

Chrostowski stopped and the policemen ordered him to get out to perform a drink-driving test, but when the bodyguard opened the car door they grabbed him, handcuffed him and gagged him, telling him as they did so, 'This is so that you don't growl during your last trip.' They pushed him into the passenger seat of their unmarked Fiat, where a man pressed a cold blade into his neck and hissed, 'Don't turn around or we'll kill you.' Chrostowski could hear the sounds of a struggle behind him as the men seized the priest, followed by Popiełuszko's surprised voice asking, 'Gentlemen, what are you doing?' Then the Fiat's boot opened, and he felt the car lurch as something heavy dropped in. The assailants climbed into the vehicle, the driver gunned the engine and they sped away to the east.

Chrostowski still kept his wits about him. A few miles down the road, he managed to open the car door and throw himself out into the night, despite being handcuffed and gagged. The vehicle was doing around 50mph at the time, and he hit the ground hard and rolled several times, breaking the cuffs. The kidnappers didn't stop: they still had their main target locked in the boot. At some point, Popiełuszko tried to force his way out. The policemen heard him, pulled over and beat him unconscious, trussing him up in such a way that any attempt to straighten his legs tightened a cord around his throat and strangled him.

Around midnight, they reached Włocławek Dam, which backs up the waters of the Vistula into a reservoir 40 miles long. They parked, attached a bag of stones to Popiełuszko's feet and heaved him into the murky water. He was probably still alive as he sank to the bottom.

The alarm went up quickly when the priest failed to return to Warsaw, not least because someone had tried to kill him only a week before by throwing a rock at his car windscreen. *Mazovia Weekly* pointed out that the communists had motive and form. In September, *Izvestia*, the Party propaganda sheet in Moscow, had attacked Popiełuszko by name, complaining that he had 'transformed his apartment into a repository for illegal literature'. 'One has the impression that he is not reading sermons from the pulpit,' the paper continued, 'but leaflets written by Bujak . . . They exude hatred of socialism.' Soon after that, the Polish regime's mouthpiece, Jerzy Urban, had launched a verbal attack on the priest, accusing him of holding 'black masses' at which Michnik was the altar boy, ringing the altar bells 'with his tail'. He didn't ask, as Henry II reputedly did before the murder of Thomas Becket, 'Will no one rid me of this turbulent priest?', but he might as well have done.

With Popiełuszko missing, tens of thousands of people came to the church to pray that he was alive and to lay offerings. Helena Łuczywo's reporters gathered accounts of eyewitnesses, who pointed the finger of blame at the security services. Wałęsa, who had been released from house arrest in November 1982 and maintained a difficult truce with the regime, warned of dire consequences if the priest was found to have been harmed. 'If even one hair falls from Father Jerzy's head someone will bear a terrible responsibility,' he said. Others applied Miłosz's description of the Party machine, blaming the 'Red Fiery Dragon' for the abduction. Workers held strikes and candlelit vigils, demanding answers. The Popiełuszko case was rapidly developing into the biggest crisis for Jaruzelski since the declaration of martial law. Something had to give. The regime had to offer up a sacrifice.

Eight days after the murder, on 27 October, Jaruzelski's interior minister, General Kiszczak, appeared on television to tell the nation they had arrested four officers for abducting the priest. Three days after that, they announced that divers had found Popiełuszko's body in the reservoir. The news that he was definitively dead provoked a new eruption of public anger. When the congregation gathered at St Stanisław's heard it, they started shrieking and weeping with grief. Polish Catholics, steeped in a tradition of martyrs and saints, began a new round of vigils. Warsaw was a city in mourning. Candles laid by the church in Żoliborz stretched for block after block. People pinned pieces of black cloth to their lapels and donned black armbands.

They buried him at St Stanisław's on a bright, chilly Saturday at the start of November. A vast traffic jam extended out from central Warsaw to Żoliborz as people queued to reach the church. Half a million came. They climbed trees and perched on rooftops and balconies to watch an event that was part canonization, part political rally. They sang nationalist songs – 'My homeland,' ran one hymn, 'so many times bathed in blood' – and held up their fingers in V for Victory salutes. A guard of honour of miners, in pit helmets and ceremonial black uniforms, carried the priest's humble wooden coffin through the crowd. Wałęsa followed with head bowed. No one from the regime dared attend in an official capacity, but opposition leaders did, including Helena Łuczywo, Adam Michnik and Jacek Kuroń, as well as a few diplomats such as the British junior minister Malcolm Rifkind and foreign journalists of every stripe.

Łuczywo, who had once seen Popiełuszko preach, thought it all 'extremely sad'. 'He really was someone,' she said, 'he was very much *our* priest.' *Mazovia Weekly*'s front page would carry an unusual, emotionally charged report from the funeral. From dawn onwards, delegations arrived in Żoliborz from all over Poland, the reporter related. They openly carried Solidarity wreaths and banners: 'Lead in love towards independence – Solidarity Białystok', read one; 'O Lord, break this sword that cuts the country – Solidarity

Starachowice', read another. Some represented factories. A banner held aloft by the Solidarity chapter at Polkolor, the Polish television manufacturer, carried the slogan 'Our heart was torn out, but we will not give up our souls'. The Roman Catholic primate Cardinal Glemp, no great ally to the opposition, used his speech to call for pluralism in Poland: 'We believe that . . . no one in our country should ever attempt to kill another human being just because they do not like the teaching he preached,' he said. Another priest asked people to pray for Solidarity, 'which has grown in the Nation like a strong tree and draws its life-giving sap from our hearts and prayers'.

When the crowd was told that Wałęsa would speak, a burst of applause rippled through the masses. He was greeted with more Churchillian V-signs and rhythmic chants of 'Sol-i-dar-ność!' He spoke quickly and directly. Father Jerzy was a victim of the very violence and hatred which he had always opposed. He was 'a good and courageous man, a great priest, a pastor and a champion of the national cause'. 'Rest in peace,' Wałęsa concluded. 'Solidarity lives because you gave your life for it.'

Even at two in the morning, the line of mourners queuing to kneel and pray before Popiełuszko's grave was half a mile long.

Had the regime ordered the killing? Or the KGB? Or had a group of hardliners taken it on themselves to do away with one of the Party's most potent critics? These questions would dominate Polish politics for years to come. The problem for the security service was Chrostowski, who, after surviving his fall from the car, had been taken into the protection of Solidarity activists, and travelled to police interrogations in company with a group of steelworkers. By allowing the bodyguard to escape, the killers had left an eyewitness who could testify that Popiełuszko had been violently abducted and that at least one of his kidnappers wore a police uniform. They couldn't simply write the priest's death off as the latest in a spate of unexplained suicides, accidents and murders by 'unidentified attackers' that had plagued the opposition.

Complicit or not, the regime's strategy was to paint itself as the victim. The murder was a 'provocation', its leaders decided, an attempt by factions within the SB to destabilize the government. As people wondered whether this meant another coup was in the offing – one backed once again by Moscow – the regime announced that the accused would stand trial in an open process, in front of the international media. This was almost unprecedented. The security service had been responsible for dozens of assassinations since the start of the Cold War, but none of the perpetrators had faced public prosecution since the mid-1950s, when several notorious killers from the Stalin era were convicted. Jaruzelski would have had to clear such a decision with Moscow, presumably on the basis that government lawyers would be given free rein to attack the church and pro-Solidarity priests, while the murderers would be sacrificed to assuage public anger. An inadvertent effect of the trial was to give Poles remarkable insight into the workings of the secret police.

The hearing began on 27 December in Toruń – a venue chosen principally for its distance from Warsaw – and lasted for six weeks. There were four men in the dock: the three officers who had been at the scene, plus Colonel Adam Pietruszka, a supervisor from SB Department IV, who was charged with having ordered the crime. The first disclosures about the nature of secret police work came from the most junior of the officers on trial, Lieutenant Leszek Pękala. Pękala, an orphan who was raised in a state children's home, cut a pathetic figure in court, cowering and hunched, with eyes downcast. He had broken down under interrogation and revealed several other plans to kill the priest, including by throwing him from a bridge and staging a traffic accident in which he would burn to death. Recalling the night of the assassination, he told the court that Popiełuszko had staggered from the trunk of their Fiat pleading, 'Save me, save me! Spare my life, you people,' before they beat him unconscious.

But it was Captain Grzegorz Piotrowski who most caught the public's attention. Tall and well dressed, swaggering and confident, he revealed details of the wealth and privilege enjoyed by the security service in a country where most people lived in poverty. Piotrowski vacationed at special interior ministry holiday camps. He had a beautiful wife and several mistresses. He drove an imported car. SB officers had special passes, he told the court, which enabled them to go anywhere they wanted, unquestioned. They stole licence plates to disguise their departmental vehicles, and celebrated successful operations with expense-account lunches at the best hotels. As for the assassination, the captain said that stopping Popiełuszko had been a 'priority assignment' for almost two years, and that his superior, Pietruszka, had told him, 'We have to shake the priest so hard that it gives him a heart attack. We have to give them a last warning.' At one moment the captain threatened the whole purpose of the trial – to sacrifice a few officers and save the regime – by telling the court he had been assured that the orders to go after Popiełuszko were authorized by 'those at the top', although in a later session he rowed back, saying he did not have concrete evidence of this.

All four defendants were found guilty and handed jail sentences of between fourteen and twenty-five years. Piotrowski's police friends celebrated his bravado with a drunken dinner in which they fired their revolvers into the ceiling. Two years after the trial, the convicted men's sentences were cut in half.

In Helena Łuczywo's view, the case showed there were dangerous rogue elements in the secret police. The killers were 'monsters', she said, who 'just thought they could do whatever they wanted, because they were not controlled. Once they started, they couldn't stop.'

There was one further important aspect of the priest's murder. The assassins had provided the CIA with a wide-open goal.

15

The Network

If I forget you, my beloved Homeland
Let me forget my right hand
Let my tongue dry to my lips.
– Jerzy Popiełuszko, Patriotic Sermons

On this earth there are pestilences and there are victims,
and it's up to us, so far as possible, not to join forces with
the pestilences.
Albert Camus, The Plague

The capture of Challot's truck and its cargo of Roneo-Vickers machines was a costly setback for Chojecki's infiltration effort, but in terms of the overall operation the loss was small and he quickly recovered. An influx of new CIA funding for Minden, combined with the millions funnelled through QRHELPFUL, meant money for new smuggling routes, which were added to the significant network Chojecki already managed. By the mid-1980s, he had partners across Western Europe, from Stockholm to Turin, each of whom had their own methods of getting contraband to trusted contacts in Poland.

The newest and most covert 'ratline' in early 1985 was overseen by Kazimierz Krawczyk, a thirtysomething KOR-era activist who had emigrated to Norway and ran a vehicle to Poland via the Baltic ferries. Minden's first use of Krawczyk came in June 1984, when he referred to 'our ultra-secret Oslo–Kraków project' in a report to Langley. Three months later, Giedroyc wrote to tell Rudzki details of 'new routes to reach the country that have opened up', including the line from Oslo: Jan Chodakowski at Polonia Book Fund had purchased a special lorry for Krawczyk, which meant that 'once a month a large transport leaves for 12 points'. The cost of the transport, including payment for the driver, was being met by Giedroyc, Chodakowski and Chojecki – all CIA assets. Giedroyc had agreed to send Krawczyk 200 copies of all his miniature editions, including *Kultura* and another Literary Institute journal, *Historical Notebooks*. Rudzki replied airily that he had known about Krawczyk's system for some time, that it was 'working well' and that the ILC would supply Oslo with 'mainly books and foreign language magazines as requested'. He had permission to pay for the books sent from Maisons-Laffitte.

Scandinavia remained the busiest, most successful smuggling route thanks to the direct ferries to Świnoujście and Gdańsk, which bypassed the difficult GDR. As well as Krawczyk, Chojecki could rely on the services of at least three Solidarity support groups in Sweden, in Stockholm (operated by the sociologist Ryszard Szulkin, among others), Lund (Józef Lebenbaum) and Malmö (Kaleta). Further south, he worked with Jan Minkiewicz, leader of the Solidarity bureau in Amsterdam, who had a regular driver shipping goods to Poland. In Cologne it was Andrzej Chilecki, who doubled up as West Germany representative of Polonia Book Fund; and in London Tadeusz Jarzembowski, aka 'Jarski', who ran a group called Solidarity With Solidarity. In Turin, Eleonora 'Nelly' Norton, a Sorbonne-educated Jewish exile of the 1968 generation, had a reliable line into the Fighting Solidarity group based in Wrocław. In Austria, Chojecki dealt with Danuta Stołecka, the sister of his friend Ewa Milewicz, and Zofia Reinbacher, who ran a bijou Polish bookstore in Vienna and regularly distributed books for Minden.

Not everyone shipped material continuously. Chojecki counted around five associates as smugglers of the top level, including Kaleta, Minkiewicz and Norton. Another thirty-five sent presses as and when they could, as Jarski did from London. Then there were individual travellers who were willing to make one-off drops, taking a single printing press at a time: Chojecki had a list of at least fifty people, many in Germany and France, who were prepared to do this. And he of course was a single asset in the ILC/CIA Polish network, which itself was just one part of the Agency's wider book programme targeting the Eastern Bloc. There were scores of others sending books or print material to Poland, including Giedroyc, Chodakowski, the Polish Library in London and émigré booksellers and distributors in the US, UK, France, Germany, Italy, Austria, Sweden and beyond.

If there was one place in Western Europe from where they didn't look to send anything it was Brussels, where the Solidarity headquarters in the West was based. The Belgian capital was a 'non-starter', Chojecki said, since everyone knew it was heavily infiltrated by Eastern intelligence.

Three days after Popiełuszko's funeral, Casey and his senior officers came together to discuss the outpouring of pro-Solidarity sentiment the ceremony had produced. The murder was 'one of the most important events in Poland since the imposition of martial law', they decided. It had 'created a martyr and an enduring symbol of opposition to the government'. They thought the killing seemed to be the work of vigilantes in the regime rather than the KGB, but whatever the truth, the Soviets bore responsibility for encouraging hardliners to push for harsher measures against the dissidents, thereby helping to create 'the climate in which such an act could occur'.

In the 1950s and 1960s, when the CIA's propaganda empire was at its peak, it could call on more than 800 news outlets, journalists and information sources around the world that were owned, subsidized or influenced by the Agency, ranging in importance from Radio Free Europe to a third-string freelancer in Quito who was able to place something in the local paper. This network, formally called the Propaganda Assets Inventory, was nicknamed 'Wisner's Wurlitzer' within the CIA, after the first chief of the Agency's covert action staff, Frank G. Wisner, who had set it up. The idea was that at the press of a button the Wurlitzer would play any tune the CIA wanted. Much of the network had been dismantled by the 1970s, but now the CIA was nurturing something similar in Poland: a covertly funded web of newspapers, publishers and media outlets, inside and outside the country, backed up by American radio stations, which was capable of pumping out the opposition message to Poles everywhere. If the new Polish Wurlitzer was more of a coalition than the old one, and less prescriptive, that was because it didn't need to call the tune, since most of the people involved were already motivated to do 'good work', as one retired CIA officer put it, to bring about the end of communism. The mid-1980s presented few greater opportunities for this system to play in concert than Popiełuszko's murder. The extensive coverage in the underground press, some of which was secretly supported by the Agency, was just one division of a Popiełuszko-related assault that was about to appear. Over the next twelve months, publishers would produce more than 300 volumes celebrating the life of the priest, in almost every European language. Not all of these were funded by the CIA, but many were.

Even before his murder, a collection of the priest's 'Homeland' sermons had been smuggled out of Poland – probably by Chojecki, Minden suspected – and reached Giedroyc's desk. Giedroyc had found them too nakedly political for *Kultura*, so he passed them on to Libella, the small press on the Île Saint-Louis. By the time the police dragged Popiełuszko's corpse from the reservoir on 30 October, *Patriotic Sermons* was almost ready to go. The next day, Giedroyc wanted to impress its significance on Rudzki. 'I think it will be very successful,' he wrote. They were already in negotiations about French and Italian translations, and he 'would like to propose an American edition . . . what do you think?'

Rudzki had not had time to reply before a new letter arrived from the Editor, written on the day of the funeral, reiterating the book's importance. News of the coming publication had been reported by both Radio Free Europe and Voice of America, so there was 'huge interest in the country' and distributors were desperate to get hold of it. 'Krawczyk in Oslo is begging for 200 copies, Chojecki for three hundred . . . I think it would be very important for you to make an exceptional purchase because of its topicality.' The ILC should get in touch with Libella directly, he told Rudzki, adding that it was 'urgent'.

Rudzki was keen: 'If this poor priest is declared a martyr or blessed by the pope, the success will be great.' A few days later he wrote again to say they had ordered additional copies of the book and would be able to supply them to Chojecki and to Oslo, although perhaps not in the quantities Giedroyc had suggested. Since Oslo usually asked them not to send too much at once, Rudzki would be grateful if Giedroyc could tell him whether Krawczyk could cope with such a large number of books in one go.

Patriotic Sermons was published on 22 November 1984. At that moment Rudzki asked Giedroyc if he could receive the shipment bound for Norway at Maisons-Laffitte and send the books north to Oslo himself, as Krawczyk's new route was so secret he didn't even want Libella to know about it. 'We treat this . . . address very confidentially,' he wrote. 'I am giving instructions today to [Libella] to deliver 150 copies to the Institute.'

When Minden arrived in Europe that month for his usual round of meetings with the émigrés, he found Popiełuszko at the top of everyone's lists. There was already 'exceptional interest' in the Libella book, he reported to the CIA, and distribution was to begin immediately. This meant that, well before the trial of the SB men captured the attention of Poles, hundreds of copies of the sermons were being trucked into the country from Norway, Sweden and every other hub in the West. Other outlets were organizing tributes, too. Chojecki's *Kontakt* magazine wore mourning black for its November issue. There were no cover lines, but a simple photograph of the priest in his vestments, small, wan, vulnerable. Inside, a message from the editors described the murder as 'a deliberate act that strikes at us all . . . [but] not an isolated one . . . it proves that political murder is a permanent feature of the actions of the representatives of the communist authorities'. Spotkania, another ILC-backed publishing house in Paris, was meanwhile working on

Fr. Jerzy Popiełuszko, Records 80–84, consisting of notes the priest had made. According to the blurb, they were a 'counterbalance to the saccharine panegyrics' and showed him to be 'a man of flesh and blood, a man of wonderful qualities and minor vices'.

In London, Minden found the Catholic publisher Veritas producing *The Price of Love: The Sermons of Fr. Jerzy Popiełuszko,* and in Rome his main Polish-language distributor reported that a young nun at the Peregrinatio ad Petri Sedem, a papal institution which helped pilgrims, was selling a Vatican edition of the priest's non-political sermons. Another of his distributors, Father Fokciński, was keen 'to receive as many copies of Libella's collection of Popiełuszko's speeches as possible'.

The symbiotic relationship between the underground and émigrés meant that books trucked into Poland from the West would be amplified by local publishers, who also worked on their own tributes. NOWa conceived *Dear Father Jurek,* a selection of letters sent to the priest during his lifetime, enlarging upon his significance for the opposition. 'What is certain', the introduction to the book began, 'is that on the day of his death he became the most important person in Poland. It is difficult the day after this terrible death, when his image, his voice, his handshake are still so luminous, to assess the weighty implications of his life and martyrdom.'

In *The Price of Loving the Homeland,* published by a Catholic group calling themselves 'the heirs of those who did not shut their mouths when it came to important matters of the nation', an anonymous poet wrote to the martyr:

> For the mother of a slain child
> You were a son,
> To the abandoned family
> You were a brother,
> To old people
> A memory of their proud youth,
> For Warsaw and Poland
> A hope and a comfort to their hearts.

With Popiełuszko's martyrdom assured – although the road to beati-
fication is a lengthy one, and the priest would only formally start the
journey in 1997 – Minden sat down with Chojecki on 23 November
to discuss another subject of growing importance to the CIA:
technology. The mid-1980s marked the dawn of the age of home
computing, with its new lexicon of hardware and software, floppy
disks, modems and BASIC. High-street stores in the West offered
a wealth of gadgets and build-your-own parts for a new generation
of garage technologists. Knowing that Soviet electronics lagged far
behind their Western counterparts, the Agency moved to exploit
its advantage. Former CIA chief historian Benjamin Fischer would
dub this aspect of their support for Solidarity 'the Radio Shack
revolution', because everything they shipped could be found at the
American high-street electronics retailer. 'We sent them Bearcat
scanners so they could monitor the police, computers, all kinds
of walkie-talkies, electronics equipment,' he said. 'By the mid-80s,
we were sending in entire libraries on floppy disk.' Even Giedroyc
embraced the revolution, naming the latest bad-tempered terrier to
occupy the villa at Maisons-Laffitte 'Fax' in tribute to the magical
new device that saved the famous man of letters so much time.

Some of the new devices were available in the Eastern Bloc, too,
including video and audio cassette recorders, which were sold in
Poland at the state-run foreign-currency outlets known as Pewex
stores, and by the mid-1980s Poles had one of the highest rates
of VCR ownership in the Soviet zone. The rise of video created a
home-cinema boom, as it had in the West, with a Polish twist. Poles,
accustomed to the 'double life' and the 'underground society', had a
tradition of gathering in private spaces for cabaret nights, lectures
and readings to escape the repressive authoritarianism outside.
Video, which slipped easily into this mix, offered an exciting new
channel for the CIA to push Polish history past the censor to an
eager, dissident audience.

Always ahead of the curve, Chojecki had been producing cassette
tapes through a new subdivision, Audio Kontakt, for some time.
Subjects for his audio documentaries would include the Soviet

invasion of Afghanistan and the history of Radio Free Europe. 'Chojecki is providing us with all the cassettes he produces,' Minden reported in November 1984. The Pole would take to video with even greater enthusiasm. Chojecki's deputy Tomasz Łabędź was a film-school graduate who regularly worked with French media companies. He was put in charge of a new department, Video Kontakt, with Mirek delivering a generous budget of $10,000 a month. It was easy to find money for film, Mirek told him, as it was 'the most promising [medium] with his sponsors'. A first tranche of 50,000 French francs ($5,000) was provided by Giedroyc, and once again it was unvouchered. Łabędź, who knew the people at Maisons-Laffitte well, was sure money for his operation came from the CIA. The first Video Kontakt production was an hour-long documentary, *Calendar of War*, which consisted of footage of anti-government demonstrations in Poland shot by Western TV news crews, starting on the day of martial law and ending with the death of Popiełuszko. The TV networks allowed Kontakt to use their images for free, and Łabędź cut them together. The last scenes of *Calendar of War* were of the priest's funeral at St Stanisław's church.

Chojecki had also commissioned a documentary about the Literary Institute, Minden discovered, entitled *Kultura*, which told the story of Giedroyc and his collaborators at Maisons-Laffitte, and, separately, a film of the life of Józef Czapski. Both were directed by the Polish film-maker Agnieszka Holland. Other historical subjects included the story of the Anders Army, Józef Piłsudski, KOR, and the Parasol group of resistance fighters with which Chojecki's mother had served. All were proscribed subjects in Poland. Not every film they would send out was made in-house. They also chose Hollywood movies, including a number from the Bond franchise, selecting those that were most anti-Soviet. Video and audio cassettes were be sent to Poland through the same ILC channels as the books and print materials.

Chojecki's video production grew rapidly. On a return visit to Paris the following year, 1985, Minden found he had moved Kontakt into a larger premises at 42 Rue Raymond Marcheron, in the southern Paris suburb of Vanves, where the basement had been converted into Łabędź's film production unit. It was 'very, very well sponsored by the Americans', Łabędź recalled, and was kitted out with the latest professional equipment. Minden spent a morning there, watching the tapes and discussing them with five Kontakt employees. Their main output at that point was a one-hour *Video Kontakt Magazine*, which they produced every two to three months. It was very political and contained 'everything that was censored in Poland', according to Łabędź. Minden thought this was probably their most useful product from the CIA's perspective. He was also shown a film on Polish cabaret, which he found forceful but 'rather crude', much preferring Agnieszka Holland's Czapski documentary, which was now finished. 'Everybody expects this video cassette to be a major success,' he reported.

Video and video-related equipment would take up a growing proportion of the CIA spend on Poland. Chojecki told Minden he didn't think the cassettes would replace literature – they were 'not as important or as prestigious as books' – but they did have certain advantages. They could be put together quickly, they could be shorter and more lowbrow, and if the authors were famous, they could reach more people. Films in particular could help build a social network of like-minded viewers who would gather to watch them together.

Minden was clearly impressed. He and Chojecki agreed to continue their arrangement of purchases and distribution: '[Chojecki] will supply our outlets with both his audio and video cassettes as they are produced,' Minden noted in his report to Langley.

As the two men parted company in November 1984, Minden reminded Chojecki of their first meeting three years earlier, on the eve of martial law. The young Pole had assured Minden then that Solidarity was in no danger from the government, which 'had lost control of the situation completely and could not use the army against the nation'. Now Chojecki recalled his naivety with a smile. He had never made another prophecy after that, he told Minden. Once again, the American was impressed by the dissident's intelligence and charm. At thirty-five, he was 'a much wiser man', the ILC boss reported. 'Of all the new Poles, he seems to be the one that has learned most from his stay in the West.'

It was true that Chojecki had made tremendous strides since the night of Jaruzelski's coup. He had achieved many things in the worlds of publishing and activism, but his masterwork was his logistics operation, the labyrinth of hidden routes he had opened up through and around the Iron Curtain. By pumping resources into Poland via this network, he had sustained a great flowering of uncensored texts, which at first had kept Solidarity alive and later provided space for uncensored political debate. The CIA kept a list of the print sites that had sprung up all around the country. Rex-Rotary and A. B. Dick presses sat behind fake walls, false chimneys and heavy wardrobes, in loft spaces above rural barns and in kitchen cellars beneath trap-doors hidden by refrigerators. The output of these printing machines was carried around in rucksacks and suitcases, or tied to men's backs beneath their coats, and dead-dropped in tree holes, under drain covers or beneath church pews. Households around Poland hid these publications under beds or beneath floorboards in case of an unannounced visit from the secret police.

Mazovia Weekly remained the most important underground paper, and in 1985 it hit its all-time peak estimated circulation of 80,000 copies. The number of uncensored books available was booming too. With Boguta back, NOWa's list grew steadily, from fourteen titles in 1983 (excluding periodicals) to twenty-seven in 1987. In all, almost 2,000 uncensored books and booklets appeared in the underground press between 1982 and 1985, each with print runs of up to 6,000. Many of these were reprints of books sent in from the West. In a survey of *Mazovia Weekly* readers conducted in December 1985, almost all respondents said they had access to independent books. The 'underground society' Giedroyc and Michnik had called for was now real, tangible.

But the SB kept up an intense campaign of shutting down under-ground publications and arresting independent publishers. Boguta found the mid-1980s one of the hardest periods of his dissident life. In May 1985, NOWa's Three Musketeers were caught. Andrzej Górski, Emil Broniarek and Tadeusz Markiewicz were betrayed by Górski's brother, who had been in the pay of the secret police all along, and they were jailed. The raid was one of hundreds on the underground press: between 1984 and 1986, police seized 36 offsets, 9 Xerox machines, 182 duplicators, 424 silkscreen frames and 225 typewriters, along with a staggering 1.3 million copies of books and periodicals. Since publishing was the main opposition activity, that was what most opposition activists were in jail for. In October 1985, a Polish human rights group estimated that the majority of the 320 political prisoners still held in the country were printers, distributors, editors or other collaborators with the social publishing movement. Punishments could be extreme. One man at that time was given an eight-year sentence for distributing a flyer.

The harshness of the struggle, and its apparent endlessness, left the underground psychologically depleted. Many people decided to abandon the 'uphill war', as activists described their fight. Some chose to emigrate, as they were encouraged to do by the regime. The pressure on the opposition spilt over into the West, where the whispering campaigns against Chojecki rose to a clamour of people calling for his dismissal. His relationship with the Warsaw Underground had been strained from the start, hampered by difficult communications and by the highly specific demands rained on him by people with little understanding of how he had to operate. His conspiratorial ways and his reputation for pulling wodges of cash out of his pockets didn't help. Some said he was alcoholic, corrupt, too busy feathering his own nest to pass on the funds he was meant to give to Poland. These lies were no doubt inflated by Polish intelligence, which always tried to sow conflict between opposition camps.

Giedroyc was angered by these attacks, particularly when it seemed that the competition for American funding threatened to spoil everything. 'I am horrified by the situation among "Solidarity" in the West,' he wrote to Nowak early in 1986. 'It is a bundle of vipers, intrigues and mafia . . . Now a large-scale campaign is being organized by these mafias against Mirek Chojecki and Kaleta. If they succeed in their aim, you can put a cross against the entire work for the country.'

The final straw came at the start of 1986, in the form of a disagreement with the Brussels bureau. Marian Kaleta had long been dreaming up a plan to send a giant shipment to Poland, with many tonnes of equipment in a single huge truck. Milewski loved this idea because he knew its success would constitute a propaganda coup and give Solidarity a boost at a time when morale was flagging. Chojecki hated it. The clever aspect of their smuggling operations was that there were too many channels to block, and each shipment was sufficiently small to be written off if it was caught. But if a giant transport of this kind was seized, it would mean the loss of hundreds of thousands of dollars' of kit. The Americans would be furious, and the full weight of the Warsaw Underground's wrath would come down on him. He would 'get his head chopped off in Warsaw' for losing so much, he told Kaleta. It was hubristic, vainglorious and, even if the goods reached the underground, hiding so much at once would be a logistical nightmare for Club B.

He refused to play along, and he was fired for it. From now on, Kaleta, the innovative, eccentric optician, with his reputation for small-time corruption and his ability to fall out with everybody, would formally take over Chojecki's role.

What could possibly go wrong?

PART THREE

RECKONING

1986–1989

16

The Regina Affair

'The worst is so often true,' murmured Miss Marple.
Agatha Christie, *They Do It with Mirrors*

Marian Kaleta and Józef Lebenbaum were polar-opposite personalities, united only by their determination to bring down the
communists. Kaleta – small, bearded, wiry – took things to the
extreme, whether it was smuggling, politics or drinking. Even his
friends found him a little too intense, a 'bit of a megalomaniac', as
one put it. Lebenbaum, fifteen years older at fifty-six, was Jewish, a
former army boxer, with a prodigious repertoire of dirty jokes and
anti-Soviet anecdotes, who made friends easily. Lebenbaum's life in
many ways told the story of Polish Jews at the hands of Hitler and
Stalin. His extended family had been killed by the Nazis, but he
had escaped east, only to be caught by the Soviets and shipped out
to Siberia, the 'prison without walls', under Stalin's policy of forced
displacement. After the war he had returned to Poland and worked
as a journalist within the Party system, but in 1968 the communists deported him again, as part of the anti-Semitic crackdown,
packing him off to Austria with a single suitcase of belongings.
He found refuge in Sweden, which was where he and Kaleta met
in the 1970s, and began sending uncensored literature to Poland
on behalf of Giedroyc and the ILC. Lebenbaum proved a highly
efficient book distributor, as well as a mine of information on East
European affairs. He got on well with Minden, who liked to fly him

out to Switzerland for extended briefings on the Polish situation. Minden would put him up in a hotel in Lausanne, and grill him at lunch over the white linen tablecloths at the Restaurant de la Gare.

Kaleta described the shipment of books and print materials he organized for the summer of 1986 as his 'Everest'. It was to be the largest, most valuable haul of contraband ever sent to Eastern Europe, a monument to the art of smuggling that would ensure his place in the history books. He had been preparing to scale these dizzy heights for years, and his inspiration was to use the global road transit protocol known as Transports Internationaux Routiers (TIR). Under the TIR system, if a truck was to carry goods from Sweden to Austria via Poland, say, it would be examined by Swedish customs, closed with a seal and not opened again until its final destination, where officials would check the cargo against the inventory made in Sweden. Crucially, the transit country, Poland, would ignore it in the knowledge that it was only passing through. But Kaleta had underworld connections, and he managed to buy TIR seals and documentation on the black market. This meant his driver could secretly unload the truck in Poland, reseal it and leave the country without the authorities knowing.

It was a clever idea, but an expensive one. TIR certification was reserved for professional hauliers with large operations, which meant Kaleta had to spend $35,000 creating a commercial front company, MSM Transporter (the acronym stood for 'Marian, Sven and Mirek'), with a fake address, fake phone number and fake accounts. Another $14,000 went on purchasing the rig, one of the largest allowed on European roads, a Scania 110 tractor with a semi-trailer. Next came the cargo: he wanted to send 11 tonnes of print equipment, electronics and books in one go. Small offset presses were increasingly rare by 1986, as Western offices had mostly moved over to photocopiers, but A. B. Dick still made a model for missionaries in Africa, and he bought fifty of these for $200,000. He stocked up on simple duplicators, too, 2 tonnes of ink and canning machinery and printed labels, so he could disguise the liquid as tins of food. To store it all, he had to rent four or five lockups around Malmö, including a whole basement just for the books he planned to send, an apartment he filled with electronics, and – after drinking too much whisky with the letting agent – an entire disused factory for heavier items such as the offset presses. A problem with the factory space was that it was on the second floor, so he also needed a crane to move in the heavier equipment. Then he hired Sven Järn's brother, Lennart, to be the Scania's driver, although he wasn't suited to the job. 'If he wanted to, he drove, and if he didn't want to, he didn't,' Kaleta admitted.

This was just the Swedish end of the attempt on Everest. More difficult was finding someone to receive his gargantuan haul in Poland. None of his usual Warsaw contacts seemed keen. Relations between the smugglers and the underground were already at a low, and the first message he sent went unanswered. Even his friend Boguta at NOWa didn't want the shipment, since he didn't have the means to store or distribute such quantities of material. In the end, Milewski told him to forget Warsaw and try Gdańsk, the Brussels bureau chief's home town. They made contact there with Jacek Merkel, who worked as a liaison connecting Bujak, Wałęsa and Solidarity's office in the West. Merkel agreed to organize the truck's reception, telling Kaleta to give him a month to prepare the drop site. After that, he would need just twenty-four hours' notice.

The mission's political aim was given extra urgency at the end of May, when devastating news reached them from Poland. After a years-long manhunt, the SB had finally worked out where Bujak would be on a particular day. Fearing that he could use his skills as a former paratrooper against them, they had blown in the door to his safe house with explosives. The same intelligence had given them addresses for Ewa Kulik and Konrad Bieliński, who were arrested at the same time. The police announced that they had found documentary evidence in Bujak's apartment showing that his activities 'were directed and inspired by Western special (intelligence) services and centres of ideological subversion'. The capture of the talismanic Solidarity leader, who had earned the reputation of a Houdini thanks mostly to Helena Łuczywo and Kulik, was a major blow for Solidarity. If ever the underground needed a morale boost it was now.

Early in June, Kaleta sent Lennart Järn on a dummy run, to check that the system worked as he hoped. The Swede boarded the ferry at Ystad, disembarked at Świnoujście, and circled back through East and West Germany without a problem. They repeated the exercise two or three times to make sure, and although they decided to abandon TIR in favour of the simpler European CMR system, which worked in a similar way, there were no major issues. By the end of the month, Kaleta was ready to go.

They loaded the Scania trailer with more than a hundred printing presses and 5 tonnes of stencils, inks, microcomputers and books, packed into twenty-one large crates. In all, the contraband was worth a quarter of a million dollars. Järn drove it to the ferry port at Ystad, where he met Kaleta on the flat, windswept concrete apron in front of the undistinguished terminal building. The driver was 'gushing with his usual optimism', Kaleta recalled. Although Chojecki had never liked the practice, Kaleta insisted on switching the truck's licence plates, since he assumed the Poles would track vehicles arriving in the country, and he didn't want them to clock the Scania as a regular visitor. Järn drove up to the Swedish border at the last minute, with the idea that the customs officials would be less fastidious when the ship was about to sail.

It was one of Kaleta's main fears that the 'Svenssons', as he derisively termed the Swedes, would discover the transport's illicit cargo on the dock at Ystad. If that happened, Lennart was to abandon the vehicle and let Kaleta deal with the fallout: he had a contact in the Swedish Säpo security service who could help out in such a situation. But Järn passed safely through customs and boarded the ferry, and the following morning he completed the checks on the Polish side without a hitch. On the way out of Świnoujście he picked up Jan Krzysztof Bielecki, a future Polish prime minister, who was overseeing security for Merkel and would guide Järn to the drop point. Bielecki had organized a few outriders to drive around Gdańsk in Fiats equipped with police radio scanners, supplied from the West, to monitor the militia channels for any uptick in activity. There were no alarms, so they continued to a village outside Gdańsk and parked the Scania at an abandoned poultry farm. A team of activists drawn from the maths and physics faculty at Gdańsk University was waiting there with an electric forklift truck to unload the goods. Merkel had given them thirty hours to unpack the cargo and despatch it to secret locations around the country.

The unloading ran to schedule. The following day, Järn telephoned Kaleta from East Germany to report that he was safe. 'A stone fell from my heart,' Kaleta recalled. 'I had made it. My dream of entering Poland in a truck loaded with equipment for the underground had come true.' Rejoicing 'like a little child', he hurried to tell Milewski.

He had reached the summit of his smuggling career, his Everest. 'I knew I couldn't do anything bigger,' he said. 'You can conquer it again, but there is no higher mountain.'

When Kaleta showed up at the Brussels office a few days later for a logistics meeting they welcomed him at the door with champagne. Milewski was in tears. The delivery was just the triumph he had been searching for. Almost immediately, they decided to go again. They had enough money to run two such transports a year, each of which would carry an even bigger load: around 150 presses, plus several tonnes of other materials. Chojecki, who had distanced himself altogether from the Scania, was horrified to learn of the risks they were prepared to take: this new shipment he reckoned was worth close to half a million dollars. But Kaleta had formally taken Mirek's job as minister for smuggling, and he and Milewski were determined to push on. Giedroyc of course didn't approve of Chojecki's being sidelined and wrote to Washington to tell Nowak about the 'most difficult . . . of the disputed matters', the transfer and purchase of equipment to Poland, which had been removed from his protégé's control and was to be dealt with by Kaleta, who, although 'Mirek's man', was now dependent on Milewski.

That summer, Kaleta was riding high on his success. He took a holiday and bought a house. He also met up with Nowak, who was passing through Sweden on a lecture tour, and asked him outright if the 'United States secret service' would buy him a second vehicle on the grounds that it was against the 'health and safety' rules to carry smuggled goods in the same truck as secret correspond-ence, as they were now doing, since it could allow the SB to tie the recipients of the messages to the contraband. Nowak demurred, telling Kaleta his ability to influence such things was limited, and no funds for a second vehicle came through. Unfazed, Kaleta returned to work, preparing for the next mega-shipment by restocking the warehouses with several tonnes more of material and painting the Scania a different colour.

On 28 November, Järn set out again. As before, Kaleta went to Ystad to watch him negotiate the ferry terminal. As before, they swapped the truck's licence plates. As before, Järn drove up to Swedish border control. Unlike before, Kaleta looked on impa-tiently as the truck stood idling for some time.

Usually there was no one in the customs booth on the Swedish side, but on this occasion there were two: an officer and his young son, whom he had brought in to work. To show the boy how smart their system was, the officer had punched the truck's licence number into his computer. He was astonished to find that the plates were registered not to this enormous articulated Scania rig, but to an old family saloon, the Volkswagen Passat from which Kaleta had taken them. Järn launched into a clumsy explanation. They were smugglers, he said, political rather than criminal smugglers. The customs man called the police. Kaleta, sitting in his car across the concourse, saw a squad car arrive and hurried to intervene. He pulled one of the police officers aside and gave them the number of his Säpo contact. But the officer didn't want to call the Säpo – why should he? Kaleta, who was always highly strung, lost his temper at that moment and started shouting. Eventually the police officer did call the Säpo, who told him to wave the truck through. The smugglers' agreed procedure was to abandon the operation in the event of the slightest issue. Given the commotion they had caused on the dock, that was what Järn should now have done. Instead, the bullish Swede drove straight on to the ferry. Kaleta didn't have a chance to stop him, and since he knew the Polish shipping lines were packed with informers, he drove back to Malmö in misery, feeling, he stated later, that he was 'going to a beheading'.

After a calm but cold crossing, the ferry disgorged its cargo in Świnoujście the following morning, 29 November. Järn cleared Polish border checks as before, but as he drove towards the exit for Szczecin he was flagged down by a group of soldiers who singled out the Scania from the stream of vehicles leaving the port. They demanded his papers and began a search. When the first crates were opened, the nature of the shipment became clear. As well as the printing presses, the truck was carrying 420 giant 2.5 kilo cans of ink, 49 photocopiers, 16 fax machines, Tandy and IBM computers, radio scanners, radio transmitter assembly kits and 5,000 copies of 'subversive' books and pamphlets.

Reinforcements were called. SB officers arrived from the capital by helicopter. Järn was arrested and the truck impounded with its cargo.

The Polish authorities brought the Scania to Warsaw, and laid out its contents in a football stadium, where they invited the media to view it. Jerzy Urban, Jaruzelski's spokesman, used the moment to try to destroy Kaleta's credibility in Swedish eyes. The shipment's size suggested it was 'a sophisticated provocation by Polish political emigrants operating in Sweden, aimed at impeding the development of Polish–Swedish relations', he said. 'The Polish Swedes were working with 'the special services of the overseas superpower which cooperate with the emigration structures of Solidarity and finance them'. Jaruzelski would personally raise the matter with the Swedish ambassador.

Where the first shipment had acted as a morale boost for the underground, the capture of the second did the opposite. 'We were crying when we heard,' Boguta said. 'The loss in terms of equipment was terrible.'

The fallout Chojecki had predicted now landed harder than Kaleta ever thought possible. The Swedish media named him as the secret mastermind behind the provocation and discovered something he hadn't known, that Lennart Järn's driving licence had been taken away for drink-driving. Even *Mazovia Weekly* blamed Kaleta, for unnecessary risk-taking and lack of common sense. His nightmare only grew worse as the year progressed. Swedish law prohibited the export of American technology to the East, so the presence in the shipment of computers made by US companies constituted a criminal offence. The authorities chose to press charges. Kaleta found this 'simply incomprehensible. We were fighting against the total dictatorship that ruled Poland, but it was us who were on trial.' The case against him would collapse when his defence attorney argued that the computers had been manufactured in Taiwan, not the US, but by that time the media exposure had left Kaleta's reputation in tatters. In April 1987 he announced the formal bankruptcy of his company MSM Transporter.

Järn, meanwhile, sat in jail. He performed well under interrogation, lying that he was supposed to deliver his cargo to a motel in western Poland, but on 16 April 1987 he was sentenced to two years, commuted to a fine of $35,000 plus forfeiture of the truck and its contents. The Brussels bureau stumped up most of the ransom payment, which the more reliable of the south Sweden smugglers, Józef Lebenbaum, was tasked with delivering. Järn was released in May 1987, after serving six months.

Theories about the shipment's capture washed around dissident circles for years afterwards. If it was the SB, who had tipped them off? It later became clear that the Swedish customs officer had sent a telex alerting his Polish counterparts to the suspicious truck. Why? Kaleta believed the officer felt his honour had been impugned in front of his son and that after going along with the Säpo's instructions he had decided to correct his mistake in allowing the Scania through. Kaleta's shouting had no doubt aggravated the situation.

The CIA had another theory. After the capture, Nowak returned to Sweden on a mission to find out how such a large amount of material, much of it bought by the Agency, had been lost. He met with Kaleta in Malmö, then went on to Lund to speak with Lebenbaum. 'The Americans thought one such loss was OK,' Lebenbaum recalled, 'but they didn't want it to happen again.' Nowak asked Lebenbaum if he wasn't suspicious about the role played by Swedish customs, and left the smuggler with the strong impression that the Americans knew 'something was wrong in the transmission line' – in other words, that someone had informed the SB. Years later, Polish secret police files would reveal that a high-ranking Polish intelligence officer had been sent to Sweden to destroy the ratline through Malmö. Some Swedish officials 'were on the [SB] payroll', Lebenbaum said. Gates at the CIA would also blame Polish intelligence for the seizure of shipments in 1986.

The capture of the huge Lennart Järn transport slowed smuggling operations almost to a standstill, but at his next meeting with Minden in Paris, Chojecki felt it best to play down the incident. The result was that the ILC boss passed a somewhat garbled account back to the CIA about the loss. The confiscation of the Scania and of the 'large delivery of books' wasn't down to SB activity, it was because the Swede 'was drunk and didn't have a driver's licence', he stated.

'[I] wasn't going to tell him all the details of what had really happened,' Chojecki said later.

After the seizure, there remained one safe channel for Brussels from southern Sweden, the one run from Lund by Lebenbaum, using an expert professional smuggler known as 'Janusz'. He at least remained discreet, trustworthy and utterly reliable. In the aftermath of Järn's capture, he would become the main carrier of messages, money and goods exchanged between the Solidarity leaders in Brussels and the underground.

Lund is a Hans Christian Andersen kind of a place, with medieval cobbled streets, half-timbered houses daubed in bright Scandinavian shades of baby blue and burnt orange, and a large student population. The main danger that lurks in these charming squares and alleyways stems from the packs of cyclists who race between the lecture halls and the coffee shops, jangling all the way. It made an unlikely place for a nest of Cold War spies, but in the mid-1980s that was exactly what Lund had become, thanks to its strategic location in southern Sweden, just 130 miles from the Polish coast. Lebenbaum, who had settled here as it was about as close as he could get to home, guessed that every third person he met in those days was working for the SB or the KGB. Decades later, when the secret police files were being pored over by historians, he would learn the cryptonyms of at least twenty-eight people who had supplied Polish intelligence with information about him, and more were coming to light all the time.

'Informers were everywhere,' he said. 'We were constantly being followed and watched. The game was going on all the time, and I was aware that I'm part of that game.'

He lived for much of the 1980s in a large, crumbling house in the north of the town, on a remote plot bounded by a railway track, a ring road and the municipal waste dump. Apart from its size and secluded location, the building's main advantage was a hidden cellar where he could keep his stash of CIA-bought books, presses and print supplies. Since he was an affable and generous host, the house became a regular stopover for travellers from Poland who were passing through, who wanted to exchange news or find a bed for the night. Some of these people were tourists; some were couriers; many were both. He offered them sandwiches, tea and coffee, and sometimes good Polish vodka. 'It was like a hotel,' he remembered. Everybody liked to smoke, and sometimes he was afraid of opening a window in case a passer-by called the fire brigade. Lebenbaum's house became so popular with Polish travellers, and he was so notorious in the minds of the state authorities, that the Polish media referred to the building as the 'CIA villa'. Lebenbaum wore this label with humour and not a little pride. His guests would head back to the Eastern Bloc carrying ILC literature, messages and sometimes printing equipment too.

In 1983, he had launched a cover for his clandestine activities, called the Independent Polish Agency (IPA). Based in an office close to the main market square in Lund, the IPA was part photo agency, part smuggling operation: its aim was to get images and information out of Poland, which he would pass to the Western media, and to get literature, messages and other material in. Photographs would reach him by a variety of odd methods and routes. One man smuggled film out of Poland in his underpants, which led Jacek Kaczmarski, the bard of Solidarity, to write the immortal lyric 'I smuggled the photos in my ass / See here the smoke, here the cops, here the gas.' Another set of negatives came hidden in a truck tyre. This must have seemed like a foolproof way of slipping the photographs out, until the tyre burst, breaking the film into pieces. When it reached Lund it was a jigsaw puzzle.

Lebenbaum published several albums of photographs, which Minden supported with purchases and distribution. The most successful was *War against the Nation*, a collection of images shot covertly in Poland which told the story of the martial law crackdown, including grainy, atmospheric photographs of the massacre at the Wujek mine on that snowy, scream-filled day in December 1981. This album even reached the White House, and Reagan wrote Lebenbaum a personal note of thanks, which the smuggler framed and hung on a wall.

It was in the IPA office that Lebenbaum had first met his trusty courier Janusz.

Lebenbaum had a theory about moving items in and out of the Eastern Bloc, which he shared with Minden in May 1983. It was all well and good to use enthusiastic idealists, he said, but there were hundreds of professional black marketeers out there profiting from the shortages in the East by shipping in Levi's, Western rock music and second-hand domestic appliances. These people had developed smuggling into a fine art. They bought off customs officials and slipped goods through the border with no questions asked. They would be perfect for moving literature and print materials, not least because in the event of capture they could pretend the shipments

were a commercial and not a political enterprise, which would draw
less attention to the émigrés.

At a meeting in the Lund office he discussed the idea of using
professionals, and as chance would have it, not long afterwards a
small, beret-wearing 'smuggler' of around forty years old made
contact with one of his associates. The associate invited Janusz to
meet the boss, and Lebenbaum thought the stranger was just what
he'd been looking for: an inconspicuous professional, with his own
vehicle and no ideological baggage. To check him out properly,
Lebenbaum gave him numerous small consignments to carry in and
out of Poland over the next year, and asked his Solidarity contacts
for references. The new courier passed every test. 'He always had
the best reviews,' said Lebenbaum. 'Always the best possible recom-
mendations. And these were from people very high up in the trade
union hierarchy, about whom I had no shadow of suspicion.'

When Janusz's probation was over, Lebenbaum began to use him
as his main channel to the country. For several years, he carried
important messages back and forth between Brussels and the
underground. After the Lennart Järn disaster, he would be given
responsibility for an extra-special shipment, a trailer full of material
of a kind they had never sent before: paramilitary equipment, for a
radical, quasi-terrorist group in Gdańsk.

The Polish opposition always spanned a political spectrum,
from communists and leftists to hard-right nationalists, from effete
Warsaw intellectuals to Gdańsk street brawlers. Periods of major
upheaval such as the strikes in the summer of 1980 had papered
over the cracks, but as the 'uphill war' continued with no end in
sight, and as the opposition grew more exhausted, the fissures in
the coalition had opened up. The CIA was well aware of this. While
an Agency assessment from the summer of 1986 continued to
support the slow and steady strategy espoused by many in Warsaw,
it noted that the underground was 'organizationally fragmented'
and 'divided over tactics'. In fact, a growing section of the opposition, including many of the émigrés, had run out of patience with
the whole 'long march' concept. Kaleta captured the spirit of this

tendency when he railed against 'Warsaw revolutionaries who sat on sofas' and 'maliciously' undermined his and Lebenbaum's hard work for the revolution.

Fighting Solidarity, founded by the physicist and underground publisher Kornel Morawiecki in Wrocław in 1982, was one of the more radical groups to have emerged after martial law. Members had to swear an oath to work for 'a free and independent Republic of Solidarity', much as Home Army soldiers in the war had sworn allegiance to the Motherland, and the group's badge blended the Solidarity logo with the old crowned eagle of pre-communist Poland. Fighting Solidarity had its own publishing operations, and even a radio station, which broadcast over 100 programmes. Its leader in the Gdańsk area was a young firebrand named Andrzej Kołodziej, who believed that all negotiations with the regime were a trap and that the security services were acting with impunity, as the killing of Popiełuszko had shown. To send a warning to Jaruzelski and the SB that they could not get away with such 'stealth murders', Kołodziej's group had begun building explosives from everyday ingredients. In February 1987, they detonated a small bomb in a skip outside the Party offices in Gdynia. The bomb wasn't meant to injure anyone, but it did raise the spectre of terrorism in what until then had been a largely peaceful resistance movement. Moderates feared that anti-communist partisans would soon be fighting the regime in the streets, with all the risks of Soviet intervention that brought. Others – including Giedroyc, Kaleta and Lebenbaum – admired the group's boldness and its attempt to break the stalemate.

Lebenbaum took the Fighting Solidarity oath himself, and on a trip to Washington early in the summer of 1987 he lobbied Brzezinski on the group's behalf. How Brzezinski responded is a matter of dispute. Lebenbaum recalled that the former national security advisor turned him down flat: 'He was very, very clear. He said don't play with them, do not get involved with them.' But SB agents who penetrated Lebenbaum's communications after the meeting heard a very different message. They reported that Lebenbaum had told Brzezinski that Fighting Solidarity needed

$100,000 to $150,000 a year, and Brzezinski suggested he approach the head of Radio Free Europe's Polish service for 'hot cash', although he said long-term aid would only be possible if he could provide full details of the organization's structure and what the money would be used for. The Americans would need reassurance that, when a 'Zero Hour' event came in Poland – meaning a major new outbreak of strikes or street protests – the subsidized organization would be 'able to take the initiative'. It would also help if the group could 'carry out some spectacular, sensational act' that would catch the attention of the American public.

Lebenbaum's subsequent moves tend to support the SB account. He threw his energy into finding backing for Fighting Solidarity, contacting Radio Free Europe, then relaying a message to Kołodziej via his trusted courier that they were ready to give money but wanted further details, including how many members the organization had, where it operated and its structure. He also asked Kołodziej when, if ever, a 'spectacular terrorist act' might take place, since the Americans wanted to know 'if it will happen, when and where'. Kołodziej replied that he understood the group had been silent 'for too long' after the bomb in Gdynia, but said the timing of the pope's visit to Poland in June had made it 'very awkward to start this kind of activity'. He went on to describe the small arsenal the group had accumulated: 'We have 8 weapons, 20 radio-telephones, about 200kg of TNT, documents and technical equipment we make ourselves, firecrackers, tear gas grenades, etc.' He reckoned they needed $1,000 a month. This money would go on people, premises, chemicals and transport. 'Explosives and weapons are bought occasionally,' he wrote.

Had the CIA's Polish remit changed? Was the Agency now moving to support militants in Poland, as it was in Afghanistan and elsewhere? Or was Lebenbaum acting on his own initiative, perhaps with Brzezinski's support? It was curious timing for the CIA, since the powerful individual who might have approved such a scheme, the 'freelance buccaneer' Bill Casey, had suffered a stroke during the Iran–Contra scandal and died that May. His replacement as director of central intelligence, the lawyerly William H. Webster, was far more cautious. Even so, the SB considered it possible that US intelligence and its émigré networks were toughening their stance, especially after they intercepted a shipment of 104 audio cassettes sent from West Germany to Fighting Solidarity's leadership in Wrocław which contained instructions in Polish for conducting a guerrilla war. According to the SB, the hour-long tapes covered three main areas: 'organization and training of underground groups', 'sabotage and terrorist activity' and 'conducting military operations'. The cassettes were 'produced in the USA' and had allegedly been sent by 'the Americans'.

If this alarmed the Polish authorities, they also recognized a golden opportunity to embarrass the opposition and its CIA sponsors. That summer, the one-star general who ran Polish foreign intelligence, Zdzisław Sarewicz, would lay a trap aimed at 'obtaining indirect evidence of participation of American-funded diversion centres in planning, preparation, financing and material support of terrorism in Poland'.

In June, Lebenbaum and Kaleta travelled to Mainz, West Germany, to meet a liaison sent by Kołodziej from Poland and discuss a special new shipment. Kaleta had money from Brussels to fund another supply of books and printing supplies to Gdańsk, and in Mainz the smugglers agreed to add two refrigerators to the transport. These would secretly contain various paramilitary items Kołodziej had asked for. Milewski knew nothing about it. No one had told him.

Kaleta returned from Germany to Malmö with his friend Krzysztof Szymański, a trusted contact who worked on the Polish ferries, carrying messages in and out of Poland. The plan was for Szymański to travel to Poland in advance of the new transport, so that he could receive it in Gdańsk from Lebenbaum's courier Janusz, but first he would help Kaleta prepare the special delivery. Mostly, this would be a typical Brussels literary-support transport, with printing machines and spares, miniature cameras, electronics and hundreds of books and journals. The really important part, the paramilitary equipment, would be fitted into the insulation in the walls of the refrigerators, so that it was all but undetectable.

Janusz would also carry correspondence from the Brussels office for various parts of the underground, as had become the norm despite breaching the 'health and safety' rules.

By late September, Kaleta and Szymański had packed the precious load into the trailer Janusz used for carrying contraband and towed it to Lebenbaum's place in Lund. The courier arrived soon afterwards, hitched it to his car and set off for Ystad. Lebenbaum had briefed him on every aspect of the delivery: where to go, what to do at each point, and a dozen contingency plans in case of problems. Some days later, Lebenbaum set out for the Frankfurt Book Fair – it was that time of year once again. He wasn't at all concerned: the courier had travelled the route dozens of times before, and the IPA boss was confident that he had planned a perfect operation. On the road south, he called his office in Lund to check everything was running smoothly.

There was nothing unusual to report. Everything seemed to be going to plan.

Everything was indeed going to plan – the SB's plan. They had known about the shipment almost from its conception, since the liaison officer Kołodziej sent to meet them in West Germany was a Polish agent, codenamed 'Diodor', who passed details of the special transport to his superiors. Most significant, Janusz, real name Jan Ostrzewski, had been a spy all along. In 1983, he had shown up at the Polish consulate in Malmö to offer his services as a snitch. The SB background checks found him to be a liar and criminal with a couple of convictions and even a jail term behind him, but this didn't deter them. They recruited him at the start of 1984. Over the years they gave him multiple cryptonyms, including 'Sab', 'Rodon' and 'Razir', but he was mostly known as 'Regina'. They trained him in intelligence techniques and sent him to Sweden to infiltrate Kaleta's and Lebenbaum's circles.

By 1987, Regina/Janusz had become the main courier for the Brussels bureau, which meant the SB knew about a whole lot more than just the connection between the south Sweden smuggling operation and Fighting Solidarity. Milewski communicated with the underground via encrypted floppy disks that were carried by Regina, and the SB had worked out how to decode them. This meant they could read almost all traffic carried between Brussels and Poland.

After crossing the Baltic and landing at Świnoujście, Regina drove the shipment straight to Warsaw, where the security service combed through the trailer's contents, finding the printing machines, paper, books and electronics devices. They were expecting to find detonators, plastic explosives and even automatic weapons, too, and when they didn't they took the trailer to Warsaw airport and ran it through the X-ray machine, which revealed the presence of seven airguns, including four that could be converted into .22 calibre firearms, along with a dozen boxes of ammunition, thirty packs of paralysing gas canisters, twenty electric shock batons and four sets of 'red dot' laser sights for snipers' rifles. Next they took the trailer to technicians at the interior ministry's 'B branch', who marvelled at the job Kaleta and Szymański had done: it was virtually impossible to extract the weapons without damaging the refrigerator walls, but the casings still looked like they were fresh from the factory. The technicians carefully removed one of the airguns and took it to a gunsmith, who showed how it could easily be converted into a lethal firearm.

With the contents of the shipment photographed and documented, the SB repacked everything and told Regina to continue his journey to Gdańsk.

The agent now had a suspicious delay to account for. Late on the evening of 29 September, he pulled into the car park of the Marina Hotel, a boxy nine-storey building on the beachfront, unhitched the trailer, let down its tyres then went off to find Szymański. He told the activist the load had been so heavy that the original trailer had broken down and he'd had to rent another, which was why he was so late. But the tyres on the rental leaked air, so he couldn't drive it from the Marina to the agreed drop point. This was all part of the SB plan to prevent Szymański taking the trailer that night, before the trap was fully set.

Szymański accepted the courier's excuses and handed over some correspondence for Lebenbaum. Regina left the scene.

Overnight, police units staked out the car park. They had to wait until eleven the following morning for their first sighting of their target, Szymański, who drove past, saw the trailer's tyres were indeed flat but didn't approach. Four hours later, he returned with three mechanics.

Andrzej Kołodziej, whose shipment it was, had spent most of the night sitting up in his apartment with a couple of radio scanners, listening to the police chatter. He heard nothing unusual, but the courier's lateness, combined with the unexpected change of drop point, gave him 'a bad feeling'. Suddenly, around 3 p.m., all hell broke loose, as the police channels lit up and the security forces descended on Szymański, the trailer and the mechanics. They were in such a rush to make arrests that they detained a random Swede who had found himself in the wrong place at the wrong time.

Hearing this cacophony, Kołodziej realized the drop had gone horribly wrong and fled the city with his fiancée and their child. They kept going for 300 miles, until they reached Wrocław, where, on the advice of Fighting Solidarity's national leader, Kornel Morawiecki, they took off into the mountains.

Szymański was brought to Mokotów jail.

It took several days for news of the shipment's capture to break in the West. Lebenbaum was enjoying cocktails with the usual group of dissident friends in Frankfurt when the phone rang. It was Axel, a Swedish colleague in Lund, who told him the TV news was reporting that a trailer filled with weapons had been seized in Poland. Journalists were calling from all over, asking to speak with him urgently. They had offered to fly anywhere in the world to meet him for an interview, Axel said.

'Tell them you don't know where I am!' Lebenbaum bellowed into the receiver. He slammed down the phone.

Over the following days he felt himself 'falling apart', 'fragmenting into pieces'. He went with Kaleta to Paris, where his internal malaise developed into a bad case of pneumonia. His temperature rose to 41.5°C.

If the capture of Järn's shipment had been mostly a financial disaster, this time the catastrophe was political. Jerzy Urban, the regime spokesman, presented the 'contraband terrorist equipment' to international journalists at a press conference on 6 October. 'Material evidence has emerged that at least some of the illegal groups that use the name Solidarity intend to bring terrorism to Poland as a method of political struggle,' he said, adding that 'the Gdańsk shipment is a signal of terrorist intentions and preparations'.

Lebenbaum was still unwell when he and Kaleta were ordered to Brussels to face the wrath of Milewski and his deputy, Joanna Pilarska. The Solidarity bureau chiefs had been reading through the transcript of Urban's press conference with mounting horror, which was captured by SB agents who had infiltrated the Brussels office. With no knowledge of what had been sent or why, Milewski and Pilarska were staggered by the extent of the disaster. The smugglers had made an 'unforgivable mistake' in taking paramilitary equipment on a Solidarity transport. It had been a 'fundamental' blunder to mix that with correspondence for other opposition leaders, whom the regime could immediately tie to 'terrorist' equipment. Among other things, the correspondence told the SB about the bad atmosphere and quarrels between national and foreign Solidarity structures – quarrels that were about to get far worse, as the seizure meant different opposition groups now tore into each other, throwing accusations of infiltration or even collaboration, stoking the animosities and resentments SB agents had been working to establish for many years.

When Lebenbaum and Kaleta reached Brussels, and walked shamefaced into the bureau on Avenue de la Joyeuse Entrée, which overlooked a famous city park, Milewski and Pilarska launched into them. The meeting was a 'massacre', according to Lebenbaum. They told him there hadn't been a catastrophe on the same scale since the 1940s, when the CIA had sent money and submachine guns to WiN, the Polish partisan group that was controlled by Soviet intelligence.

Lebenbaum, who was still struggling with pneumonia, tried to calm them. 'If you keep shouting at me in this way,' he said, 'I'm going to go off and find a hotel because I just can't listen to any more.'

He and Kaleta were so worried about the fallout from their failed shipment that when they made their way home to Sweden they avoided the main Copenhagen–Malmö ferry crossing and took the quieter northern route via Helsingborg instead.

The affair of Regina and the fridges would reverberate for months. In Mokotów jail, interrogators confronted Syzmański with a mountain of evidence. They quickly found their prisoner's weak spot: his wife, with whom he had two daughters, was an Indian national. The police gave him an ultimatum: if he didn't cooperate he would rot for an eternity in prison while his family was deported. He wouldn't see his daughters for years.

Szymański broke down. He admitted carrying letters and publications between Poland and the West more than a dozen times, often between Kaleta and the Gdańsk Solidarity leaders Jacek Merkel and Bogdan Borusewicz. He had also acted as the recipient for Regina in Poland, picking up floppy disks, money, duplicators, an IBM typewriter and radio scanners sent by Kaleta and Lebenbaum. Szymański's extensive evidence led to the arrest and interrogation of a slew of activists in Gdańsk and put everyone in the underground on high alert. Within four months of the transport's seizure, the SB had found and arrested Morawiecki and Kołodziej. To avoid a trial, the regime expelled them to the West.

Lebenbaum still hadn't worked out who the mole in the midst of his organization was. After two weeks, Janusz resurfaced in Sweden, where he made a great show of being furious. Asked where he had been, he said he had only escaped Poland with great difficulty and had gone to hide in Berlin. When he knew it was safe, he had made his way to Sweden to find out what had gone wrong. It was clear that Szymański had been a Polish informer all along, he said, but it was Lebenbaum who was to blame for everything.

'He said that it was on my initiative that he had transported such treacherous goods,' Lebenbaum recalled, 'and that if he had been caught they would have executed him for terrorism.'

The IPA boss felt so guilty he even gave the courier 3,000 kronor ($500) to compensate for the loss of the trailer. Janusz was soon back in business, carrying materials 'secretly' to Poland on Lebenbaum and Kaleta's behalf.

17

A General, a Lowly Recruit and All Ranks In Between

But you do know, as you stand alone, handcuffed, with your eyes filled with tear gas, in front of policemen who are shaking their guns at you . . . that the course of the avalanche depends on the stone over which it rolls. And you want to be the stone that will reverse the course of events.

Adam Michnik, *Letters from Prison and Other Essays*

The string of catastrophes in 1986–7, culminating in the Regina affair, left the Polish opposition demoralized and angry. Émigré incompetence combined with the years-long SB campaign to penetrate the Solidarity networks in general and the Brussels bureau in particular had enabled Polish intelligence to take control of the enemy's main East–West communication channel and expose and humiliate dissidents at home and abroad. General Sarewicz could hardly contain his glee. The seizure of the Fighting Solidarity transport had led to 'deepening of mutual animosities, resentment, embitterment and an atmosphere of suspicion between activists of both domestic and foreign Solidarity structures', he reported to Jaruzelski. Those in the opposition were turning on each other, with activists in the underground demanding that those responsible for the 'organizational incompetence' in the supply chain must 'face the consequences'. It was agreed that Kaleta should never again be allowed to run smuggling activities, and a motion had been put forward to dismiss Milewski from his post. Worse still for the opposition, the Brussels office had conducted a thorough analysis of transports to date, which – thanks to some interference by SB agents in the bureau – found that the smugglers had been providing false information about their activities and embezzling money, stirring the recriminations ever more fiercely. It was likely, General Sarewicz believed, that the Swedish authorities would clamp down on smuggling from their territory in future. He also anticipated a 'negative reaction of the American sponsors of Solidarity'.

He was right about that. Nowak wrote to Giedroyc in October 1987 to tell him that the Americans believed this latest, third bust was down to 'a reprehensible lack of precautions'. Kaleta had proved himself 'absolutely unfit to be Minister of Smuggling' after Chojecki's removal and had always been under surveillance by Warsaw counter-intelligence, 'which does not let him out of its sight'. Milewski, meanwhile, was 'completely burned . . . both the [US] administration and the unions treat him as persona non grata', and the idea that he had sent the most secret letters with a transport of printing equipment, air pistols and electric-shock batons was 'shameful'. (To be fair, this hadn't been Milewski's fault.) When the unfortunate Brussels bureau chief showed up at the AFL-CIO conference in Florida, he wasn't welcomed or even allowed to speak, and Nowak no longer felt able to defend him, he wrote.

Such a pall of gloom hung over Maisons-Laffitte that Giedroyc didn't answer this letter for weeks. He finally replied in late January the following year, agreeing that everything 'looks as bad as it can'. He, too, would not defend Milewski from the increasingly loud calls for his impeachment, although no one could agree who should replace him. The fiasco had further disrupted deliveries of printing equipment, which were already at a low ebb. 'Kaleta has withdrawn,' he wrote. 'Sweden is, after all, burnt out despite Lebenbaum being a great optimist. To a certain extent he is also responsible for the last slip-up, sending such careless letters.' The crisis had damaged opposition politics inside Poland too. 'The country is completely divided,' Giedroyc wrote. Wałęsa was recognized by everyone, but increasingly criticized. Bujak was 'a man of good will and full of enthusiasm', but also 'very naïve and manipulated by the so-called Warsaw salon headed by [Adam] Michnik'.

The obvious solution was to turn back to Chojecki. Mirek wasn't one to gloat, but the lesson of the Swedish disasters was that he had been right all along. His unflashy, small-scale approach to smuggling materials had been by far the best way to operate, while his extraordinary knack for subterfuge had kept him safe from the worst SB predations. He was 'a conspirator by nature', a friend of his told Minden, who would 'persist in conspiratorial tactics long after they have ceased to be useful'. He was also one of the few Solidarity émigrés the Americans and their allies seemed genuinely to trust. Nowak continued to have 'great confidence' in him, while Giedroyc valued and liked him 'very much'. There remained the issue of his difficult relationship with Warsaw, where there was a 'kind of campaign against him', Giedroyc wrote. But people from Poland continued to approach him with all kinds of requests, and although it was clear that there were many things he couldn't arrange or sort out, he always tried his best to be helpful: 'He cannot refuse [them].'

Minden continued to rate him too, writing approvingly about him to the CIA. In their meetings over the years, the ILC president had documented the dissident's development from the 'very self-assured young freedom fighter' he had first met in 1981 to 'a much better informed, skeptical, and careful exile opposition leader' – one who could admit, for instance, that Jaruzelski was 'far from stupid' and that his spokesman Jerzy Urban 'had considerable debating skills'. Unlike many émigré dissidents, who easily fell out with one another, often launching bitter vendettas against their peers, Chojecki seemed measured. Overall, the ILC president found him a mature political analyst, whose judgement was 'far better than that of most of the other exiles'.

For much of this period, Helena Łuczywo was absent, visiting the United States on a year-long peace fellowship organized by a friend,

Joanna Weschler, and her husband Lawrence, who wrote for the *New Yorker*. As much as anything it was a rest cure. While she enjoyed *Mazovia Weekly*'s camaraderie, and most of the staff were her friends, like others she had been ground down by the open-ended nature of the conflict. She remembered walking through an empty construction site in the Ursynów quarter of Warsaw, where the regime had planned a metro station it couldn't afford to build, and seeing that people had divided up the open land into little plots where they were growing vegetables. 'What do they care about us,' she thought, 'or about Solidarity? They're more interested in their little gardens.' She didn't mean this as a criticism, but found it disheartening to see others getting on with their lives when the underground appeared stuck. Popular support was ebbing, safe apartments were increasingly hard to find and the regime showed no sign of collapsing any time soon. It seemed likely that she would still be working in secret decades hence, when she reached her seventies. So she had accepted the offer of a year-long place at Radcliffe College in Cambridge, Massachusetts. The regime still had nothing on her, and anyway preferred dissidents to be abroad rather than in Poland.

Once in the West, she took time to travel to Maisons-Laffitte, to interview Giedroyc, 'the greatest Polish editor', for *Mazovia Weekly*. She found the villa that served as her main sponsor's billet and headquarters to be 'incredibly wonderful' and 'extremely important', but she was shocked by something the Editor told her, which was that Solidarity would not be able to defeat the communists without shedding blood. She found these sentiments 'totally unacceptable'. It fed into her fear that Polish extremists would bring the country to civil war. She wanted to tell her sponsor that it would be her blood and that of her friends that would be spilled, not his, but she didn't say it because she was being polite.

She returned to Poland late in 1987, to pick up where she had left off. For several months it seemed that nothing had changed. But at the end of that year, even as the SB revelled in their counter-intelligence triumphs, another crisis was brewing for Jaruzelski.

The central problem was the same one faced by communist leaders everywhere, including the new, reform-minded general secretary in Moscow, Mikhail Gorbachev: the Eastern economies, which had been struggling for decades, were on the brink of collapse. The Soviet system produced a society in which a few things functioned well, but many things barely functioned at all. Working practices were inefficient, managers corrupt, conditions dangerous and output shoddy. Gorbachev planned to address these with *perestroika* ('restructuring') and *glasnost* ('openness'), which meant moving towards a more transparent, enterprise-based system, and he encouraged the East European nations to do the same. But creating a market economy in a poor country with a political culture that had been designed to stamp out business enterprise would prove a near-impossible task.

In February 1988, the Party chiefs in Warsaw were forced once again to increase state-controlled prices. The costs of food, rent and petrol went up by half, electricity doubled, coal tripled. Poles were used to shortages, and to scrimping and hustling, but they now faced absolute poverty: by spring, almost four in ten would describe themselves to government surveyors as 'impoverished and needy'. 'Pressures and hardships in social and economic life are very high,' the survey team reported. Tolerance for violence was growing. Michnik realized how bad things had become when he heard a famous Polish actor complain that her apartment block hadn't been heated for five days. If she and her husband were cold, he thought, so was everyone else. 'I realized that this was what Gorbachev was facing,' he said. 'The radiators had gone on strike.'

The outcome was a new round of labour unrest, beginning in April, which centred on the giant Nowa Huta steelworks outside Kraków. Employees began a sit-in which spread to half the plant's workforce of 32,000. A sympathy action erupted in the Lenin Shipyard, then copycat strikes broke out around the country. The latest round of popular dissent was led by a new generation of Polish workers, younger than those who had gone on strike in 1980, but some factories called for the release of Solidarity-era detainees, and in Gdańsk the strike leaders invited the star of the 'Polish August', Lech Wałęsa, to join their action. He agreed.

The regime responded as it always had, with sackings, a propaganda campaign vilifying the workers' leaders, intimidation and the threat of force. On the night of 4–5 May, it sent elite 'Tiger' anti-terrorist troops into Nowa Huta. Black-clad special forces soldiers caught the strikers asleep, seized control of the plant and arrested thirty-eight people. The Zomos threatened a similar action at the shipyard in Gdańsk, which was enough to end the strike. But if the regime thought this would solve the problem, it was quickly proved wrong. As one Western diplomat said at the time, this was a terrible mistake, the worst thing the authorities could have done.

Later that month, the CIA war-gamed a full Polish meltdown. A secret National Intelligence Estimate conjured three extreme scenarios, the most likely of which was 'popular upheaval'. This would take the shape of a 'broad-based challenge to party supremacy and ultimately Soviet control'. Unaware that Gorbachev had ruled out military intervention, the analysis stated that 'In extremis . . . there is no reason to doubt [Gorbachev's] willingness to intervene to preserve party rule and decisive Soviet influence in the region.' In spite of this risk, the US-backed opposition continued its work to destabilize the regime. Strikers used CIA-bought radio equipment to communicate with workers at other plants, while Polish-language broadcasts from the West continually carried news of the industrial unrest into the country. One SB analysis reckoned Radio Free Europe's Polish service devoted 90 per cent of its content to the subject: 'Just as in 1980–1981, the broadcasts aim to encourage and shape ongoing events,' the intelligence agency warned, 'in some cases by putting Polish opposition activists on the air to mobilize the broad mass of Polish society to radicalize pay demands and spread the strikes.'

Wałęsa's re-emergence at the Lenin Shipyard had captured the imaginations of the new generation of activists, and the opposition once again coalesced around the rotund electrician with the handlebar moustache. In August, he led a new walkout in Gdańsk, joining a fresh wave of unrest around the country. The strikers had one major demand: the re-legalization of Solidarity.

These stoppages, according to the CIA, would constitute 'potentially the worst crisis for the government since the imposition of martial law in 1981'.

No one had anticipated the August strikes. Helena Łuczywo at that moment was hiking through the beautiful Beskid mountains of southern Poland with her daughter and nieces, touring from one refuge to another, carrying everything she needed on her back. Since mobile phones hadn't yet reached the country, she was blissfully out of reach. In fact the entire staff of *Mazovia Weekly* were on vacation in mid-August as the newspaper took its regular summer break, enforced by the absence of the college students who did most of the distribution. Anna Bikont was at the seaside. Piotr Pacewicz, another editor, was visiting the Mazurian lakes. The only senior staffer left in Warsaw was Joanna Szczęsna, who had been looking forward to a relaxing staycation, which she planned to fill by seeing friends and soaking up a little culture.

When the first strikes broke out in the mines in Upper Silesia on 15 August, Szczęsna told herself they were no big deal. 'So what,' she thought, 'I'm on holiday like everyone else. Nobody's around. What can I do?' The only way to speak with Łuczywo would have been to get her somehow to a local post office, yet there was no way to do that. As the unrest spread, however, her conscience kicked in. 'A strike that is not publicized cannot gain strength or be effective,' she told herself. She had to act. The consequences of this decision would lead her to one of the most intensive periods of work in her life, as she tried to organize an emergency edition of the underground newspaper.

A few colleagues heard about the strike action and rang in to speak to her, but since the phone lines were all tapped these exchanges could only be conducted by euphemism. When Pacewicz rang, several days in, they had a 'ridiculous, stupid conversation', Szczęsna said, which sounded more like a 1950s melodrama than a work call. It ran something like this:

Pacewicz: 'I wonder how much you miss me.'

Szczęsna: 'I can't live without you . . . I thought you were supposed to come back sooner. You promised you'd be back.'

Pacewicz entirely failed to pick up the important message within the innuendo, which was that they needed to produce a newspaper *right now* and he had to *hurry back to Warsaw to help*. She understood after putting down the phone that if there was going to be a special strike issue of the newspaper she would have to do it solo. She would have to be 'a general, a lowly recruit and all the ranks in between', she said.

She gave herself the better part of a week to research, write, edit, print and distribute it, then embarked on an insane shift that would last 120 hours, five huge days in which she barely slept. She found she was forced to take ever-greater risks with her underground 'health and safety' protocols, as she had none of the usual communications or liaison network. Since security procedures also cost time she didn't have, she took the brave and strategically momentous decision to work in the open. 'We are the free press,' she told herself.

Despite the wiretaps, she began giving striking workers her home phone number and told them to call her there, and when she heard news from Silesia that miners were threatening to blow themselves up, she even took the extreme risk of ringing friends in Paris to pass on the information, knowing they would take it to Radio Free Europe. If protesters were prepared to adopt such drastic measures then she had a duty to spread the news, she thought, even if it meant she would be arrested.

She allowed two days for reporting, touring the striking plants and coal mines, and two more days to write the articles in Warsaw. Then she had to find someone to print it. She managed all of this in the allotted time, and at last the issue went to press. Finally, she could sleep! She was soon woken by a man who arrived with the message that a belt had snapped in the offset machine they were using for the edition and there was no replacement. The entire print run was threatened.

She asked the messenger to write down the model of the press and the name of the part, then she went to all the underground publishers in Warsaw – NOWa, CDN, Krag, PWA – to try to find a spare. She didn't know the people who ran most of these houses personally, but she broke her anonymity when she asked to speak to them, and even if the person she contacted wasn't aware that she was an editor for *Mazovia Weekly*, practically all the people at the top knew. 'It meant I wasn't just someone coming off the street,' she said, 'and they weren't worried that I would inform on them.'

She went from group to group, asking if they had the particular type of offset machine her printer used, and met a string of negative responses.

'Shit,' she thought, 'this is not good.'

Finally, she found a publisher who had the same machine. She asked where it was and who ran it. Earlier in the 'state of war', it would have been unthinkable that anyone in the underground would have asked for such information, never mind given it, but Szczęsna's reputation preceded her. 'I got the name of the printer,' she said.

She still had to find him. She was told he attended a patriotic mass at a certain church, and she went there to look around,
although she didn't know what he looked like. Finally, someone
brought him to her.

'Listen,' she told him, 'I am Joanna Szczęsna, don't ask me from
where, but I have access to such and such an offset machine, and I
need you to lend me a belt for it.'

The man gave her a pitying look. 'Guess what,' he said. 'I'm the
person printing *Mazovia Weekly* for you. It's my machine's belt that
has broken.'

Szczęsna almost collapsed. After the enormity of producing the
paper alone, she had been running around Warsaw – 'so much
effort, so many meetings' – at great personal risk, only to catch her
own tail. She had also unlocked many of the secrets of the entire
Warsaw Underground printing network in the space of a few days.

Luckily *Mazovia Weekly*'s head of production returned from
holiday at that moment to save the edition. By this point Szczęsna
had resorted to pouring water over herself to stay awake. Pacewicz
arrived around the same time. He was mortified when he understood what she'd been trying to tell him on the phone and that she'd
produced the whole issue alone. 'Oh my God,' he said, 'I thought
you meant you needed me for the *next* edition!'

The special strike issue of *Mazovia Weekly*, No. 260, was published
on Thursday 25 August 1988. Szczęsna received several thousand
copies, and since she still had no distribution channels she took
them personally to drop-off points next to pro-Solidarity churches,
where she knew they'd be handed out, and grabbed friends,
acquaintances and anyone else she could catch, telling them, 'You're
going to Szczecin and you're going to take these copies. You're going
to go to Gdańsk, you're going to give them these . . .'

She would never claim her single-handed *Mazovia Weekly* made
a difference – she had no idea if it prolonged the industrial action
or not, she said – but the strikes of August 1988 marked a turning
point in the 'uphill war', as the regime realized it no longer had the
resources to crush every demonstration that broke out in Poland.

The day after the edition emerged, 26 August, Interior Minister Kiszczak appeared on television to make an official announcement. 'I have been authorized [. . .] to meet the representatives of various social groups and labour,' he said. 'These meetings may take the form of a "round table".'

Five days after that, Wałęsa sat down with Kiszczak for high-level negotiations aimed at finding a way forward, and on 1 September the union leader called the strikes off. The price he had exacted was a series of secret preliminary discussions about the 'Round Table Talks', in which he hoped to legalize Solidarity.

A coda to Szczęsna's open reporting was that on 10 October the police finally raided a *Mazovia Weekly* editorial meeting. The team had relaxed some of their 'health and safety' rules, and were working in the apartment of one of the editors when the police burst in, confiscated money and electronic equipment, including a computer, and took several journalists back to their own homes to conduct searches there. It was the first time in six and a half years of operation that the security services had worked out where and how the newspaper functioned. Even though General Kiszczak had appointed an operational group whose aim was to liquidate *Mazovia Weekly*, they never succeeded in interrupting its publication. Szczęsna and Łuczywo ascribed some of the police failings to sexism: 'They thought that *Mazovia Weekly* was being prepared by men all the time,' said Szczęsna. 'And that the women were somewhere at the end of the process to do with distribution, some minor [aspect of it].' By the time the SB finally caught them in the act, it was too late. Despite finding ample evidence of illegal activity, and large quantities of uncensored publications in the editors' apartments, they couldn't arrest anyone because they didn't want to upset the secret negotiations with the opposition.

After the raid, the newspaper returned to normal operations.

It was clear that the political atmosphere was changing, and the system the opposition had spent most of their adult lives working against was starting to disintegrate. 'We knew that this was the end,' Łuczywo said.

Grzegorz Boguta understood this when the secret police came to arrest him for what he reckoned was the tenth time. They hand-cuffed him as usual and pushed him into the back seat of their car. Sitting between the officers as they drove towards the interior ministry, one of them turned to him and said: 'Mr Boguta, I hope that when you defeat communism you will hire us?'

It could have been a joke, but Boguta didn't think so. The police more than anyone knew the trajectory Poland was on. If the people who gained most from communism were demoralized, what chance did it have? 'I knew that something was coming,' he said.

Michnik knew, too. The Russian-speaking oracle of the 'Warsaw salon' kept a close eye on the Moscow papers. He recognized what the Polish authorities, the émigrés and even the CIA didn't: that Gorbachev's changes weren't a ploy but were a genuine movement. In 1981, the hardline Soviet leadership had forced martial law on the Poles to protect the communist bloc. Now the ageing hawks of the Brezhnev era were dead or in retreat, and the messages reaching Warsaw from Moscow were of openness and reform. In that situation, even the most popular communist leader would have struggled to justify a hardline position to the people, and Jaruzelski was never that.

One day, Boguta went to see Michnik at his apartment and found him with Russian newspapers and books spread all over the floor.

'You will see,' Michnik told him, 'you will see. It will come from Russia.'

18

Television Free Europe

Intellectual freedom is essential to human society – freedom to obtain and distribute information, freedom for open-minded and unfearing debate and freedom from pressure by officialdom and prejudices. Such a trinity of freedom of thought is the only guarantee against an infection of people by mass myths, which, in the hands of treacherous hypocrites and demagogues, can be transformed into bloody dictatorship.

Andrei Sakharov, 'Thoughts on Progress, Peaceful Coexistence and Intellectual Freedom'

It thus appears to be impossible to reform a Stalinist-type system by means of a liberal policy pursued by a leading group of the Party which, while granting more freedom to the people, is the sole body to lay down the limits within which it may be exercised.

Jiří Pelikán, *The Socialist Opposition in Eastern Europe*

By 1988, the Polish authorities had spotted a strange new phenomenon. White discs, close to 6 feet across, had begun to appear on buildings all around the country. The first few had arrived secretly, smuggled in by entrepreneurial black marketeers, and most people, including the police, had little idea what they were for. But by the late 1980s these large parabolas, always white, always pointing skywards, were springing up all over the place, on the walls of people's houses and on the roofs of apartment blocks. 'Cosmic television', or 'space television', as it was sometimes called, had arrived.

Ironically, communications sent via space were a Soviet creation. Moscow had launched the first satellite, Sputnik 1, in 1957, and ten years later had created the first national satellite television system, Orbita, which allowed the Soviet authorities to deliver their programming even to the remotest parts of the Siberian steppe. It wasn't this turgid, censored, propaganda-heavy offering Poles were intrigued by in the late 1980s, however, but TV from the West. With a large dish pointed in the right direction, Poles could pick up the forbidden fruits of American, British and European popular entertainment. The first European television satellite, EUTELSAT I-F1, whose footprint covered parts of the Eastern Bloc, carried a wide array of news, education and cultural channels, all free of ideological interference from the Main Office. Super Channel, owned from 1988 by NBC, featured everything from *Doctor Who* to soap operas, pop music and major sports events. Dutch-based broadcaster Filmnet was a major draw, not least for its soft-core porn offering: adult entertainment was as big a driver of traffic in the 1980s as it would later prove for the internet. Rupert Murdoch's Sky Channel screened classic British game shows such as *The Price is Right* and *Sale of the Century*, while Worldnet, run by the US Information Agency, provided American news bulletins and even programmes in Polish, Russian and Ukrainian.

In the early 1980s, dishes had been prohibitively expensive in Poland, since they had to be imported, but the high cost only increased satellite TV's desirability, and the few dealers in the new technology were mobbed wherever they showed their wares. Soon, people devised ways around the hefty price tag. One way to cut the cost was by sharing: neighbours would go round to each other's apartments to watch programmes, much as they did with VCRs, and if a wealthy individual in one block installed a dish they could offer the signal to anyone else in the building who bought the decoder box. Social institutions, especially churches, started to install their own systems too, with large screens, and crowds of congregants would watch programmes together. Enterprising hobbyists and craftsmen also began to build copycat parts from Polish materials: in Szczecin, a whole satellite-TV cottage industry grew up, using concrete, aluminium or fibreglass boat-builders' resin to knock out cheap dishes.

At first the authorities tried to ignore the phenomenon – what was the point in regulating satellite TV when only a handful of złoty millionaires could afford it? But by the late 1980s alarm over the effect 'satellite imperialism' might have on the fragile political views of the citizens meant the technology was too important to overlook. In 1987, a defence ministry publication, *Guest from Space or Space Invader?*, proclaimed that the 'Western apparatus of ideological sabotage' was using the system as 'a tool of information warfare'. The risk of direct reception of this material by Poles should be regarded as 'a threat to the informational sovereignty of the state'. But they weren't able to block the signal, so what could they do? One answer was to try to sate the desire for Western programming with a show of curated highlights on terrestrial Polish TV. *Closer to the World*, which consisted mostly of bloopers and moments of low comedy, gravely discussed in the studio by a panel of international correspondents, proved immensely popular, not least because it often concluded with a clip of scantily clad women from *The Benny Hill Show*. But the regime's main solution to the satellite problem was to stick a great mountain of socialist bureaucracy in the way. To get permission to own a receiver you had to fill out piles of forms for the State Radio Inspector, the Main Customs Office or the Ministry of Communications, setting out your need and guaranteeing that no unauthorized person would see it. Installing a dish required a separate application, and everyone who applied had to be cleared by the interior ministry, taking into account 'considerations of security and public order'. In fact there was such a huge black market, and officers had become so demoralized by this time, that the police often turned a blind eye. Despite official figures that showed only 920 private users had dishes in 1988, a survey conducted that summer found that more than 100,000 Poles had access to the medium.

The CIA, always looking to exploit the technological gulf between East and West, would help turn satellite communications into a new weapon in the ideological arms race. Once again, Chojecki led the way. He and his Paris-based cell had made great inroads with film and video, and now they turned their attention to space.

Chojecki first discussed the new medium with Minden in November 1987, as the ILC president reported back to Langley: '[Chojecki] would . . . like to find money for the broadcasting via satellite of a TV educational program for Poles in Germany and France that could also be seen in Poland.' A year later, when they met again in Paris, the project was close to fruition. It would be called Euro TV Kontakt, and was conceived as a kind of Television Free Europe. He put together a team of experts and eminent broadcasters to manage it, including Zdzisław Najder, a former head of Radio Free Europe's Polish service. Łabędź, Chojecki's point person for all things video, would oversee day-to-day operations. Advice and financing came from multiple sources, including Jiří Pelikán, an ILC-distributed author who had run Czechoslovakian TV until the Soviet invasion of Prague in 1968 and whose actions in the West were 'directed and subsidized by the CIA', according to the Czech secret service. Chojecki's friend at the PTTI union, Stefan Nędzyński, who was supplying him with regular CIA cash payments from a Geneva bank, also helped with funding.

At the end of 1988, the team were almost ready to air their first programme when fate, in the shape of François Mitterrand, presented them with the perfect story. The French president had invited Lech Wałęsa to Paris to celebrate the fortieth anniversary of the adoption of the Universal Declaration of Human Rights on 10 December. The declaration, driven through the UN in 1948 by a tireless Eleanor Roosevelt, stood as the most widely recognized statement of the freedoms to which every person on the planet was entitled, a yardstick by which to measure governments from Moscow to Warsaw to Pretoria. To mark the anniversary, President

Mitterrand invited two Nobel Peace Prize laureates: the famed Soviet defector Andrei Sakharov, whose work the CIA had long promoted, and Wałęsa. For Chojecki it was an unmissable opportunity to present the Solidarity leader to Poles as a statesman on the world stage, against the backdrop of the very thing they were all fighting for: liberty. The fact that the regime agreed to let Wałęsa travel told of its need to appease Western financiers, as well as Gorbachev's spirit of *glasnost* and the forthcoming Round Table Talks, which were scheduled to begin in February. Wałęsa by this time had also been interviewed by state media and invited to take part in an uncensored televised debate. As he said at the time, 'Nothing like this has ever happened [before].'

Broadcasting via satellite was a highly technical operation that required careful diplomacy with the French authorities, who had rules against transmitting political propaganda. Negotiations with the government would be handled by Łabędź, who had to get permission from Mitterrand's office for a frequency the Poles could use and find time on a satellite. He spoke with contacts at the French channel TV5, which broadcast via the EUTELSAT. The Polish plan was controversial. 'At the beginning, the French didn't want a political programme to be on just after the official television,' Łabędź said. The satellite company said the same: 'EUTELSAT is an international European institution, and they don't rent out their frequency for propaganda. And we were going to broadcast pure propaganda. It was an exception in the history of satellite television, that we broadcast a purely political programme.' It was only thanks to Łabędź's friends at the Élysée that their plan was allowed to go ahead: 'Mitterrand's staff were very, very pro-Polish.'

TV5 told him there would be free bandwidth on the satellite after their late-night news bulletin, from midnight to 1 a.m. If the Poles could find the money to pay for it, it was theirs. The slot was hugely expensive, roughly $10,000 for an hour, but Chojecki found the cash from his backers. It was 'a big, big, big video event', Łabędź recalled, 'with a big, big budget'. The next job was to instruct the Polish audience on how to set up their dishes to receive the signal. For this

they turned to their allies in the Western broadcasters, Radio Free
Europe, the BBC and Voice of America, who gave out the information on all the Polish services. The satellite dishes in the churches
were a key part of the strategy. With the high levels of Polish VCR
ownership, it would also be possible to record the broadcast and
send out hundreds of copies on VHS cassettes. Lech Wałęsa's priest
in Gdańsk, Henryk Jankowski of St Brygida's church, ran a Pastoral
Centre for Documentation and Dissemination of Video which spe-
cialized in this form of distribution.

With Wałęsa's visit confirmed, Chojecki and Łabędź hired five
camera crews to shoot in different locations, as well as several vehicles. They would be given special access to the events, and they put
Solidarity stickers on all their equipment so that the French police
knew who they were. The broadcast was to go out on 13 December,
the anniversary of the declaration of martial law.

Now all they had to do was await the arrival of their star.

Wałęsa landed at Paris's Orly airport on 9 December 1988, and for
the next three days he enjoyed the sort of welcome reserved for
heads of state from France's more powerful allies. The union leader,
a little jowlier than he had once been, with a greying moustache and
a Solidarity pin, was put up in a luxury Paris hotel, sped through
the capital in a motorcade of black limousines with police sirens
blaring and guided past the salutes of the ceremonial Republican
Guards – with their sabres, gold lace and steel helmets polished into
mirrors – to grand receptions in some of France's most glorious
buildings. Everywhere he went, a scrum of journalists and flashing
snappers followed. Chojecki's camera crews filmed Wałęsa's every
move, including some events, such as the private meeting with the
West German foreign minister Hans-Dietrich Genscher, where no
one else was allowed.

Sunday night found the union leader regaling 3,000 Parisian
Poles who had gathered in the chapel of the Catholic Pallottine
order with anti-communist stories and jokes. 'The men slap their
thighs,' reported Le Monde's correspondent, 'the nuns are red with

laughter.' Giedroyc was there, on a rare outing from Maisons-Laffitte, as was Yves Montand, although Simone Signoret had succumbed to cancer three years earlier. Chojecki and the Solidarity leader shook hands in a brief, unplanned moment. They did little more than exchange pleasantries, but it was a sign of the changing times that the two great Solidarity campaigners could meet face to face, when a genuine chance of ending Soviet domination over Poland seemed almost within reach. It was incredible, Mirek said later, to witness the Solidarity leader receiving such treatment after seven years of military rule, in which Wałęsa had been under house arrest and Chojecki in exile. 'I could only see him in photos before that,' he said.

The Kontakt team rushed the footage of Wałęsa's triumphal progress through Paris to their video editing suite in Vanves by motorbike. The clips were catalogued as they arrived, and when the final frames were in, Łabędź raced to cut it all into a sixty-minute film. He worked night and day for forty-eight hours, and when it was done, he hurried with the tape to Radio France, which had

agreed to send the transmission on Kontakt's behalf. He arrived five minutes before the film was due to air, but they managed to broadcast *Wałęsa in Paris* to Poland on schedule, at midnight on 13 December, the seventh anniversary of martial law.

It's impossible to say how many people saw Euro TV Kontakt's inaugural broadcast, although Chojecki and Łabędź knew that a lot of churches had set up screens especially. There was an issue with the sound, which meant EUTELSAT agreed to repeat the broadcast for free the following night. Fr Jankowski in Gdańsk managed to record it and called Chojecki afterwards to tell him they had distributed 500 copies of the film on VHS. Robert Gates at the CIA would claim this first satellite television broadcast into Poland a success for US intelligence. 'CIA arranged the first satellite telecast into Poland from Western Europe,' he wrote. 'We got a strong, positive reaction from Solidarity leaders.' The Agency doubtless played a major role, but the triumph surely belonged to Łabędź and Chojecki.

Chojecki saw a big future in satellite. After Euro TV Kontakt's success with *Wałęsa in Paris*, they started to plan ways to build on their achievement. Chojecki would find a lot more money, enough to enable them to broadcast an hour-long show every night, consisting of political films and documentaries. Łabędź began preparations. He rented a studio in the suburbs of Paris and had a set built, then started auditioning professional news anchors. He hired five journalists, including two from the French state broadcaster Radio France Internationale, which ran a Polish-language service. There were four or five camera operators too – at least fifteen people in total. 'It cost a lot,' he remembered, 'but Mirek assured me that the financing would come because the cast was excellent.' Łabędź never specifically asked Chojecki where he sourced the funds, but he was given around $20,000 a month to play with. 'It was a big, very professional studio,' he said.

In early 1989, they were ready for launch. By that time, however, events in Poland had started to move very quickly.

19

High Noon

A crack has appeared in the fortress and, it could be assumed, the disintegration of the whole monstrous empire has begun. Undoubtedly, this could bring with it many terrible and tragic events: it would be impossible for the kingdom of evil to fall without a sound.

Irina Alberti, *Russkaia Mysl*

Plurality is the condition of human action because we are all the same, that is, human, in such a way that nobody is ever the same as anyone else who ever lived, lives, or will live.

Hannah Arendt, *The Human Condition*

One day at the end of the winter in 1989, Helena Łuczywo stood in the Viceroy's Palace in Warsaw, staring through a window at the mob of protesters who had gathered outside. They were there to demonstrate against the ongoing Round Table Talks, begun on 6 February, where Łuczywo was serving as a negotiator. The main meeting of fifty-seven people – including communist officials, Solidarity leaders and a few members of the Catholic church – sat in the Column Hall, around the great wooden 'O' of the purpose-built round table, which was 40 feet across. Hundreds more delegates would meet in breakout groups around the palace to debate areas of specialist concern. They returned day after day, to hammer out the future of the Polish state.

Łuczywo was assigned to the mass communications group, but at that moment she was captivated by the protesters outside. A range of opposition parties wanted to stop the talks. Some thought they were a secret service plot. Others denounced them as treachery. The Fighting Solidarity leader Kornel Morawiecki, who had smuggled himself back into the country in disguise, said there was nothing to negotiate as long as there was still repression in Poland and political prisoners in Polish jails. Others said that after so many state-sponsored killings the only place the people should meet the communists was in a courtroom. Łuczywo had grown used to being attacked by extremists in the opposition, but still she found the protests 'extremely weird'. What did they want, these people? Fighting in the streets? Morawiecki in particular she thought was 'an idiot'.

Future historians would compare the Round Table Talks to Caesar's crossing of the Rubicon: it was a no-going-back moment, which would end with the demise of a political system. But nothing about the situation seemed inevitable at the time, apart from the fact that Poland could erupt any day. Shortly before negotiations began, a CIA analyst wrote that the stage had been set for 'a major confrontation between the Jaruzelski regime and Solidarity', as radicals bayed for revenge and the security forces tried to work out how to protect themselves from reprisals. Wałęsa captured this fear with a typically folksy anecdote in Paris. 'Take my dog,' he said. 'He sits there all day in his kennel. When I let him out in the evening, he's so happy and he runs so fast that he can't turn the corner and sometimes he bangs his head against the wall.' It was the same with people, he said, 'when they have been kept in a cage and are suddenly let loose'. He saw negotiation as the only way to avoid chaos and civil war, but it required a distasteful compromise, in which the former prisoners would have to sit down with their jailers and torturers, while being heckled from their own side as traitors.

General Kiszczak, a key architect of martial law, led the government side at the talks, while Wałęsa headed the Solidarity team, although the main issues would be negotiated by a close circle of

Wałęsa's advisors, including Kuroń, Michnik and Bujak, whose politics had been shaped by uncensored literature and who owed their authority to the underground press. They were well versed in Poland's political problems, as they had been reading, writing and thinking about them for decades.

NOWa and *Mazovia Weekly* representatives dominated the opposition side of the mass communications subgroup, with Michnik and Boguta working alongside Łuczywo. Jerzy Urban, the regime mouthpiece, sat across the table. Michnik spoke out against censorship, demanding to know why books by such writers as Orwell and Miłosz were banned and describing the state's actions against independent publishers as immoral and unnatural. Łuczywo insisted that if the people were to feel they had any oversight of their government they needed access to uncensored mass media: it was clear that Solidarity should be able to produce its own legal publications, as it had in 1981. Boguta argued for an end to the state monopoly on publishing and called for the legalization of the underground press: paper supplies should be made available to all, and there should be a free market for printing equipment. Urban countered with his usual sardonic wit that NOWa and other independent publishers could become legal as long as they obeyed the censors and paid their taxes.

The talks ground on through February and March, in an atmosphere of deep mistrust. At the start of April the state's own trade unionists – acting with the support of Party hardliners – threatened to kibosh the whole thing, insisting their members shouldn't bear the brunt of new, free-market policies. For a moment, the talks balanced on a knife-edge, and Wałęsa once again warned that failure to reach an agreement would lead to chaos and civil war. But it was in neither party's interest to let them fail, and the unions were brought around. On 5 April, the parties signed the Round Table Agreement. The government accepted the re-legalization of Solidarity in return for its participation in semi-free elections. Both sides could describe this as success. For the regime, it meant it had co-opted the moderate opposition into government, which would neutralize some of its critics and placate some of the people. For Solidarity, however, this was a moment of dizzying triumph. Its main goal had been legalization, but here was a path to democracy too.

Poland was to hold partially free elections for the first time since the war, and the old one-party system would be replaced by a new, two-chamber legislature, consisting of the existing lower house of parliament (the Sejm) and a new Senate. Thirty-five per cent of the seats in the lower house would be freely contested, along with all 100 seats in the Senate. A president, elected by parliament, would act as the country's chief executive in place of the general secretary of the Polish Communist Party. There were victories for freedom of speech as well as democracy. Solidarity would be allowed a television broadcast of no less than thirty minutes per week, and a sixty-minute radio broadcast. Repression of the independent press was to stop, and, from January 1990, all publishers would be able to buy paper supplies on the open market. Censorship was to continue for the time being, although in a less severe form. Crucially, Solidarity would be allowed a new, independent national daily newspaper.

Great as these victories were, no one gave Solidarity any chance of prevailing in the elections. The first round of the vote was just two months away, on 4 June, and whereas the Party had a large machine with an established bureaucracy, Solidarity was starting from scratch. It had no candidates, little money, no campaign structure and few members compared with its Carnival peak of ten million. Its broadcast media allocation was small, which meant the only real weapon on the campaign trail would be the daily newspaper it had been allowed but which didn't yet exist. If this publication was to have any effect on the June vote, Solidarity needed to launch it now. But how? Wałęsa handed this problem to Michnik, and Michnik came straight to Łuczywo. He'd had a simple, brilliant idea: recruit the entire team of *Mazovia Weekly*.

At first, Łuczywo and her editors were sceptical. Michnik had the reputation of being headstrong: he liked things to be done his way or not at all. This conflicted with *Mazovia Weekly*'s collaborative culture. They arranged a meeting, in which the editors told Michnik they didn't want to work in an undemocratic fashion. But Adam was nothing if not persuasive, and Helena found the idea of working on the first legal independent daily in the Soviet Bloc 'irresistible'. They consulted everyone, from the editorial board to the distributors, and agreed to move across to the new title en masse. Łuczywo would serve as the editor, with Michnik as editor-in-chief. Anyone who had contributed to *Mazovia Weekly* in any way was offered a job.

Within days, they had shuttered the old paper. The last issue, number 290, appeared on 12 April, with an editorial explaining why they had decided to take a leap despite the great uncertainty involved:

> We know very well how frail and unstable the present political structure is . . . how we cannot trust the declarations of the authorities, how high the risk is that we will lose what we had without getting anything in exchange . . . [and yet] to wait and see would mean giving up new, far greater chances to act in the name of the ideals we have fought to achieve for years – the ideals of Solidarity.

Mazovia Weekly had exerted a profound influence on Polish politics. It was unique among the underground papers in having a nationwide character, and it had led the way in arguing for negotiations with the regime. Years later, Michnik would pay tribute to this, the most important publication of the 'Polish Underground Republic'. During all the years he had spent in prison, *Mazovia Weekly* had been 'a source of strength, a source of hope, a source of faith that there would be a free Poland . . . we could taste it in every issue'. For the journalist Paweł Smoleński it was 'a miracle of conspiracy', 'a taste of free Poland in times of enslavement' and 'a word of truth for the hundreds of thousands of Poles who waited for those few A4-size sheets'. Everyone was too polite, of course, to mention that it had been funded by the CIA, and that its largest income stream had come through Giedroyc, aka QRBERETTA.

Łuczywo was typically unsentimental about closing the weekly she had created. In any case, she was entirely taken up with the mad scramble of launching the new paper. The *Mazovia* team possessed vast experience of working underground, but a large-circulation daily threw up problems of a wholly different magnitude, most of which had to be solved right away. Needing office space, they moved into a former kindergarten, which was unbearably cramped. They held editorial meetings around a children's sandbox, and journalists wrote stories at low nursery tables, sitting in chairs designed for infants. To recruit more staff, Łuczywo arranged a meeting at Warsaw University's Institute of Psychology – which happened to be next to the Umschlagplatz, in the old ghetto, where Polish Jews had been forced to board the freight trucks that took them to the death camps. Crowds of people came to the meeting, and she picked out the ones she thought were best, telling them to show up at the kindergarten. The editors brought their few computers from *Mazovia Weekly* to the new paper, but now they needed more, and more money, since they no longer received Giedroyc's subsidies. 'We just closed that chapter of our lives,' Łuczywo said. They found they could secure loans against future paper sales, and more help came from abroad. A couple of friends who ran the *New York Review of Books* loaned her the huge sum of $100,000. A French designer from *Le Monde* sketched out how the new paper would look.

One area they no longer had to worry too much about was printing. Since this was an official newspaper, they were allowed to use the state-owned printworks, DSP, and the state distribution system, which meant they could shift close to half a million copies a day. The downside was that the paper's galley proofs had to go through the censor who still worked at the printing plant, something Łuczywo found 'disgusting, disgusting, disgusting'. She had daily quarrels with this woman, but as censorship had weakened significantly since the Round Table, she won the arguments most of the time. The censor's objections were mainly about the way they covered the Soviet Union and other countries in the bloc.

Always a workaholic, Łuczywo lived in those weeks on adrenaline. When she finally tried to get to sleep, the problems of the newspaper would flood into her thoughts. She took to keeping Post-it notes on her bedside table, and every night covered it with ideas scribbled on little stickers. One by one, the difficulties were resolved, and in the first week of May they were ready to launch. They had given the newspaper a straightforward name: *Election Gazette*. The first issue hit the streets on 8 May, less than a month after *Mazovia Weekly* closed. It was a thin product at first, eight pages of greying Polish paper, but it had been a phenomenal achievement to launch a daily paper in such a short time.

Election Gazette began 'more than modestly', Michnik recalled, but soon they 'took off headlong into the sun'.

Even with the launch of *Election Gazette*, no one believed Solidarity would win the vote. At one point the ruling party discussed how they might manage the international fallout if the union failed to collect any seats at all, since it wouldn't look good for their baby steps in democracy, or to the bankers preparing to release $1 billion of desperately needed loans. In fact neither side was accustomed to the idea of campaigning publicly in a genuinely open contest, and it took time for them to get to grips with the knockabout nature of an election that mattered, conducted through a partially independent media.

The CIA continued to fund Solidarity throughout the campaign via QRHELPFUL, and Chojecki's role was to give as much support as he could. He had been able to hold open, direct phone conversations with Poland from Paris for several months now, and was in continuous contact with the head of the Solidarity campaign committee, Henryk Wujec, whom he had known since the 1970s. The authorities had further relaxed border controls after the Round Table Talks, and he could ship in pretty much anything they wanted direct from Paris with humanitarian aid transports, which continued to run through the Iron Curtain. All he had to do was declare that it was campaign material for the elections and it would go straight through customs. They weren't sending printing equipment by this time as the country was awash with it: he even heard that people were selling their offset machines, which went for between $3,000 and $5,000 apiece. In any case, Solidarity had access to state presses to print election materials. What it needed was cash, communications equipment and lots of self-adhesive paper to make stickers. Chojecki reckoned he sent fifty fax machines, in batches of five or ten at a time, and overall he contributed $105,000 worth of CIA-funded material. Other émigré groups were supporting Solidarity from Brussels, West Germany and Norway. With help pouring in, the opposition soon began to find its feet, mounting, according to the CIA, a 'Western-style campaign complete with brass bands, bumper stickers, and stump speeches'. Buses in major cities were 'festooned with opposition placards' and 'Solidarity lapel pins were widely visible'. Thousands of citizens went to opposition rallies and bought Solidarity coupons to help finance the election effort. The Party in contrast never shed its stilted, rigid style. By the middle of the campaign, it was clear that the regime's candidates were struggling.

The defining image of the summer was a poster based on *High Noon*, the 1952 western starring Gary Cooper as a small-town marshal who walks out alone to confront a gang of killers. Tomasz Sarnecki, a shy, third-year graphic design student at Warsaw's Academy of Fine Arts, thought the marshal's story provided the perfect metaphor for Solidarity as it took on the communists. He adapted the promotional poster produced for the movie, replacing Cooper's gun with a ballot paper, giving him a Solidarity name badge and adding the union's logo and the words 'High Noon: 4 June 1989'. When Sarnecki showed the campaign committee his design they weren't keen, since it depicted Solidarity as an individual rather than a collective, but a visiting trade union delegation from Italy saw it and immediately spotted its potential. They told Wujec they could take it to Italy, run off some copies and send them back. Soon 10,000 *High Noon* posters were winging their way to Poland. They reached the capital in the early hours of 4 June, just in time to be plastered on the buses waiting in the Warsaw depots before they headed out into the capital's streets.

The *High Noon* posters would be reprinted in the country for the second round, on 18 June, using funds provided by the CIA.

Long before the results were in, the regime had begun to teeter under the rain of blows landed by the increasingly open, pluralistic Polish civil society. What Miłosz called the 'culture of monolithic uniformity' produced by Stalinism was rapidly giving way to the kind of environment of which Hannah Arendt, another ILC favourite, would surely have approved. The seizure of illegal books and presses hadn't entirely stopped, but the wall of censorship was crumbling, and emboldened publishers of all stripes were launching a cavalcade of new editions of works that had been blacklisted, selling them openly at book fairs and on street stalls, even within a few minutes' walk of the Main Office on Mysia Street.

W SAMO POŁUDNIE
4 CZERWCA 1989

Boguta was one of twelve underground publishers invited to the Warsaw International Book Fair, held in Stalin's totemic Palace of Culture and Science in mid-May. The NOWa stand was mobbed. 'Three years ago I never could have imagined that events would take this course,' he told a reporter from the *Washington Post*. 'But here we are, and people love it – the crowds at our stalls have been tremendous.' More remarkable even than NOWa's presence was that of Jerzy Kulczycki, owner of the London-based Orbis bookstore, who had worked for decades with Minden and the Polonia Book Fund. Kulczycki arrived in full expectation that the police would move in and close him down, and for that reason had booked an open return flight from London. Instead, when the doors to the fair were unlocked he watched a mob of eager Poles push past the official stands to get to his. The centrepiece of his offering was the 500th issue of *Kultura*, fresh off the press, which Giedroyc had sent with other Literary Institute publications to signal his approval of Orbis's attendance. Around a hundred books from the stand would be stolen over the next frenzied days, but Kulczycki was delighted. On his return to London he invited Minden to his house for a full briefing, including a screening of the film footage he had shot. He hadn't been allowed to sell his books directly, only take orders, but he had succeeded in distributing many thousands of catalogues for Kultura, Polonia, Puls and Orbis, for which Minden paid.

It wasn't only the independents who were now prepared to take risks. In June, the official publishing house Czytelnik launched a new edition of Jerzy Kosiński's 1965 novel *The Painted Bird*, which addressed the issue of anti-Semitism in the country, and which an official publication had previously labelled a 'vicious libel on the Polish nation and the Polish state'. Czytelnik sold all of its 100,000 first print run in a few hours. The same house published 30,000 copies of Gustaw Herling-Grudziński's Gulag memoir *A World Apart*, which had existed only in underground editions until then, and considered an edition of *The Gulag Archipelago*, but decided against it because the book was so long it would require an enormous quantity of paper which would be lost if the authorities decided to pulp it: these were still uncertain times. PIW, another state-sanctioned publishing house, had already issued Orwell's *1984* and planned to reproduce Pasternak's *Doctor Zhivago*. All of these works had been promoted by the CIA.

Boguta and Chojecki were reaching the point where they felt the official publishing houses were giving the independents unfair competition.

It was clear by the eve of the 4 June vote that Solidarity would put in a good show, but what would happen afterwards? The US ambassador in Warsaw, John Davis, cabled Washington that day to tell them that while a 'historical force of a vast and powerful current is about to transform Poland's topography forever', a military response from the regime could still not be ruled out. Davis's fears were realized that night, not in Poland, but in another country where a communist dictatorship was struggling to control pro-democracy protesters: China. The government there sent tanks and armoured vehicles to disperse the crowds in Beijing's Tiananmen Square. They killed many thousands. If the Poles needed any further warning of the direction events could take, China had provided it.

Łuczywo was horrified by Tiananmen, but she no longer feared a great shedding of blood in Poland. Although she rarely left the *Election Gazette* office, on the day of the poll itself she went to Freta Street, in the Old Town, where the Solidarity electoral committee was based, in the company of a friend, the British historian Timothy Garton Ash. It soon became clear that Solidarity had performed spectacularly well, and she felt an intense happiness as she and Garton Ash wandered around. She knew something truly profound had taken place and that after the elections Poland 'would never be the same'.

Not everyone was so optimistic. The full results showed that the union had won all of the 161 seats open to it in the Sejm, and an astonishing 99 out of the 100 available in the Senate. The victory was so overwhelming that people feared communist diehards in the security forces might launch a coup and seize control. Wałęsa warned of chaos once again, telling the Americans that this scenario could lead to 'Tiananmen in the middle of Europe'.

On 23 June, US Ambassador Davis had been canvassing the thoughts of a group of newly elected Solidarity parliamentarians in Warsaw. The only way to manage a peaceful transition of power was to keep Jaruzelski in office, they argued. 'If Jaruzelski is not elected president,' Davis reported in a secret cable to the State Department the following day, '[Solidarity believes] there is a genuine danger of civil war, ending in most scenarios with a reluctant but brutal Soviet intervention.' But how could the new deputies in the Senate and the Sejm remain credible if they voted for Jaruzelski to become president, when they had promised their voters they would keep him out? Resolving this dilemma was doubly urgent for Davis, given that President Bush was due soon in Warsaw, to show Washington's support for Poland's reforms. 'There have probably been few occasions when an American president has arrived for an official visit in a more fluid and fast-moving political situation than the present one in Poland,' Davis concluded.

It was Łuczywo and Michnik, now speaking from the pulpit of their 450,000-circulation daily *Election Gazette*, who plotted a route through the political maze. On 3 July, the paper put forward a compromise, written by Michnik and captured by Łuczywo in the headline 'Your President, Our Prime Minister', which proposed a temporary alliance of the democratic opposition with the Party's reformist wing. Tadeusz Mazowiecki, the former editor of *Solidarity Weekly*, would take the post of prime minister, but the presidency would go to Jaruzelski. Michnik, writing with all the moral authority of the years he had spent in the regime's jails, argued that people needed to have patience to secure 'a way out of totalitarian communism' that would not end in bloodshed. The only major obstacle now was Jaruzelski himself, who had gone into a sulk, announcing that he was unwilling to run since he didn't believe he could win and he didn't want to suffer another humiliation.

Air Force One touched down in Warsaw on 9 July, and Bush spent the first morning of his visit trying to persuade the general to become president of the new, semi-democratic Poland. The alternative, he said, was serious political instability. The irony was not lost on Bush, who had once led the CIA, that 'here was an American president trying to persuade a senior Communist leader to run for office'. Reluctantly, Jaruzelski agreed to put himself forward. Many Solidarity leaders in the new parliament abstained, but a week later the general was elected president with a fraction more than 50 per cent of the vote in the Senate. He would remain in office for a little over a year, a symbolic president, no more. On 24 August, Mazowiecki took up his post as prime minister, with a Solidarity-led government sworn in on 13 September. This was the first democratically elected administration in Poland for fifty years, and the first non-communist government in the Soviet Bloc.

Rebuilding the state from the ruins of communism would take years, but decades of underground literary activity gave the new Polish leaders a head start. All that effort spent working to develop a parallel civil society, with its own publishing concerns, libraries and universities meant that, unlike in other states emerging from Soviet rule, there was a readymade administrative class who had already thought through the major policy issues facing the country. As Seweryn Blumsztajn put it, 'the publishing movement had played a huge role in developing and also maintaining the Solidarity myth, so that by 1989 we had an elite ready. It was that elite that enabled Poland to execute the fundamental economic transformation, self-government, and above all enable it to join Nato and the European Union.'

As 1989 progressed, the wishes Łuczywo, Michnik and Boguta had expressed at the Round Table Talks were gradually granted. *Election Gazette* thrived, rapidly becoming Poland's most influential daily. The state monopoly on paper supplies ended. The Main Office for Control would not shut its doors for good until the spring of 1990, but after the Round Table Agreement, censorship 'just burst open', Michnik said.

The secret police, on the other hand, would remain in their posts for some time, busily covering their tracks and settling what scores they could with their long-standing enemies.

20

Bloody Feliks

I saw a huge steam roller,
It blotted out the sun.
The people all lay down, lay down;
They did not try to run.
My love and I, we looked amazed
Upon the gory mystery.
'Lie down! Lie down!' the people cried,
'The great machine is history!'

Kurt Vonnegut, *Mother Night*

Our day of victory will also come. One day the sun will shine on crowds of singing and dancing people drunk with joy in the streets of Warsaw. The free soul of Poland will survive until that day.

Jan Nowak, *Courier from Warsaw*

Tomek Łabędź was the first to hear about the fire. It was 19 July 1989, and he was working as usual in the Video Kontakt studio in Vanves when the police called to say there was a blaze at Chojecki's flat. Mirek lived at that time with Jolanta and their young children in a social housing block in Saint-Germain-en-Laye, ten minutes from Maisons-Laffitte. He wasn't in the office himself: after years of living in attic rooms and tiny apartments, he had decided to build himself a house and had bought a plot for this purpose in a village

10 miles south of Versailles. He was at the building site that day, so Łabędź jumped in his car and raced to tell him the news. By the time they reached Saint-Germain-en-Laye, the fire trucks had gone, but police were still at the scene. The ground-floor flat was filled with black ash and wrecked by smoke from the blaze and water from the hoses. The police thought it was arson and showed Chojecki the evidence. Someone had broken a window to get in, there were dead matches scattered about the place, and accelerant had been squirted on the beds to get them burning quickly. Chojecki immediately thought it was communists. Luckily no one had been at home, as Jolanta and the children were away in the south of France.

The family moved into a hotel, and the DST French security service offered them protection for a few days while investigators tried to find the culprits. A few weeks later they arrested a couple of young pyromaniacs who liked to set rubbish bins alight. The youths said they had been approached by a man they didn't know, who offered them 10,000 francs (around $1,600) to start the fire. When they agreed, the man had supplied the Chojeckis' address and a downpayment of half the money, along with a special lighter fluid you couldn't buy in the shops, which implied it was a professional job. The boys had done as asked, but the man had never returned to pay them the rest of the cash.

Jolanta was convinced the SB or KGB were behind it, not least because of two other events that happened the same day: in Poland, Jaruzelski was finally installed as president, and in London, the leader of the Polish government-in-exile, Kazimierz Sabbat, died suddenly of a heart attack. She didn't believe such things would happen together by chance. 'I think it was a very suspicious coincidence, and with communists, there are no coincidences,' she said. Mirek was more inclined to think French or international communists were behind the arson attack. A Marxist newspaper had recently published a photograph of Maisons-Laffitte with an arrow pointing out Giedroyc's villa and a caption that read 'this is the house where Anders fascists live', which made him realize the émigrés were being picked out as targets. But they would never entirely be able to rule out SB involvement, since that autumn the security service began destroying all the files relating to Polish espionage activities in the West, which went under the umbrella codename 'Snakes'. It would take months to get through all of the Snakes operations, but on 10 November they began on 'Anaconda', which dealt with 'foreign Solidarity offices in France', and on 13 December it was the turn of 'Python', which aimed to disrupt 'new emigration structures in Western Europe', both of which would have targeted Chojecki.

Even as late as the summer of 1989, the communists had good reason to want to shut Chojecki down. With change arriving rapidly in Poland, he was determined to press home his advantage on new fronts, and when Minden took him out for a long lunch meeting soon after the second-round vote, they discussed his priority of that moment, which was to export the Polish revolution to other nations in the Eastern Bloc. Before the birth of Solidarity, Chojecki had organized groups of dissidents from other countries to come to Warsaw for instruction on underground printing, and in Paris they ran regular training sessions on the Kontakt presses. They had an especially strong relationship with Hungarian activists, whom they taught to screen-print. But it was his new obsession, TV and video, that Chojecki wanted to work on that summer. He planned to start with Romania, the country of Minden's birth, which had been ruled since the mid-1960s by the communist despot Nicolae Ceauşescu.

'[Chojecki] feels that he should help foment a feeling of solidarity among East Europeans and create an East Central European bloc opposing the Soviet Union,' Minden reported. Mirek needed a Romanian to lead the video project, and Minden recommended the historian Dinu Giurescu, who had recently defected to the West. He would make a great fit with Chojecki's own preferred candidate, the militant anti-communist Mihnea Berindei.

This plan, like that to broadcast Euro TV Kontakt regularly, would soon be overtaken by events, which were moving faster than anyone had foreseen, as the spirit of Solidarity spilled over into other countries at breakneck speed.

Gorbachev had declared that any interference in the domestic affairs of other states was 'inadmissible' and made it clear that Moscow itself would not intervene. Robert Gates at the CIA read this as an acceptance of the political changes taking place, and, as Brzezinski had forecast, with the lid of the Soviet threat removed, a wave of revolutions swept across Eastern Europe, from the Baltic to the Black Sea, as the 'captive nations' threw off communist rule. In June, Hungary started its own Round Table Talks, based on the Polish model. They would lead to the country's first free elections since the war. Hungary also began dismantling the 150-mile stretch of the Iron Curtain that guarded its frontier with Austria, and thousands of Czechoslovak and East German citizens took the opportunity to cross over to the West.

In August, the former crown prince of Austria, Otto von Habsburg, helped organize a 'Pan-European picnic' in a meadow on the Austro-Hungarian frontier, during which a border post would be held open for three hours. The event was designed to test Gorbachev's reaction to a breach in the Iron Curtain. Leaflets inviting people to the picnic were distributed all over Hungary, and on the day itself music was played, speeches were made and there was wine, beer and goulash. Although the picnic was aimed at Hungarians and Austrians, East Germans crashed the party in large numbers, as the organizers knew they would, and made a dash for the West. Hungarian border guards did not intervene; nor did the 80,000 Soviet troops stationed in the country. More than 600 East Germans fled that afternoon, in the largest breakout from the GDR since the Berlin Wall was built in 1961.

As summer turned to autumn, tens of thousands more Germans fled through Hungary and Czechoslovakia, forcing the Berlin regime to close all borders with its Warsaw Pact neighbours. But even the fearsome German Democratic Republic was about to crumble. On 9 November, people from the East overwhelmed border guards at

the Berlin Wall and broke through. They were met on the other side
by their Western counterparts, who offered flowers and champagne.

Dissidents across the East were now pushing at an open door.
The communist regime in Bulgaria fell three days later, followed
by those of Czechoslovakia and Romania. Many of the instigators
of the Eastern European revolutions were associates of Minden or
Chojecki, or readers to whom they had sent books and journals.
Otto von Habsburg had worked with Minden, and once wrote
to him to express thanks for all he had been doing 'in favour of
European freedom'. Chojecki had come to Habsburg for help with
the satellite TV project, and even made a film about him for Video
Kontakt. The Czechoslovakian playwright Václav Havel, who would
become the country's first democratically elected president, had been
promoted by the ILC for years. Gábor Demszky, who would serve
as mayor of Budapest for two decades, owed his underground
publishing skills to Chojecki and his team.

In the midst of the tumult, American legislators invited Wałęsa
to Washington, where he became only the fourth foreign citizen
who was not a head of state to address a joint meeting of Congress.
He was introduced in the same way as an American president before
the State of the Union address. 'Mr Speaker, the leader of Solidarity,'
the doorkeeper announced. As he made his way down the centre
aisle of the chamber he disappeared beneath a mob of representatives who struggled to get close and to shake him by the hand. From
the rostrum, in a speech that was broadcast on Polish Radio, the
Solidarity leader thanked the American people for their support
during the years of persecution. '[Americans] sent us aid,' he said,
'and thanks to them the people of Solidarity were never alone.'
He also thanked the 'many, many Americans' including members
of Congress, the AFL-CIO and the institutions and foundations
'who lent us support in our most difficult moments', and those who
'through the airwaves or printed word' had 'spread the truth', and
singled out the émigrés, whose support 'was always priceless for us'.

At the end of his speech, he recalled the days of August 1980 in
Gdańsk, when he had slipped over the Lenin Shipyard fence to join

his colleagues in their sit-in and been appointed their leader. 'When I recall the road we have travelled I often think of that jump over the fence,' he said. 'Now others jump fences and tear down walls. They do it because freedom is a human right.'

The Congressmen and women leapt to their feet. Cheers rang round the room. Sitting in the chamber was the Soviet ambassador to Washington, who was seen applauding vigorously.

The eight years Chojecki had spent in the West had exhausted him, as martial law had exhausted most opposition leaders. In 1989 you could read it in their lined and aged faces. On the night of 13 December 1981 he had been thirty-two years old, a young activist with fire in his veins. In the intervening years, the freedom fighter had become a *comandante*. His mane of red-brown hair had mostly gone, the moustache was flecked with grey. The once open, steely gaze was hooded.

Others had decided to settle in the West, in Washington, Chicago, New York, London and Paris, but this had never been Chojecki's intention. 'The date I decided I would return to Poland was the first day I found myself in exile,' he said. He liked France, but he didn't have a gift for languages, and had never put down roots in the French media or the scientific community. It took him a long time to get used to the idea that the communists were truly done: even late in 1989, he refused to believe that this wasn't some sort of ploy. But after the former editor of *Solidarity Weekly* was installed as Polish prime minister and Chojecki recognized that his purpose in the West had evaporated, he decided to go home.

One major hurdle stood in his way: he was still wanted by the Polish police for crimes he had allegedly committed when a member of KOR. His colleagues from that period had been arrested on 13 December 1981 and had served time in internment, and the cases against them had eventually been dropped, but since he was never caught, the charges against Chojecki were outstanding. He would be imprisoned as soon as he arrived on Polish soil. The only way around that was to obtain a so-called 'iron letter' from the government guaranteeing his safe passage. So he went to the Polish embassy in Paris to request that the new Solidarity justice minister, Lech Kaczyński, declare on a piece of paper that the warrant against him should be ignored. Kaczyński, who would be Polish president one day, obliged. He also sent Chojecki a phone number to call in case he ran into difficulty at the border.

Chojecki caught a flight to Poland, and when he arrived at the crumbling, overcrowded terminal at Warsaw's Okęcie airport, the guards started to go through the huge ledgers containing the names of all the people who were wanted by the police or had been banned from entering the country. They found Chojecki on their lists and told him he was under arrest.

Chojecki produced the 'iron letter', which bore an official government stamp, but the border guards had never seen a document like it. It could easily be a fake, something he had put together himself. They handcuffed him.

His last resort was the phone number. He told the guards he could clear the matter up with one quick conversation. They refused to let him make the call, but he persisted, and at length one of them said he would dial the number himself.

Chojecki watched as he picked up the phone. He saw the border guard stiffen to attention. A brisk conversation followed.

'Of course, Mr Minister,' the guard said, then replaced the receiver.

The number he had been given was the direct line for General Kiszczak, who still served in the government, still responsible for the SB. For decades this man had led the organization that had made Chojecki's life hell. Now he had ordered the border guard to allow him to enter Poland unmolested.

Tomasz Łabędź was waiting for Mirek in the arrivals hall. He had driven there from France and after watching the other passengers from the Paris flight file through he had spent the best part of two hours wondering what on earth had happened to his friend.

They drove into the city together. Nothing much seemed to have changed. As Chojecki had discovered, the same communist politicians were in the government. The same sounds and smells of two-stroke engines and cheap fuel hung in the air. He recognized the same potholes, the same broken-down fence by his mother's apartment, the same missing paving slab. Warsaw felt as familiar as an old pair of shoes.

But beneath the surface, seismic changes were sweeping the country, as the old political system was replaced by another. This came home to Chojecki when he heard that the statue of Feliks Dzerzhinsky, the Polish founder of the Cheka, the forerunner of the KGB, was to be pulled from its plinth. He decided he should record this moment on film. Knowing that the state broadcaster had a department that loaned out camera equipment, he decided to approach them.

'I went to the director,' he remembered. 'I said I wanted to borrow a camera for three hours. "Wonderful," the director said. "Go to the secretary, she will help you."

'I went to her, and she said, "Yes of course, no problem. We have a small private business here that has the equipment, and you can hire it straight away." '

The business turned out to be in the same building. All they had done was move the state-owned camera equipment from one room to another, and now they were renting it out for private profit. After the extremes of totalitarian communism, Poland was about to be subjected to an extreme form of capitalism in which everything was up for sale.

'They took what didn't belong to them, said they were the owners and organized their own enterprises using government materials,' he said.

He turned down the chance to hire the camera, but went to witness the secret policeman's fall anyway. It was 17 November, a bright, cold Warsaw day, when the city lay beneath a spotless dome of ultramarine sky. Dzerzhinsky stood in a large square a few hundred yards from the KSMO police headquarters where Chojecki had been brought on that fateful night in March 1980. The giant bronze likeness of the secret police founder, whose agents had deported and murdered hundreds of thousands of Poles, had

surveyed his compatriots from a high pedestal here since 1951. But on this day he was finally to get his comeuppance. 'I was there to see it, and I was very happy,' Chojecki recalled.

He watched from among the large, cheering crowd as the yellow arm of a 25-tonne crane extended towards Dzerzhinsky. Workmen passed a rope around his chest, a diesel engine revved and the caped figure was dragged reluctantly from his plinth. For a few seconds he seemed to struggle in the air, then something happened that no one had expected. The great communist fell apart. His legs broke away first, in a shower of dust, then his torso, leaving his head and shoulders dangling in the noose.

'Bloody Feliks' had not been made from bronze at all, it turned out, but from humble, fragile concrete.

Epilogue

The Best-Kept Secret

Do not make a cheap demon out of me. I will be on the side
of human order to the end of my days and in dying as well.
Witold Gombrowicz, *Diary*

The CIA moved rapidly after the Polish elections to pull the plug
on QRHELPFUL. Celia Larkin had to sever so many relationships
in Paris that she began referring to herself as 'The Terminator'.
Many CIA staffers thought that cutting off people so quickly was
a mistake: the Agency had behaved in much the same way with
the Afghan mujahideen, leaving heavily armed groups of militants
squabbling over diminishing resources, and look where that was
going. Still, they had to do as they were ordered.

Minden continued to lead the ILC for a couple more years,
although money was tight and many of his associates were moving
their activities to Poland, where printing was cheap and the audience close, and there was nothing now to stop people publishing
freely. He spent his 1990 tour of Europe winding operations down,
closing bank accounts and retiring the long-serving employees of
various front organizations. In Paris, he found that the Librairie
Polonaise had fallen into financial difficulty, having received so
much CIA business in the past, and warned the Agency that it
might have to close its doors, which would be a great shame. It's
unlikely anyone in Langley was too concerned about that. Minden
had happier news from London: the new Polish prime minister,

Tadeusz Mazowiecki, had visited the ILC's main outlet there, the Polish Library in Hammersmith, and made a point of thanking them for the books they had sent him over many years.

On 30 January 1991, Minden wrote his final report, entitled 'ILC: A short description of its structure and activities', which served as a summary of his career. The ILC teams had been distributing books, magazines and cassettes to Poland, Czechoslovakia, Hungary, Romania and Bulgaria for roughly thirty-five years, and to the Soviet Union for approximately thirty years, he wrote. The number of items sent east in that time was close to ten million, and recently they had been running at around 300,000 per annum, at a cost to the CIA of $2.7 million: in the ILC's final year they had distributed 316,020 books. His staff had been so diligent in documenting their shipments that they had records of all the titles distributed and the names of almost all the people who had taken them. Minden was instructed to send the files to Washington, where they remain classified.

With the ILC wound up, Minden resigned, sending two undated letters to the CIA, one addressed to the 'board of directors', the other to a PO box in Washington, DC. For the next decade, as he lived out his retirement, the book programme's existence remained hidden. For the former CIA historian Benjamin Fischer, it had been the 'best-kept secret' of the Cold War: despite so many people being on the payroll, 'everybody just sort of looked the other way'.

Gradually, however, a few details began to leak out. In 2003, John Matthews, who had worked for Free Europe Press in the 1950s, revealed the programme's existence in an article for the *International Journal of Intelligence and CounterIntelligence* entitled 'The West's Secret Marshall Plan for the Mind'. Minden didn't talk to Matthews for the article – he would never discuss his work publicly – but when it was published he showed it proudly to his sons, John and Paul, giving them their first clear sense of what he had achieved. Following Matthews, further details of the CIA activity in Poland began to dribble out, often in the memoirs of former officers. In 2004, William J. Daugherty wrote about QRHELPFUL, without revealing its codename or any details, describing it as 'perhaps the most successful covert action program, regardless of standard of measure'.

Minden died at the age of eighty-five in 2006. The *New York Times* ran an obituary which described the International Literary Centre as 'something of a personalized book club' and disclosed that it had been financed by the CIA. Around that time, Minden's family found more than 500 pages of his written reports, documenting European field trips between 1973 and 1990, which they gave with other papers of his to the Hoover Archive at Stanford University. Some of the details from these documents were used by Alfred Reisch, another programme veteran, in his 2013 account *Hot Books in the Cold War*, which focused on the early post-war years. It had been 'ideological, political, cultural, and psychological warfare all wrapped up in one', Reisch said, which used 'enlightenment and persuasion by means of the printed word'.

Within the CIA, however, the book programme and QRHELPFUL were given little credit. In Langley it was the Agency's action in Afghanistan, Operation Cyclone, that took the plaudits for bringing about the end of the Cold War. There were two reasons for this. First, the Afghan operation was enormously expensive. Where QRHELPFUL cost $18.6 million over five years, and the book programme's latterday budget stood at around $2 million–$4 million annually, Operation Cyclone by 1987 was running at a cost of $700 million a year, taking up 80 per cent of the overseas budget of the clandestine service. Given this tremendous outlay, it was politically expedient to give the Afghan action all the credit.

Fischer also believes that Cyclone suited the image US intelligence leaders liked to project of the CIA, of an organization packed with spooks and paramilitaries who fought in war zones, in sharp contrast to the more intellectual pursuit of sponsoring books and publishing. 'The bottom line was that it didn't fit their image of themselves as CIA operators who went around recruiting spies,' he said. 'The operators, the spy guys, think covert action is a waste of time, waste of money,' he said. The result was that some of the people who worked on Polish operations were not properly recognized for their work, despite being 'heroes of the story', as Fischer puts it. Richard Malzahn, who ran QRHELPFUL from Langley, was one of those who suffered. Far from being promoted, he was packed off to be a lowly analyst.

Strangely, it may have helped Minden for the ILC to have been viewed as a backwater within the Agency, as it gave him a degree of independence. 'I think Minden ran his own show from beginning to end,' said Fischer. 'The really clever ones knew they had the upper hand. If you found out what they were doing, it was usually after the fact.'

There were some people on the National Security Council, however, who had a clear understanding of what the book programme had achieved. Walter Raymond Jr, a former CIA officer who worked as special assistant to President George H. Bush, wrote to Minden on his retirement to tell him that he should take 'a great deal of personal pride in all the valuable quiet work that you were able to do on behalf of the freedom of thought and the expression of independent ideas so desperately sought by millions'. He had made a 'genuine difference' by 'keeping the links open to the millions whose principal misfortune was to be located in the eastern half of Europe'.

Matthews, too, believed that the programmes had 'intimately affected . . . hundreds of thousands of educated people in Eastern Europe and the former Soviet Union', while Reisch wrote that the project had played 'a decisive role' and 'contributed to the West's ideological victory'. Minden's one-time 'rabbi' at the CIA, John Richardson, compared the books the ILC sent to food denied to needy people by their oppressors. 'I sometimes wondered whether those books in the hands of the intellectual elites of Central and Eastern Europe might not rival or even exceed Radio Free Europe in influencing the course of history,' he told Minden. Even some of the CIA's numerous critics would place this unusual operation near the top of American intelligence success stories. Tim Weiner, whose

Legacy of Ashes catalogues the disastrous foreign interventions Bill Casey oversaw in the 1980s, found the political-warfare programmes to support dissidents in the Soviet Union, Poland and Czechoslovakia 'among the most important CIA operations of the Cold War'.

The most valuable assessments may come from the people most directly affected: the Poles who were sustained by it. For Joanna Szczęsna, part of the job of uncensored literature was to give Poles access to information they were not allowed to have, about suppressed aspects of their history. 'We didn't want to accept that somebody is going to tell us how we should see everything,' she said. But that was only part of the picture. Literature also nourished the soul, and gave them a sense of a broader human context. 'Books gave us the tools to understand this world,' she said. 'We read poetry and literature. It showed us that there are likeminded people who are above nationality, who we can empathize with, who admire beauty, who admire virtue.' Adam Michnik, who spent so much time in jail, found literature a compass by which to live. It gave him a perspective and values, he said. 'It allowed you to look at and assess your own country's history from a contemporary point of view. And you could feel after reading a book that your spine would be straightening up. And you knew then that you can tell the state "No". And I still know that today.' Wiktor Kulerski,

for many years Bujak's deputy in the Warsaw Underground, would compare the printing machines they received in the aftermath of Jaruzelski's crackdown to weapons. 'The importance of the press cannot be overemphasized,' he has said. 'The printing presses we got from the West during martial law might be compared to machine guns or tanks during war.'

Perhaps the highest tribute to the book programme came from Aleksandr Solzhenitsyn, who, after moving to the US, became a distributor of ILC books himself. When Minden retired, the great author thanked him personally in a copy of his book *The Red Wheel: A Narrative in Discrete Periods of Time*. 'To George Minden with gratitude,' he wrote, signing it: 'Sasha'.

This book is now in the possession of Minden's sons. 'I think George and Solzhenitsyn were on a shared mission,' said John Minden. 'To make the world a better place.'

Acknowledgements

I began research for this book in January 2020, a few weeks after the Covid-19 virus was first identified in China and a few days before the first lockdown in Wuhan. This exquisite timing and the years of disruption that followed meant I had to rely more than ever on the generosity of strangers, and I was fortunate to encounter several kind individuals early in the process. One was the late A. Ross Johnson, a renowned expert on Radio Free Europe and Radio Liberty, whose enthusiasm convinced me there was an untold story here worth relating. Another was the Polish historian Paweł Sowiński, who shared his knowledge freely along with many of his contacts. Then there was Jan Chodakowski, who regaled me at his home in Earl's Court with accounts of his time at Polonia Book Fund. It was Jan who introduced me to Yolanta Łodzińska, my fixer, translator, driver and – in periods when travel was impossible – stand-in interviewer. Without Yola this project would have been far more challenging and the outcome, I have no doubt, far worse.

Since this is in large part an oral history, I would like to thank the many people who gave their time freely to endure my questions. (At least one interviewee said I reminded them of their communist-era interrogators.) Key among these were Mirek Chojecki and Helena Łuczywo, whose memories have formed the backbone of the narrative. Of the many others who submitted to shorter interviews or provided information, I would like to mention Seweryn Blumsztajn, Teresa Bogucka, Grzegorz Boguta, Magda Boguta, Jacky Challot,

Tomasz Chlebowski, Chris Gremski, Tomasz Łabędź, Irena Lasota, Witek Łuczywo, Adam Michnik, John and Paul Minden, Jan Axel Stoltz, Andrzej Świątek and Joanna Szczęsna. Several people will find that in order to focus the story I have downplayed their roles, and I apologize for that. Józef Lebenbaum is one. Józef was kind enough to invite us to Sweden, to spend many hours touring the sites from which he waged his campaign for a free Poland. I hope one day he will get the biography he deserves. The printer Andrzej Zieliński is another. As well as submitting to lengthy questioning, Andrzej took me to the tiny, secret print shop above an apple barn outside Warsaw where he had spent many nights producing illicit copies of *Mazovia Weekly*. Incredibly, the shop he built is still there. Zofia Reinbacher is a third. She took days out to show me around her bookstore in Vienna, and to relate all she could remember about her meetings with Minden and how the ILC system worked.

For much of the writing process, I have been glad to have had the expert advice and support of Benjamin B. Fischer, the former CIA chief historian, and the only author ever to have written a book and made a film about QRHELPFUL based on the classified sources. Hopefully his book and movie will one day be released, but for now they are themselves classified. For legal reasons, Ben was unable to share too much of what he knew, but I am grateful to him for advising me on aspects of the story, and for reading the manuscript.

I would further like to express thanks to the people who help me navigate the archives. These include Tinotenda Nyandoro, who copied the Minden Papers at the Hoover Institution on my behalf when it was impossible for me to get to California; Anna Bernardt, president of the Kultura Literary Association and custodian of all things Giedroyc, who helped me find important documents from the Editor's collection during my visits to Maisons-Laffitte; and Witold Bagieński, historian at the Institute of National Remembrance, who swiftly produced the most relevant secret police files from the IPN archive whenever I asked him for help.

At times, researching and writing a non-fiction book during a pandemic felt like an 'uphill war' in itself, but I have been able to draw encouragement from a regular group of friends. They include: Ian Katz, Sam Wollaston, Ben Macintyre, Katherine Fleming, Pascal Wyse, Tom Campbell, Ingrid Karikari, John Rogers, Bruce McKernan, Nick O'Toole, Julian Borger and Paul Hamilos.

As ever, I am hugely thankful to my publishers, Arabella Pike at William Collins and Hilary Redmon at Random House, who kept faith in this at times challenging project. I would also like to mention Peter James, who helped polish the manuscript in its latter stages, and Eve Hutchings and Sam Harding of HarperCollins.

The further I travel on my non-fiction career, the more indebted I am to my agents, Stuart Krichevsky and Felicity Rubinstein, whose sage advice I carry wherever I go.

Finally, I would like to thank my family: my mother, Barbara, in whose giant footsteps I tread; my brother, Hugh, whose support I feel even from afar; and the four individuals I cherish most in the world, Harry, Arthur, Eddie and Lucy.

Captions

PART ONE: HOPE (1980–1981)

PART TWO: WAR (1981–1985)

PART THREE: RECKONING (1986–1989)

Notes

On Language

I've opted to use English translations of Polish titles in the main text, to improve the narrative flow for Anglophone readers. So *Tygodnik Mazowsze* is rendered as *Mazovia Weekly*, *Biuletyn Informacyjny* becomes *Information Bulletin*, and *Gazeta Wyborcza* is *Election Gazette*. In two important cases, those of *Kontakt* and *Kultura*, I have retained the Polish titles, partly because their meanings in English seem obvious, partly because I felt Giedroyc's famous journal lost something when rendered simply as *Culture*. To help direct readers to the correct sources, however, I have used Polish titles in the Notes – along with English translations at the first mention in each chapter – and in the Bibliography. Similarly, the Instytut Literacki, known in Paris as the Institut Littéraire, is referred to as the Literary Institute in the main text, but is Instytut Literacki/Institut Littéraire in the sections below.

On Sources

This story is largely based on hundreds of hours of interviews conducted in Poland, Sweden, the US, France, Austria and the UK over a five-year period from 2020 to 2024. This was the best and perhaps only way to piece together the full story of the CIA book programme in Poland, since almost all the files relating to it remain classified. There are a few important documentary sources in the public domain, however. The most valuable of these are George Minden's notes from his meetings with book network contacts in Europe. Minden wrote contemporaneous aide-memoires, which were typed up when he returned home by his wife Marilyn, a *New York Times* journalist. These reports can now be found with other early book programme documents in the George Capuțineanu Minden Papers (abbreviated below as GCMP) in the Hoover Institution Library & Archives at Stanford University. Further sources from the US, including some declassified intelligence documents, are available through the CIA's online reading room, the Wilson Center Digital Archive and the Ronald Reagan Presidential Library. For the Polish side, there are two invaluable collections of material: the Archive of the Institute of National Remembrance (abbreviated to AIPN), which holds vast quantities of files created by the SB; and the library of the Instytut Literacki/Institut Littéraire in Paris, which contains the fruits of Giedroyc's lifetime of letter-writing. The British Library meanwhile has an extensive collection of Polish underground publications from the period.

There are also several published books and articles on the subject of CIA activity in Eastern Europe and Poland that I found myself turning to again and again. These included Alfred Reisch, *Hot Books in the Cold War*; Seth Jones, *A Covert Action*; Paweł Sowiński, *Tajna dyplomacja* [Secret Diplomacy]; Gwido Zlatkes, Paweł Sowiński and Ann M. Frenkel (eds), *Duplicator Underground*; Siobhan Doucette, *Books Are Weapons*; Shana Penn, *Solidarity's Secret*; Benjamin B. Fischer, 'Solidarity, the CIA, and Western Technology'; and John P. C. Matthews, 'The West's Secret Marshall Plan for the Mind'. You will find details of these and other important works in the Selected Bibliography.

Front Matter

vii. The quote from Adam Michnik, 'We should build a monument to books,' is from an interview with the author in October 2021.

vii. Jerzy Kulczycki's entreaty that the Poles should 'tell it like it was' is from his memoir, *Atakowac książką* [Book Attack].

Prologue: Teresa's Flying Library

3. My outline of Teresa Bogucka's stewardship of the Warsaw Flying Library is based on interviews with Bogucka conducted in Warsaw in October 2021 and February 2022. I'm also indebted to Róża Sułek, of the University of Warsaw, who made the connection between Teresa Bogucka and the copy of *1984* in the university's Library of the Institute of Applied Social Sciences. Sułek, who has conducted her own research, believes a significant part of the early collection was put together by the sociologist Jakub Karpiński, and that many of the first books were sent from the West by Konstanty Jeleński. For more on Jeleński, see p. 140.

6. 'free, honest thinking': 'mailing operations Monthly Report #14', dated 25 October 1957, cited in Matthews, 'The West's Secret Marshall Plan for the Mind'.

6. The selection of titles sent is compiled from various book-distribution reports, including 'IAC Semiannual Report on Book Distribution, January 1 to June 30 1972', GCMP.

7. 'I'd almost take money from the devil himself': author interview with Józef Lebenbaum, September 2020.

Chapter 1. A Snaggle-Toothed Thought Machine

11. Many details of Mirosław Chojecki's arrest and detention are from his account 'Rękopis więzienny' ['Prison manuscript'] and 'W obronie Mirosława Chojeckiego i Bogdana Grzesiaka' ['In defence of Mirosław Chojecki and Bogdan Grzesiak'], as well as author interviews with Chojecki conducted between 2020 and 2023.

12. Christlike, 'only somehow bolder': Marian Brandys's description, from *Moje przygody z historią* [My Adventures with History].

12. 'SB security service': the SB (short for Służba Bezpieczeństwa, meaning 'Security Service') was the main secret police organization in Poland. The nickname for SB functionaries, 'Ubek', derived from the Urząd Bezpieczeństwa ('Security Office'), which the SB replaced in 1956. The acronym KSMO meanwhile stands for Komenda Stołeczna Milicji Obywatelskiej ('Metropolitan Headquarters of the Citizens' Militia'). The MO Citizens' Militia, which worked closely with the SB, was the main uniformed police force in communist Poland.

12. Details of the weather that day are from weatherspark.com.

13. around fifty dollars: the actual amount was 7,600 złoty. The złoty's value is difficult to estimate because exchange rates varied wildly between the black market and the bank rate. According to Paul Lewis, 'The Lure of the Dollar in Poland', *New York Times*, 9 October 1981, at the end of 1981 the official rate was 34 złoty to the dollar, while the black-market rate was around 320 złoty per dollar, but this represented an increase of 100 per cent on the start of the year. I have assumed an approximate exchange rate of around 160 zł/$ in 1980.

13. Harassment, assault, imprisonment: details of the beatings meted out to Chojecki, including a subcutaneous haemorrhage inflicted at Radom courthouse, can be found in Jan Józef Lipski's *KOR: A History of the Workers' Defense Committee in Poland, 1976–1981*. Although many files relating to Chojecki's activities in exile have been destroyed, the Institute of National Remembrance (IPN) holds many more that detail SB attempts to investigate Chojecki before he left Poland, including numerous short-term arrests.

14. a house of terror: my characterization of Mokotów jail, and the methods of torture used by the security service, is based on a tour of the prison in October 2023 with an IPN guide. Mokotów now houses a Museum of Cursed Soldiers and Political Prisoners of the Polish People's Republic, which details the horrific treatment of prisoners.

15. Conversations between Chojecki and prison staff are recorded in 'Rękopis więzienny' ['Prison manuscript']. Chojecki gives several details about his hunger strike, such as that by day 8 he had lost 7.7 kilos, that the pipe the doctor used was 1.5 centimetres in diameter and that the amount of food they force-fed him was 0.75 litres.

17. 'The beaten prisoner': Solzhenitsyn, *The Gulag Archipelago.*

19. *Courier from Warsaw* was one of the best books they had ever produced: author interviews with Chojecki. The book was especially important to Poles because it revealed suppressed details about Stalin's betrayal during the Warsaw Uprising.

19. Maria Stypułkowska-Chojecka, who died in 2016, recalled details of her life and wartime experiences with the 'Parasols' for the Warsaw Uprising Museum's oral history project, available at https://www.1944.pl/archiwum-historii-mowionej/maria-stypulkowska-chojecka,468.html, accessed September 2024. Although the Germans arrested and shot several hundred people in reprisal for Operation Kutschera, the Nazi official's assassination is widely believed to have reduced the levels of terror on Warsaw's streets. See e.g. https://polishhistory.pl/operation-kutschera/, accessed September 2024.

20. as large as the population of Switzerland: this estimate is from Miłosz, *Native Realm*. Tadeusz Piotrowski, in *Poland's Holocaust*, states that six million Poles were killed in the war, mostly by Hitler's and Stalin's genocidal regimes. Of these, only 600,000 were combatants.

20. The Warsovian joke about the Palace of Culture was related by Józef Lebenbaum, in interviews.

20. The term 'spit-spattered dwarf of reactionary forces' (*zapluty karzel reakcji* in Polish) was used on a 1945 communist propaganda poster to describe the Home Army.

21. Apart from Krystyna Starczewska, other famous activists produced by Warsaw High School Number Seven included Adam Michnik and Jan Józef Lipski. Starczewska related her encounters with the Polish security services, who also threatened to run her over in the street, as part of the oral history project Memory of Nations, available at https://www.memoryofnations.eu/en/starczewska-krystyna-1937, accessed September 2024. Fideism, the offence for which she was sacked, refers to the view that faith can be superior to reason in religious or philosophical matters.

22. The description of Poland's system of censorship is drawn from Jane Leftwich Curry, *The Black Book of Polish Censorship*, which describes censorship apparatus in the 1970s as being 'one of the most complex and developed bureaucracies of media control in the world'. Gaweł Strządała, in 'Censorship in the People's Republic of Poland', details the publications that were prohibited in 1951, including the book about growing carrots. Miłosz reports in *The Captive Mind* that *1984* was 'difficult to obtain and dangerous to possess'.

25. 'We were living in Orwell's world': author interview with Zofia Reinbacher, February 2020.

25. 'dog-eared copies of *Animal Farm*': Timothy Garton Ash, 'Orwell for our time', *Guardian*, 5 May 2001.

26. Chojecki's realizing as he grew up that Poles were excluded from their own history is in Anna Belkiewicz, 'Nowa przed sądem' ['NOWa before the court'], *Biuletyn Informacyjny* [Information Bulletin], No. 4/38 (June 1980). The dissident journalist who told him they had a duty to fight for independence was the Auschwitz survivor and resistance fighter Władysław Bartoszewski (author interviews with Chojecki).

26. Marcin Zaremba has written an exceptional summary of the Polish experience of the 'Year of Revolutions', including the government's propaganda campaign against the Jews, in '1968 in Poland: The Rebellion on the Other Side of the Looking Glass'. For the regime it was, he says, 'a Pyrrhic victory', as a number of politicized students from March 1986 would join the Workers' Defence Committee (Komitet Obrony Robotników, or KOR) in 1976.

27. 'It was simply a moral decision': Lynn Darling, 'Outside Looking Back', *Washington Post*, 18 December 1981.

27. For an account of the events of 1976 and KOR's role in supporting the workers, see Lipski, *KOR*. Lipski describes Chojecki as 'the initiator, the creator, and then the excellent director of NOWa'. Further details of the founding of the independent publishing house can be read in Chojecki, 'Jak powstała NOWa' ['How NOWa was created'], in Wojciech Borowik (ed.), *N jak Nowa: Od wolnego słowa do wolności, 1977–1989* [N for NOWa: From Free Speech to Freedom, 1977–1989].

28. 'to lift society out of the state of apathy': John Darnton, 'Polish Underground Publisher Flouts Censor and Thrives', *New York Times*, 28 May 1980.

29. 'In a country that was so tightly, hermetically closed': author interview with Andrzej Świątek, July 2021.

29. For a list of NOWa's publications, see Borowik (ed.), *N jak Nowa*. Early titles included *Nierzeczywistość* [Unreality] by Kazimierz Brandys; *Pochodzenie systemu* [Origins of the System] by Marek Tarniewski (a pseudonym for Jakub Karpiński); and *O pewnych przemianach etyki walki* [Certain Developments in the Ethics of Combat] by Maria Ossowska. See also Darnton, 'Polish Underground Publisher Flouts Censor and Thrives'.

29. 'NOWa showed the way': Lipski, *KOR*.

29. Details of Tomasz Strzyżewski's leak are reported in Curry, *The Black Book of Polish Censorship*, which contains many excerpts from the documents he smuggled into Sweden.

30. 'tastiest parts': author interviews with Chojecki.

30. 'truly amazing': Leo Łabędź, 'The finely-tuned machinery that selects what Poles may read' and 'How the blue pencil can be blunted', *The Times*, 26 and 27 September 1977 [two-part series].

30. 'Do you think, Mirek, that you'll be able to bring down the communist system with your little books?': author interviews with Chojecki.

Chapter 2. Our Friends Down South

31. Abbott Washburn, executive vice president of the Crusade for Freedom, recalled the August 1951 balloon operation in 'Freedom Crusade Sends Nine Million Balloon Messages', *Chronicle-Express*, 20 September 1951.

32. 'TO THE PEOPLE OF CZECHOSLOVAKIA': from Herbert A. Friedman, 'Free Europe Press Cold War Leaflets'. Friedman has created a valuable online resource for the balloon operations, which can be found at https://www.psywarrior.com/ RadioFreeEurope.html, accessed September 2024. Note that, while I state that the 'Winds of Freedom' was the brainchild of the Free Europe Committee, at that time the organization still went by its original name, the National Committee for a Free Europe.

33. For a detailed history of the 'radios' and their origins, see A. Ross Johnson, *Radio Free Europe and Radio Liberty: The CIA Years and Beyond*.

33. The statistics that more than half a million balloons were launched and 300 million leaflets dropped, including 260,000 copies of *Animal Farm*, are from Friedman, 'Free Europe Press Cold War Leaflets', and from Peter Finn and Petra Couvée, *The Zhivago Affair: The Kremlin, the CIA, and the Battle over a Forbidden Book*.

34. The angry response of communist states to the balloon operations is recorded in Alfred Reisch, *Hot Books in the Cold War: The CIA-Funded Secret Western Book Distribution Program behind the Iron Curtain*. Reisch also states that the operations were 'not as effective as initially conceived'. They were terminated in 1956 after an objection was lodged by the West German government.

34. The launch of the mailing project is documented by John P. C. Matthews in 'The West's Secret Marshall Plan for the Mind', which gives credit for the idea to Sam

Walker, director since 1952 of
Free Europe Press (FEP), a newly
created sister of Radio Free Europe.

34. Details of Minden's life are drawn
from author interviews with his
sons, John and Paul, conducted
in July and November 2021;
from Martin Douglas, 'George
C. Minden, 85, Dies; Led a Cold
War of Words', *New York Times*, 23
April 2006; and from Reisch, *Hot
Books in the Cold War*.

35. 'reduce the efficiency of the
communist administration':
Matthews, 'The West's Secret
Marshall Plan for the Mind'.

35. 'an offensive of free, honest
thinking and accurate information':
ibid.

35. 'our friends down south': ibid.
According to Matthews, this
was how the Free Europe
Press employees referred to
their 'overseers in the Central
Intelligence Agency'.

35. For details of titles sent by the
mailing project, see the annual
reports from the book-distribution
programme, GCMP. Matthews,
'The West's Secret Marshall Plan for
the Mind', gives a detailed account
of the mailing of *The Hundred Years
of American Painting*. According to
him, Sam Walker and the CIA were
'so won over by Minden's change of
direction that they decided to give
him virtually free rein'.

35. 'All book distribution is politically
significant': George C. Minden,
'Some Additional Notes on the
Current State of Book Distribution',
10 November 1969, cited in Reisch,
Hot Books in the Cold War.

36. For a full list of publishers and
distributors who acted as 'sponsors',
see GCMP.

36. Poland's exceptionally positive
response to the books is recorded

in e.g. Reisch, *Hot Books in the Cold
War*, in which Poland is referred
to as the programme's 'crucial
country'.

36. Paweł Sowiński has documented the
early years of the Polonia Book Fund
in 'Promoting diversity: The Polonia
Book Fund, Ltd. Transnational
Network, 1958–1963', *Advance*, 4
October 2019, and in 'Cold War
Books: George Minden and his Field
Workers 1973–1990'. Minden took
charge of Stypułkowski's person-to-
person mechanism in 1963.

37. 'to place as high a number as
possible of books': George Minden,
'Response Patterns of the FEP
Mailing Operation behind the Iron
Curtain, as of September 1958',
cited in Reisch, *Hot Books in the
Cold War*.

Chapter 3. The French Connection

39. Further details of Chojecki's time
in jail and his release are from
his 'Rękopis więzienny' ['Prison
manuscript'].

40. Details of the campaign to free
Chojecki are from Darnton, 'Polish
Underground Publisher Flouts
Censor and Thrives', *New York
Times*, 28 May 1980, and from 'W
obronie Mirosława Chojeckiego i
Bogdana Grzesiaka' ['In defence
of Mirosław Chojecki and Bogdan
Grzesiak'].

41. 'one of Poland's most influential
publishers': Darnton, 'Polish
Underground Publisher Flouts
Censor and Thrives'.

41. My account of Jan Walc and Zenon
Pałka's print job is derived from
the account Walc wrote in June
1980 for *Biuletyn Informacyjny*
[Information Bulletin], which was
translated and republished as 'We,
the Free Drum'n'Roller Press' in
Gwido Zlatkes, Paweł Sowiński and

Ann M. Frenkel (eds), *Duplicator Underground*. The climatic conditions that day are from weatherspark.com.

47. Accounts of Chojecki's day in court were carried by *Biuletyn Informacyjny*, No. 4/38 (June 1980), in two pieces: Anna Belkiewicz, 'Nowa przed sądem' ['NOWa before the court'], and 'Wystapienie Mirosława Chojeckiego' ['Statement by Mirosław Chojecki'].

Chapter 4. An International Spider Web

52. 'appalling that these excellent programs should have fallen into such jeopardy': 'Memorandum from Paul Henze of the National Security Council Staff to the President's Assistant for National Security Affairs (Brzezinski)', Washington, DC, 2 June 1980, in US Department of State, *Foreign Relations of the United States, 1977–1980*, Vol. VI: *Soviet Union*, available at https://history.state.gov/historicaldocuments/frus1977-80v06/d280, accessed September 2024.

52. For the impact of the invasion of Afghanistan, see e.g. Office of the Historian, Foreign Service Institute, United States Department of State, 'The Soviet Invasion of Afghanistan and the U.S. Response, 1978–1980', available at https://history.state.gov/milestones/1977-1980/soviet-invasion-afghanistan, accessed September 2024.

52. 'ground-pounders' vs 'knuckle-draggers': author interviews with Benjamin B. Fischer, October 2021 and February 2023.

52. 'Real men don't sell books': ibid.

53. For Brzezinski titles that were distributed, see e.g. 'IAC Semiannual Report on Book Distribution, January 1 to July 31, 1973', GCMP, which shows that in the first half of that year alone the CIA were promoting no fewer than four of his works: *Between Two Ages*, *Dilemmas of Change in Soviet Politics*, *The Fragile Blossom* and *Unity or Conflict*.

53. Brzezinski's desire to grow the ILC's budget can be seen in a memorandum he sent to Carter on 28 February 1977, in which he argued that 'this [books] program should probably be expanded'. 'Editorial Note', *Foreign Relations of the United States, 1977–1980*, Vol. XX: *Eastern Europe*.

53. 'probably not actually given this . . . any serious thought': 'Memorandum from Paul Henze of the National Security Council Staff to the President's Assistant for National Security Affairs (Brzezinski)', Washington, DC, 23 January 1979, in *Foreign Relations of the United States, 1977–1980*, Vol. XX: *Eastern Europe*.

54. 'I will back it strongly': 'Memorandum from Paul Henze of the National Security Council Staff to the President's Assistant for National Security Affairs (Brzezinski)', Washington, DC, 2 June 1980.

54. New York's 1980s crime wave is widely documented. The idea that CIA officers would refuse to visit was relayed to me in author interviews with Fischer.

54. Details of the rules Minden liked to live by were related by his sons in interviews, along with a description of the office they sometimes visited. Chris Gremski, an ILC veteran, provided a floorplan showing the internal layout of the organization. Further details about the staff, the functioning of the desks and

relations with readers in the
Eastern Bloc are from Reisch, *Hot
Books in the Cold War.*

57. Pope John Paul II's birth name,
Carol Wojtyła, appears regularly in
Minden's distribution reports, such
as in an appendix listing 'Notable
recipients of PSPD [Press and
Special Projects Division] books' in
the 1969 'Annual Report', GCMP.

57. The book centre's issue with
the New York Post Office is
documented in Reisch, *Hot Books
in the Cold War.*

58. 'a complex organization': from
Minden, 'ILC: A short description
of its structure and activities', 30
January 1991, GCMP.

58. 'huge international spider web':
Reisch, *Hot Books in the Cold War.*

58. Adam Rudzki's important role in
the ILC has been attested to by his
son, Marek, in 'Akcja masowych
przekazów książek do Polski w
latach 1956–1994' ['The campaign
of mass book transfers to Poland in
1956–1994'].

59. Overviews of Giedroyc's life can
be found in Marek Żebrowski, *La
Maison Kultura – le guide* [The
Kultura House – A Guide]; in 'Jerzy
Giedroyc: Biografia najkrótsza'
['Jerzy Giedroyc: the shortest
biography'], *Kultura Paryska,*
at https://kulturaparyska.com/
pl/people/show/jerzy-giedroyc/
biography, accessed September
2024; and in Jerzy Giedroyc,
Autobiografia na cztery ręce [An
Autobiography in Four Hands].
Adam Zamoyski, in 'Obituary,
Jerzy Giedroyc', *Guardian*, 19
September 2000, reported that
the Editor was said to have saved
Polish literature from extinction,
while Miłosz (cited in Benjamin
B. Fischer, 'Repudiating Yalta')
opined that he was 'sometimes no

less than credited with the abolition
of communism in Poland'. The
naming of 2006 as the 'Year of Jerzy
Giedroyc' can be found in Rod
Fisher, *A Cultural Dimension to the
EU's External Policies.* Czapski's
prison-camp lectures on Proust can
be found in *Lost Time: Lectures on
Proust in a Soviet Prison Camp.*

61. 'The situation was clear to me':
Żebrowski, *La Maison Kultura –
le guide*, citing Giedroyc in
the documentary *Kultura* (dir.
Agnieszka Holland, 1985).

61. '*At every step I saw*': Józef
Czapski, *Inhuman Land: Searching
for the Truth in Soviet Russia,
1941–1942.*

61. 'fresh bread rolls': author interview
with Joanna Szczęsna, February
2022.

61. 'a legend that shines': Robert
Kostrzewa (ed.), *Between East and
West.*

62. 'The future of *Kultura* is at stake':
letter from Giedroyc to Melchior
Wańkowicz, 9 March 1949, in
Aleksandra Ziółkowska-Boehm,
'Correspondence: Jerzy Giedroyc
and Melchior Wańkowicz'.

62. '[He] is mad at me': letter from
Giedroyc to Wańkowicz, 8 March
1950, ibid.

62. Frances Stonor Saunders has
thoroughly documented the
activities of Josselson and the
Congress for Cultural Freedom in
Who Paid the Piper? She describes
the congress as 'one of the most
ambitious secret operations of the
Cold War'.

62. 'a most interesting individual,
exceptionally intelligent and very
strong minded': this description of
Josselson, who was working for the
Office of Policy Coordination, the
covert operations wing of the CIA,
is in Jerzy Giedroyc, *Autobiografia*

na cztery ręce. In the same passage Giedroyc described meeting Irving Brown, an individual with whom he 'maintained a very good relationship'. For more on Brown, see p. 171.

62. Details of the deal agreed between Giedroyc and the CIA are from Jones, *A Covert Action*. Jones reports that the Poles met two officers from the OPC, who offered an annual subsidy of 'nearly $10,000' – roughly $130,000 in 2025 prices – from the spring of 1950. 'Support to Kultura was one of the CIA's early political covert action operations,' Jones writes, 'and it was given the cryptonym QRBERETTA.' Benjamin J. Fischer, in interviews with the author, said Giedroyc's longstanding work for the CIA 'was an open secret . . . but everybody agreed just not to talk about it because he was doing God's work. Leave him alone.' According to Paweł Sowiński ('The Paris "Kultura" in the Light of the Newest American Studies), Giedroyc's deal with the CIA symbolized the beginning of the book programme for Eastern Europe since it predated by several years the Free Europe Committee's experiments with sending literature across the Iron Curtain.

63. 'proprietorship': see 'Paper Prepared in the Central Intelligence Agency for the Special Activities Working Group', Washington, DC, 4 February 1977 (*Foreign Relations of the United States, 1977–1980*, Vol. XX: *Eastern Europe*). This states that 'It is doubtful that they [the Polish journal, i.e. *Kultura*] would be permitted to continue operation . . . if U.S. proprietorship were acknowledged.'

63. 'Go tell BERETTA': author interview with sources.

63. 'I had always maintained': Giedroyc, *Autobiografia na cztery ręce.*

63. On increasing Agency subsidy over the years, see e.g. 'Paper Prepared in the Central Intelligence Agency for the Special Activities Working Group', 4 February 1977, in *Foreign Relations of the United States, 1977–1980*, Vol. XX: *Eastern Europe*, which refers to the CIA giving $115,000 in 1977 to 'a literary institute in France which publishes a monthly Polish language magazine and selected books directed at Polish intellectuals and youth'.

63. 'What bothers me about this project': 'Memorandum for Chief, SA, Subject: QRDYNAMIC', 20 April 1973, available at https://www.cia.gov/readingroom/, accessed September 2024.

Chapter 5. They Will Crush Us Like Bugs

65. Both Arthur M. Schlesinger Jr and his father, Arthur M. Schlesinger Sr, wrote about the oscillation theory of history, but it was Jr who worked more closely with the CIA. A 1968 book-distribution report lists two works of his that were being distributed by the Agency that year, *The Politics of Upheaval* and *The Age of Roosevelt*, Vol. III. He was also involved with the Congress for Cultural Freedom, and his work was published by the CIA-funded journal *Encounter*.

65. Chojecki's movements that August were recounted in interviews with the author.

66. Details of the 1970 events in Gdańsk are drawn from Timothy Garton Ash, *The Polish Revolution*, and Neal Ascherson, *The Polish August.*

67. 'A commotion had suddenly erupted': Kazimierz Brandys, *A Warsaw Diary, 1978–1981.*

67. 'To the workers of the Gdańsk Shipyard': 'Odezwa Komitetu Założycielskiego Wolnych Związków Zawodowych Wybrzeża i redakcji *Robotnika Wybrzeża* . . . do pracowników Stoczni Gdańskiej' ['Proclamation from the Founding Committee of the Free Trade Unions of the Coast and the editors of *Coastal Worker* to the workers of the Gdańsk Shipyard'], from the Karta library, available at https://dlibra. karta.org.pl/dlibra/publication/3709/ edition/3548/content, accessed September 2024. Siobhan Doucette, *Books Are Weapons*, states that Borusewicz had about 12,000 flyers printed and several posters.

68. 'Remember me?': Garton Ash, *The Polish Revolution.*

68. 'sit in the corner and drink his tea': author interviews with Chojecki.

68. 'internal charisma': ibid.

69. 'If you abandon us we'll be lost': Garton Ash, *The Polish Revolution*, and 'Ukazała się biografia Henryki Krzywonos' ['A biography of Henryka Krzywonos has been published'], PAP [Polish Press Agency], available at https:// dzieje.pl/aktualnosci/ukazala-sie- biografia-henryki-krzywonos, accessed September 2024.

69. 'Close the gates!': from Dorota Karaś, 'Anna Walentynowicz i Alina Pienkowska. Buntowniczki, które przestały byc przyjaciółkami' ['Anna Walentynowicz and Alina Pienkowska. Rebels who ceased to be friends'], *Gazeta Wyborcza* [Election Gazette], 13 August 2021. Biographical information about Pienkowska is from Arkadiusz Kazański, *Alina Pienkowska-Borusewicz.*

70. 'in solidarity': author interviews with Chojecki. Chojecki said he toured other plants that evening with the activist Andrzej Gwiazda.

71. 'You know what happened when they abolished censorship in Czechoslovakia?': Garton Ash, *The Polish Revolution.*

71. 'Respect for the freedom of speech': ibid. The full list of twenty-one demands is at https://en.wikipedia. org/wiki/21_demands_of_MKS, accessed September 2024.

71. The editor-in-chief of the Gdańsk *Solidarity Strike Information Bulletin* was Konrad Bieliński. In interviews, Chojecki said that at first they hadn't wanted to use the shipyard print shop because 'we shouldn't break any locks . . . we're honest strikers, you know, not criminals', but Andrzej Kołodziej at the Paris Commune yard showed them the way. Details of the bulletin's content and print run are from Doucette, *Books Are Weapons*, as are the activities of NOWa printers during the strike.

72. The moment Alina Pienkowska stood up and called for Chojecki's release can be seen in the documentary *Robotnicy '80* [Workers '80], directed by Andrzej Chodakowski and Andrzej Zajączkowski. Details of Chojecki's conversation with prison officers were provided by Chojecki in interviews with the author.

73. Details of the scene when the agreement was reached – including the statue of Lenin and Wałęsa's oversized pen, are from Garton Ash, *The Polish Revolution*, and Ascherson, *The Polish August.*

74. 'the most significant development in Eastern Europe': Garton Ash, *The Polish Revolution.*

75. Grzegorz Boguta attested that it was impossible to raise a toast in Chojecki's apartment. Author interviews, October 2021 and February 2022.

75. 'I had argued that the masses in Poland were passive': Brandys, *A Warsaw Diary, 1978–1981*.

75. 'the notion of "illegal" publishing': Barańczak, cited in Doucette, *Books Are Weapons*.

75. The post-Gdańsk Agreement boom in independent publishing in Poland is documented by Doucette, ibid. She also states that the first unabridged *Gulag Archipelago* in the Soviet Bloc was published by Toruń Independent Office and has details of the NOWa gathering in October 1980.

76. For the activities of Marian Kaleta and Captain 'Edek' Waszkiewicz see Kaleta's memoir *Emigrancka spółka 'Szmugiel'* [The Émigré Smuggling Company].

Chapter 6. The Deal

79. Chojecki related details of his journey to Frankfurt in interviews with the author.

79. Frankfurt hosted Germany's most important book fair from the fifteenth to seventeenth centuries, and the fair was revived in 1949. My portrait of it in the 1980s is informed by author interviews with Chojecki, Boguta, Józef Lebenbaum, Tomasz Łabędź and Felicity Rubinstein, and by Nicole Zand, 'La 33e Foire du livre de Francfort', *Le Monde*, 26 October 1981. See also Brigitte Weeks, 'Letter from the Frankfurt Book Fair', *Washington Post*, 23 October 1983.

81. 'handbook used by Poland's censors': John Tagliabue, 'Dissidents' Books at Frankfurt Fair', *New York Times*, 15 October 1981.

82. 'the number one issue in the world': Kaleta, *Emigrancka spółka 'Szmugiel'*.

82. Kaleta describes the funding of the independent publishers' stand, ibid., stating that 'The Frankfurt Fair was always arranged by Andrzej Chilecki together with Polonia Publishing House, headed by Andrzej Stypułkowski.' Chilecki was West Germany representative for Polonia, a CIA front. Kaleta continues: 'All the big underground publishers were represented: NOWa, of course, Spotkania, ABC from Kraków, Krąg, and Bratniak from Gdańsk. Andrzej Chilecki had special funds to help them, and I distributed the money.' For more details of the links between Minden and the Polish Cultural Foundation, Aneks (run by Eugeniusz Smolar), and Odnowa (run by Jerzy Kulczycki), see GCMP.

82. NOWa reprinting Literary Institute titles: Giedroyc wrote to Jan Nowak-Jeziorański on 22 October 1981: 'At present there are already over 50 [Kultura] items reprinted by independent publishing houses [in Poland].' Jan Nowak-Jeziorański and Jerzy Giedroyc, *Listy, 1952–1998* [Letters, 1952–1998].

82. 'the boss': The full quote, given by Chojecki to the author in February 2021, is: 'I believe that America and Reagan, who was the boss at the time, so head of it all . . . in the fight between these two big interests [East and West] . . . I am on the side of democracy.'

83. 'one of the few people in whom I have confidence': Giedroyc letter to Nowak-Jeziorański, 10 August 1981, in Nowak-Jeziorański and Giedroyc, *Listy, 1952–1998*.

83. 'lower than in Hong Kong': Giedroyc to Nowak-Jeziorański, 22 October 1981, ibid. The $20–$30 average wage is calculated at black-market exchange rates.

84. 'fundamental breakthrough in the relations between the émigré and national opposition': Giedroyc to Nowak-Jeziorański, 22 October 1981, ibid.

84. 'arrange publishing issues': Giedroyc to Nowak-Jeziorański, 10 August 1981, ibid.

84. On arranging Chojecki's permission to enter the US without a valid passport, Chojecki (author interviews) said he flew first to Canada, where his entry was arranged by a friend who worked at the Polish Canadian Association. His journey to Washington from there was assisted by Nowak or Brzezinski or both. He also said his flight to America was paid for by Giedroyc.

84. Minden described his Paris visit in October–November 1981, and his preferred accommodation in general, in his European Trip Reports, GCMP.

85. The Librairie Polonaise's role in CIA book distribution is detailed in Minden's European Trip Reports, 1980–90, GCMP, and in 'Report by Gen. Bryg. Zdzisław Sarewicz, Chief of Polish Foreign Intelligence on the Use of Paris-Based Polish Bookstore by the CIA-Funded International Literary Center', 12 February 1984, History and Public Policy Program Digital Archive, AIPN, collection number IPN BU 0449/32/5 cz. 2, available at http://digitalarchive.wilsoncenter.org/document/121673, accessed September 2024. Poles could also order deliveries, which the bookstore disguised by calling itself 'Bookstore 123' on the official forms.

86. 'Boguta and Chojecki live at Maisons Laffitte!': For this and Minden's other notes on the Chojecki–Boguta meeting see European Trip Reports, 1981, GCMP.

87. 'I offered Minden a better deal': author interview with Grzegorz Boguta, February 2022.

88. 'We had different histories': ibid.

Chapter 7. The Night of the General

91. 'Pietrek, what sort of man are you': this poem, written a few days after the pacification operation at Wujek, was first published anonymously in Tygodnik Mazowsze [Mazovia Weekly], 15 December 1983. It is included in Anna Bikont, 'Kopalnia Wujek Miners', in Jacek Kołtan and Ewa Konarowska (eds), European Solidarity Centre Permanent Exhibition: Anthology. Bikont identifies the author as Michał B. Jagiełło, a teacher and translator from Łodz.

91. The Łuczywos' movements on 12 December and after are drawn from author interviews with Helena and Witek conducted between 2021 and 2023.

91. 'Dark Circles': Shana Penn, in Solidarity's Secret.

92. Climate conditions are from weatherspark.com.

92. As well as to the author, Witek Łuczywo told the story of the elastic in Zlatkes, Sowiński and Frenkel (eds), Duplicator Underground.

93. Many details from that night, including the goings-on inside the Mazovia Solidarity building, are drawn from Gabriel Meretik's La Nuit du général, and from Tomasz Urzykowski and Jerzy

S. Majewski's hour-by-hour account of the night, 'Niedziela, 13 grudnia 1981' ['Sunday, 13 December 1981'], *Gazeta Wyborcza* [Election Gazette], 13 December 2021.

93. had raided a cinema: Meretik, *La Nuit du général*, reports that two or three hundred Zomos were seen at the Klub cinema around 3 p.m.

93. 'The Zomos are here!': ibid.

94. 'Why on earth would I go back?': author interviews with Helena Łuczywo.

94. *Captain Blood*: Witek (in interview) was specific that he thought of this French-Italian swashbuckler from 1960 while hiding from the police.

94. Paweł Śpiewak: a Polish sociologist, and co-founder in 1979 of the underground quarterly *Res Publica*.

95. Primate's palace: it would take roughly an hour to walk from Helena's parents' building to the palace, on Miodowa.

95. let the Poles crush Solidarity themselves: a full insider's account of the negotiations and planning for martial law was provided by Ryszard Kukliński in an interview first published in *Kultura* in 1987. It was reprinted as 'The Suppression of Solidarity' in Robert Kostrzewa (ed.), *Between East and West*. See also Mark Kramer (ed.), *Soviet Deliberations during the Polish Crisis, 1980–1981*.

96. the final order to go: timings are from Meretik, *La Nuit du général*. See also Andrzej Paczkowski, 'The Night of the General', in Kołtan and Konarowska (eds), *European Solidarity Centre Permanent Exhibition: Anthology*.

96. even the odd Party member: arrested communists included Edward Gierek, the Polish premier through the 1970s. Garton Ash, *The Polish Revolution*.

97. 'I have already been . . . in Auschwitz': this was said by Professor Klemens Szaniawski, cited in Tomasz Urzykowski, 'Rzucały się na nas wilczury na smyczy' ['We were threatened by wolves on leashes'], *Gazeta Wyborcza*, 13 December 2021.

97. Jerzy Zieleński: the account of his death is in Meretik, *La Nuit du général*.

97. Boguta had been out for dinner: author interviews.

98. Adam Michnik arrested: Urzykowski and Majewski, 'Niedziela, 13 grudnia 1981', and Meretik, *La Nuit du général*.

98. 'They thought they were going to their deaths': Urzykowski and Majewski, 'Niedziela, 13 grudnia 1981'.

98. The Monopol, Grand and Heweliusz: Meretik, *La Nuit du général*. Other details of the Gdańsk arrests are from Michael Kaufman, *Mad Dreams, Saving Graces*.

98. Jacek Kuroń's mock execution: Meretik, *La Nuit du général*.

99. 'Once resistance had meant taking up a gun': Kaufman, *Mad Dreams, Saving Graces*.

100. *This is Polish Radio Warsaw*: there are several versions of Jaruzelski's speech online, including excerpts in 'Text of Polish martial law declaration', UPI, available at https://www.upi.com/Archives/1981/12/13/Text-of-Polish-martial-law-declaration/5129377067600/, accessed September 2024. The speech can also be found on YouTube. The line *We shall consistently purge Polish life of evil* is in Garton Ash, *The Polish Revolution*.

101. 'socialist allies and friends': Gregory Domber, in *Empowering Revolution*,

states, 'Brezhnev called Jaruzelski [on 13 December] to congratulate him, and he expressed "his warm feelings towards [Poland] and stated that we have effectively engaged the fight against the counterrevolution. They were difficult decisions, but appropriate ones".' Jaruzelski himself said his public announcement had 'met with high acclaim' in Moscow.

102. 'What a beautiful day': These were the words of the journalist Hanna Krall, cited in Meretik, *La Nuit du général*.

102. IBM typesetting machine: Witek called this their 'biggest treasure' in interview.

103. 'weakening the defence preparedness': new crimes and punishments were set out in Council of State of the Polish People's Republic's 'Obwieszczenie o wprowadzeniu stanu wojennego ze względu na bezpieczeństwo państwa' ['Proclamation of martial law for reasons of national security'], 13 December 1981.

103. The Łuczywos' daughter, Łucja: Helena recalled details of the arrangements she made with her mother, Dorota, in interviews with the author.

104. Meeting in Żoliborz: several details of this and the establishment of the Damska Grupa Operacyjna are from Penn, *Solidarity's Secret*.

105. 'a brilliant manager': author interviews with Helena Łuczywo.

105. 'hang an axe in it': Tomasz Chlebowski, unpublished memoir.

105. 'That's our ammunition': This and much of the detail of the first *Solidarity Information* newsletter are from an author interview with Joanna Szczęsna, February 2022.

106. 'You Who Wronged': this 1950 poem can be found in Czesław

Miłosz, *The Collected Poems, 1931–1987*.

106. 'If your name is public': author interviews with Helena Łuczywo.

107. 'find the men': Penn, *Solidarity's Secret*.

107. Brutal clashes in Silesia: see Bikont, 'Kopalnia Wujek Miners', and Andrzej Paczkowski, 'The Night of the General'. Other sources include Robert Ciupa and Sebastian Reńca (eds), *Wujek '81. Relacje* [Wujek '81: Accounts].

108. one young man was killed: this was Antoni Browarczyk, who was hit in the head by a militia bullet on 17 December.

108. Bujak and Kulerski: a detailed account of Ewa Kulik's operation to recover the two leaders is in Penn, *Solidarity's Secret*.

Chapter 8. This Is Big Casino

111. 'Martial Law Carol' by Joseph Brodsky: cited in Agnieszka Niegowska (ed.), *It All Began in Poland*.

111. Nowak met Chojecki at the airport: interviews with the author.

112. 'This is independent Poland': apart from Chojecki's recollection, details of the house at that time are in Paul Hendrickson, 'Sorrows of Another Poland', *Washington Post*, 24 September 1982.

112. They married on the thirty-seventh day: Jan Nowak-Jeziorański, *Courier from Warsaw*.

112. Pope shaving to RFE broadcasts: for this and other anecdotes from Nowak's life, see 'A Knight Passes', by Nowak's friend George Weigel, available at https://eppc.org/publication/a-knight-passes/, accessed September 2024, and Radio Free Europe's obituary, 'Legendary RFE Polish Service Director Jan Nowak Dead at

91', 21 January 2005, available at https://about.rferl.org/article/legendary-rfe-polish-service-director-jan-nowak-dead-at-91/, accessed September 2024.

112. 'Uncle' and 'Aunt': this detail, along with accounts of his visits to the State Department, was recalled in Chojecki interviews with the author.

113. 'a feverish intensity': Lynn Darling, 'Outside Looking Back', *Washington Post*, 18 December 1981.

113. 'No way will there be martial law': Chojecki interviews with the author.

113. On the night of 12 December 1981, Chojecki was visiting his friend Tadeusz Walendowski, who lived in Arlington, VA. He recalled this and other details of the night in interviews with the author.

114. Kaleta's recollections of the night are captured in *Emigrancka spółka 'Szmugiel'* [The Émigré Smuggling Company].

115. 'I just thought I've got to do something': author interviews with Lebenbaum.

115. '[Chojecki] would be our beacon': Kaleta, *Emigrancka spółka 'Szmugiel'*.

115. 'Psychologically unbearable': this description and other details are from the transcript of an interview with Chojecki by Maciej Piotr Prus, 27 June 1987, Instytut Literacki/Institut Littéraire, Paris.

115. Helsinki Watch press conference: see Dan Collins, 'Polish dissident says Polish crackdown harsher than Nazi occupation', UPI, 15 December 1981, https://www.upi.com/Archives/1981/12/15/Polish-dissident-says-Polish-crackdown-harsher-than-Nazi-occupation/4332377240400/, accessed September 2024.

116. 'hollow from the news': Darling, 'Outside Looking Back'.

116. his name appeared in the *New York Times*: Associated Press, 'Unionists and Dissidents Reported Held in Poland', *New York Times*, 17 December 1981.

116. he flew to Switzerland: according to Gregory Domber, in 'The AFL-CIO, the Reagan Administration and Solidarność', Chojecki travelled to Zurich on 19 December, and to Brussels for 8–9 January for a second meeting with those caught abroad during martial law. Trade unions were heavily involved by this stage. The Zurich meeting, Chojecki said in an interview, was organized by Stefan Nędzyński, a Polish survivor of Stalin's labour camps, who led the Postal, Telegraph and Telephone International labour union (PTTI), and by Jan Kułakowski, a veteran of the Warsaw Uprising, who in 1981 was general secretary of the World Confederation of Labour (WCL). The Brussels trip in January was paid for by AFL-CIO, which gave Chojecki $575 to make the round trip. This, according to Domber, was AFL-CIO's 'first direct payment to support [the New York Solidarity committee's] more conspiratorial activities'. During the first year of the Brussels Solidarity office's operations, the AFL-CIO would provide around $200,000.

116. newsletters . . . were already reaching them: according to Meretik, *La Nuit du général*, the first train left Warsaw for Paris on 16 December, carrying images of the crackdown which a young photographer had hidden in a sandwich and placed in a rubbish bin. Polish friends searched the

train at the Gare du Nord and found the images.

116. gave evidence to Congress: see United States Congress, Commission on Security and Cooperation in Europe, 'The Crisis in Poland and its Effects on the Helsinki Process'.

117. 'Everybody was obviously very kind': author interviews with Chojecki.

117. US government in disarray: the locations of key administration officials are drawn from Meretik, *La Nuit du général*.

118. 'was one of the people from Solidarity who misled the government': Jonathan Kwitny, *Man of the Century*. Chojecki said he did not remember the Pipes call.

118. highest-placed spy in the Eastern Bloc: Tim Weiner, in *Legacy of Ashes*, describes Kukliński as 'the highest-ranking source that the agency had behind the iron curtain'. According to the CIA's Robert Gates, Kukliński's information was 'critical to us all through 1981' (*From the Shadows*).

118. 'The Polish Government appears to be prepared': Intelligence Information Special Report, 'Current Status of Preparations for Martial Law in Poland', 7 October 1981, available at https://www.cia.gov/readingroom/docs/1981-10-07.pdf, accessed September 2024.

118. Evacuating Kukliński: details of the operation are from Ben Weiser, *A Secret Life: The Polish Colonel, His Covert Mission, and the Price He Paid to Save His Country*, cited in Michael Keller, 'Kukliński: How the CIA's Best-Placed Cold War Spy Escaped the Eastern Bloc', culture.pl, July 2017, available at https://culture.pl/en/article/kuklinski-how-the-cias-best-placed-cold-war-spy-escaped-the-eastern-bloc, accessed September 2024. Huw Dylan, David V. Gioe and Michael S. Goodman's *The CIA and the Pursuit of Security* has a good assessment of Kukliński's impact.

119. Kukliński's sons would be killed in separate, mysterious accidents: one was run down by a truck with no licence plate; another drowned after his yacht capsized in a quiet sea.

119. dinner at the Nowaks': my reconstruction of this evening is based on interviews with Chojecki.

119. 'absolutely surprised': this and other remarks about Casey's appointment are in Weiner, *Legacy of Ashes*.

119. 'Wild Bill' Donovan: for a potted biography, see Central Intelligence Agency, 'The Legend of Wild Bill: How Donovan Got His Nickname', available at https://www.cia.gov/stories/story/the-legend-of-wild-bill-how-donovan-got-his-nickname/, accessed September 2024.

120. 'freelance buccaneer': this was coined by Admiral Bobby Ray Inman, who served as Casey's deputy, cited in Weiner, *Legacy of Ashes*.

120. 'screw it up': Gates, *From the Shadows*.

120. real anger in Washington: according to Pipes, cited in Gregory Domber, *Empowering Revolution*, 'Real rage dominated after the declaration of martial law . . . The president erupted. It was a fantastic meeting.'

120. 'the first time in sixty years': National Security Council Meeting minutes, 21 December 1981, available in Executive Secretariat, NSC, NSC 00033, Box 91283, Ronald Reagan Presidential Library.

121. speech to the nation: Ronald Reagan, 'Address to the Nation about Christmas and the Situation in Poland', available at https://www.reaganlibrary.gov/archives/speech/address-nation-about-christmas-and-situation-poland, accessed September 2024.

122. He was relieved: author interviews with Chojecki.

122. the tree in front of Rockefeller Center made him morose: ibid.

122. Soros's typesetter: ibid.

122. 'I feel terrible in America': Chojecki letter to Jerzy Giedroyc, 31 December 1981, Instytut Literacki/Institut Littéraire, Paris.

122. two job offers: ibid., and author interviews with Chojecki. Stypułkowski had died on 25 November 1981. Chojecki described the individuals who offered him the Polonia job as 'people who didn't speak Polish, only English', and said the offer was made in New York. He said he didn't know for certain that Polonia was a CIA front at the time, but 'that's what I presumed'. The Radio Free Europe offer came via the writer and RFE cultural commentator Tadeusz Nowakowski.

123. 'What do you think of or know about Andrzej Stypułkowski's connections?': Chojecki letter to Jerzy Giedroyc, 31 December 1981, Instytut Literacki/Institut Littéraire, Paris.

123. 'Chojecki – stipend': Jerzy Giedroyc, diary entry, 6 January 1982, Instytut Literacki/Institut Littéraire, Paris.

Chapter 9. Citizens versus the Secret Police

125. 'And Tomorrow You'll Not Even Find a Trace' by Natalya Gorbanevskaya: *Poetry*, July 1974, available at https://www.poetryfoundation.org/poetrymagazine/browse?volume=124&issue=4&page=27, accessed September 2024.

125. wasn't the type to cry often: author interviews with Helena Łuczywo. Her memory of it being a cold winter is borne out by weatherspark.com and by the fact that an ice-jam blocked the Vistula that year.

126. snitches had been reinvigorated: Marek Nowakowski, *The Canary and Other Tales of Martial Law*, first published in Polish as *Raport o stanie wojennym* [Report on Martial Law] by the Instytut Literacki/Institut Littéraire, Paris – contains accounts of police informants working after December 1981.

126. 'I won't be able to manage': author interviews with Helena Łuczywo.

127. 'the jobs no one else wanted to do': Penn, *Solidarity's Secret*.

127. 'Flying Universities': see Jan Józef Lipski, *KOR*, which states that this tradition dated from the turn of the twentieth century. The name reflected the fact that the university had to move from place to place in order to hide from the Russian secret police.

127. worked and slept in the same place: Penn, *Solidarity's Secret*.

128. Hosting wasn't something people did lightly: author interview with Joanna Szczęsna, February 2022.

128. 'Wherever I went in hiding, people would welcome me': ibid.

129. The Łuczywos' marriage would not survive: author interviews with Helena Łuczywo.

129. 'I was a woman, educated, and a well-known oppositionist': Penn, *Solidarity's Secret*.

130. Details of Tomasz Chlebowski's life in the underground are drawn from an author interview, November 2021, and from Chlebowski's unpublished memoir.
131. *The Little Conspirator* (Polish: *Mały konspirator*) by Czesław Bielecki, Urszula Sikorska and Jan Krzysztof Kelus was translated by Roman M. Boreyko and André YaDeau and published in *Conflict Quarterly*, Fall 1986. CDN is the Polish acronym for 'To Be Continued'. *Little Conspirators* published in the West included a reprint in London in the journal *Puls* [Pulse], No. 18, June 1983. *Puls* was originally a NOWa quarterly which resurfaced in London after being shut down by the security forces.
132. 'stupid little moustache': Penn, *Solidarity's Secret*.
132. Bujak's make-up sessions: Chlebowski, unpublished memoir.
132. fewer than 5 per cent of the uncensored periodicals produced in 1981 would survive to 1982: Siobhan Doucette, *Books Are Weapons*, states that 'of the estimated 1,896 independent periodical titles published in 1981, only 82 were still in print in 1982'.
133. SB operations against the church: see Antoni Dudek and Andrzej Paczkowski, 'Poland'. The SB's Department IV was established in 1962 to dealt with the Catholic church and other religious organizations.
134. they had to take the chance: author interview with Witek Łuczywo.
134. the 'Three Musketeers': author interviews with Grzegorz Boguta. See also Maciej Radziwill, 'Trzech wolnych drukarzy' ['Three NOWa printers'], *Gazeta Wyborcza* [Election Gazette], 6 January 2022.

Chapter 10. Raphael
135. 'Our nation's like a living volcano': from the Charles Kraszewski translation of Mickiewicz's *Forefathers' Eve*.
135. the Poles and the French: further evidence of their connection can be found in the Polish national anthem, 'Poland Is Not Yet Lost', where Napoleon is the only non-Pole referenced. The lyric runs: *Dał nam przykład Bonaparte / Jak zwyciężać mamy*, 'Bonaparte has given us the example / Of how we should prevail.'
136. A quarter of a million people marched: Meretik, *La Nuit du général*.
136. barely a couch to sleep on: Kaleta, *Emigrancka spółka 'Szmugiel'* [The Émigré Smuggling Company]. Chojecki was put up by Marc (sometimes Marek) Franciszkowski, whom Minden described as a 'young Paris businessman'.
136. Solidarity in Paris: author interviews with Tomasz Łabędź, 2021 and 2022, and with Seweryn Blumsztajn, 2021.
136. Communications with Poland: interviews with Łabędź and Blumsztajn, ibid. As well as using the trains, the Paris Poles would receive messages through the diplomatic bag, sent by a cultural attaché Blumsztajn knew, and via travelling journalists.
137. 'Everybody knew what I did before': author interviews with Chojecki.
137. On Giedroyc's help finding him finance, Chojecki said: 'Giedroyc took it very seriously to make sure that I had some sort of financial support.'
137. 'extremely depressed': Rudzki letter to Giedroyc, 21 December 1981, Instytut Literacki/Institut Littéraire, Paris.

138. 'pure Soviet agent': Rudzki letter to Giedroyc, 21 January 1982, Instytut Literacki/Institut Littéraire, Paris.

138. heart problems: Rudzki seems to have become aware of his heart condition in March or April, and informed Giedroyc. In a letter of 29 April 1982 (Instytut Literacki/Institut Littéraire, Paris), the Editor wrote, 'I was very upset to hear of your illness and the need to postpone your annual pastoral visit.'

138. Giedroyc dispensed significant amounts: on the question of where this money originated, the former CIA chief historian Benjamin Fischer stated that it is 'a reasonable assumption to make that he was acting as a "cut out" [CIA intermediary] at this time'. At one moment Minden, who had a sometimes spiky relationship with the Editor, complained to the CIA about the way he dispensed money, writing in his trip report in June 1982, 'How can Giedroyc give prizes to the friends of Kultura out of the money he receives to help Poland?' GCMP.

138. '5,000d for Bujak': Giedroyc diary entry for Thursday 15 April 1982, Instytut Literacki/Institut Littéraire, Paris.

138. 'an incredible, *incredible* amount of money': author interviews with Helena Łuczywo. According to Chojecki, $25 was a monthly salary in Poland at that time. For more on exchange rates, see note to p. 13. Witek Łuczywo said he thought *Tygodnik Mazowsze* [Mazovia Weekly] received more than $1,000 a month because he remembered distributing an additional $500 monthly to printers. On the methods Giedroyc used to transfer funds to Poland, the SB noted, in a Carter-era intelligence assessment:

'The Instytut Literacki finances the activities of a significant proportion of anti-socialist elements in the country. It does so through direct payments (on the occasion of stays of "opposition activists" in the West, or transfers of substantial sums of money to Poland by third parties), and also indirectly – inspired by J. Giedroyc – in the form of the granting of literary and artistic prizes by the institute and other Western foundations, honoraria for manuscripts received by the editorial office, material assistance in the form of parcels, as well as the arranging of scholarships and trips abroad.' 'Główne kierunki działania wrogich ośrodków dywersji ideologicznej przeciwko Polsce' ['Main lines of action of hostile centres of ideological diversion against Poland'], IPN BU 0 1738/36, AIPN.

138. 'awful things': in Chile, the CIA supported the military coup which overturned the election of Salvador Allende, leading to Allende's death and the long-running dictatorship of General Augusto Pinochet.

139. 'we probably got the money from the CIA': author interviews with Helena Łuczywo. For more on the CIA's funding of *Tygodnik Mazowsze*, see Jones, *A Covert Action*, which states that the underground paper received 'covert assistance' from the CIA, support that continued under QRHELPFUL. Fischer, in 'Repudiating Yalta', states that 'CIA money also went to *Tygodnik Mazowsze*, a four-page weekly newspaper with circulation of 50,000 that provided excellent cover because of paid subscriptions.'

139. 'Mr. Editor, the matter is banally simple': Kaleta, *Emigrancka spółka 'Szmugiel'*.

139. instructed him to set up a monthly magazine: author interviews with Chojecki.

140. Rudzki agreed to regular purchases: on 23 April 1982 Rudzki wrote to tell Giedroyc he had received a request from Chojecki to buy *Kontakt* and had sent his response.

140. 'All the people who were active in Kontakt': author interviews with Chojecki.

140. Polish Publishing and Culture Fund: a handwritten sketch of the plan is in the Instytut Literacki/ Institut Littéraire, Paris.

140. *Preuves* 'was unmistakably the house organ of the [Congress for Cultural Freedom], giving it a voice as well as advertising its activities and programmes', according to Stonor Saunders, *Who Paid the Piper?* She states that the CIA had 'an involvement' in publishing Jeleński's *History and Hope: Progress in Freedom.*

140. 'a long-time collaborator': 'Główne kierunki działania wrogich ośrodków dywersji ideologicznej przeciwko Polsce', IPN BU 0 1738/36, AIPN.

140. Francis X. Sutton in Paris: see Konstanty Jeleński, 'Fundusz pomocy niezależny literaturze i nauce polskiej / Informacji bieżące do wiadomości ścisłego Komitetu Wykonawczego /' ['Fund to assist independent Polish literature and science / Current information for the attention of the close Executive Committee /'], 1 April 1982, Instytut Literacki/Institut Littéraire, Paris.

140. $28,000 a year: this was in 1984, listed as 'Stipend for Fund's secretary, Mirosław Chojecki',

with additional allowances for travel, stationery, phone calls, etc, in 'Financial Statement, Final Report', 26 December 1984, Instytut Literacki/Institut Littéraire, Paris.

141. Was Ford a channel for CIA money? According to Rudzki's son, Marek, the Ford Foundation was happy for the ILC to use their name to send books to the east (Marek Rudzki, 'Akcja masowych przekazów' ['Mass transfers action']). Stonor Saunders, *Who Paid the Piper?*, details other Ford links with the CIA.

141. 'knows nothing about the economic side': 'Plan for Cultural Defence', 10 March 1982, Instytut Literacki/ Institut Littéraire, Paris.

141. CIA funding from the PTTI: in interviews, Chojecki set out how he collected money from the bank in Lignon, Geneva. He said he didn't know this cash was from the CIA at the time, but only later, when Nędzyński told him that was the case. Philip Agee, *Inside the Company*, names Joseph Beirne and William Doherty as principal US intelligence agents inside the PTTI.

141. Foundation for European Mutual Intellectual Assistance: the SB described the foundation as having been established on the initiative of 'the CIA-funded "International Association for Cultural Freedom"', and its officer, Konstanty Jeleński, as 'a long-time collaborator of the CIA' ('Główne kierunki działania wrogich ośrodków dywersji ideologicznej przeciwko Polsce', IPN BU 0 1738/36, AIPN).

141. 3,000 French francs: author interviews with Chojecki.

142. 'honeypot': Kaleta, *Emigrancka spółka 'Szmugiel'*.

142. 'small explosive devices': 'Spis rzeczy, o ktore prosi Gdańsk' ['List

of items requested by Gdansk'], February 1982, Instytut Literacki/Institut Littéraire, Paris.

142. 'golf ball' typing heads: author interviews with Łabędź.

143. Radio Solidarity: author interviews with Chojecki. Gates, in *From the Shadows*, said the CIA 'sponsored' Radio Solidarity. Andrzej Friszke (ed.), *Solidarność Podziemna, 1981–1989* [Solidarity Underground, 1981–1989], details the origins of the station.

143. humanitarian supplies: the estimate of 1,500 charitable transports is from Kaleta, *Emigrancka spółka 'Szmugiel'*. In interviews Chojecki set out how he worked with the transports and how he used a falsified Swedish passport.

144. A shopping list: message from 'Witek' to Kaleta, 10 August 1982, Instytut Literacki/Institut Littéraire, Paris.

Chapter 11. Ideas for Getting Out of a No-Win Situation

147. 'If we are to believe': from Kuroń's essay 'Tezy o wyjściu z sytuacji bez wyjścia' ['Ideas for Getting Out of a No-Win Situation'], published variously in *Tygodnik Mazowsze* [Mazovia Weekly], 31 March 1982, in the January/February 1982 issue of *Kultura*, and in *Aneks*, No. 27 (1982).

148. interview with Bujak and Kulerski: Chlebowski, unpublished memoir.

149. Details of the production cycle are largely from author interview with Witek Łuczywo, February 2022. Witek said the press was located in Radość; other sources, such as Wojciech Borowik (ed.), *N jak Nowa* [N for Nowa], say Falenica, but these suburbs are very close.

151. 'What is a pole?': Jan Olaszek, ' "Tygodnik Mazowsze" – prasa

w konspiracji' ['*Mazovia Weekly* – press in conspiracy'], *Polityka*, 4 March 2012, https://www.polityka.pl/tygodnikpolityka/historia/1524447,1,tygodnik-mazowsze---prasa-w-konspiracji.read, accessed September 2024.

151. 'Absent from the funeral': 'Słowo o Jerzym Zieleńskim' ['A word about Jerzy Zieleński'], *Tygodnik Mazowsze*, 11 February 1982.

151. 'to create basic connections': 'To było jedno z naszych wielkich powstań narodowych' ['It was one of our great national uprisings'], ibid.

152. Michnik's smuggling: author interview with Adam Michnik, October 2021. For Minden's promotion of Michnik see e.g. European Trip Reports, 19 November 1987: 'I told [Barbara Torunczyk] . . . that we would also buy at least 200 copies of Michnik's book.'

153. 'You needed thousands of people': author interviews with Helena Łuczywo.

153. 'I don't mean that there weren't independent groups': Bujak is cited in Penn, *Solidarity's Secret*.

153. eclipsing other newsletters: titles such as *Tygodnik Wojenny* [War Weekly] were 'increasingly pushed to the background', according to Andrzej Friszke (ed.), *Solidarność Podziemna, 1981–1989* [Solidarity Underground, 1981–1989].

153. multiple publishing houses: author interview with Witek Łuczywo. Witek said by summer 1982 there were 'probably a couple of hundred people' working on the paper, which was being printed in fifteen or sixteen plants.

153. circulation: estimates vary widely. Witek believed at its height they were printing 70,000–80,000 copies.

A set of accounts sent to Giedroyc in 1987, which Helena Łuczywo thinks is reliable, states that the circulation was between 8,000 and 12,000 ('*Tygodnik Mazowsze* – zarys funkcjonowania poligrafii i rozliczenie finansowe obejmujace okres od IX 1986 do VIII 1987' ['*Tygodnik Mazowsze* – outline of the operation of the printing works and financial accounts covering the period from September 1986 to August 1987'], Instytut Literacki/ Institut Littéraire, Paris).

154. 'basis of our existence': 'Aprawozdanie finansowe za rok 1987' ['Financial statements for 1987'], Instytut Literacki/Institut Littéraire, Paris.

154. bookkeeper: this was Krystyna Gawarska.

154. 'Giedroyc told us': author interview with Joanna Szczęsna, February 2022.

154. a textbook example of bringing citizens to heel: Mark Kramer, 'The Rise and Fall of Solidarity', *New York Times*, 12 December 2011.

154. 'Ideas for Getting Out of a No-Win Situation': Kuroń, 'Tezy o wyjściu z sytuacji bez wyjścia'.

155. Łuczywo's and Szczęsna's argument: Olaszek, ' "Tygodnik Mazowsze" – prasa w konspiracji'.

155. Forming the TKK: Helena Łuczywo, in interview, said, 'the thing that I was most afraid of was that some people would use violence . . . so it was extremely urgent that they announced that they are the body that coordinates all the actions underground'.

156. 'any confrontation must lead to tragedy': Adam Michnik, *Letters from Prison and Other Essays*.

156. 'The most dangerous spot': Penn, *Solidarity's Secret*.

156. Chojecki formally appointed: Kaleta, *Emigrancka spółkà 'Szmugiel'*.

157. Brussels an obvious target for Eastern spies: See also Patryk Pleskot (ed.), *Solidarność, 'Zachód' i 'Węże'* [Solidarity, the West and Snakes].

Chapter 12. HELPFUL

159. 'Poland is not bounded': cited in Robert Kostzrewa (ed.), *Between East and West*.

159. Casey on the charge: Gates, in *From the Shadows*, writes of his former boss, 'Casey never stopped coming up with ideas – or forwarding those of others – for waging the war against the Soviets more broadly, more aggressively, and more effectively.'

160. Top Kremlinologists in the State Department included Mark Palmer. Jones, in *A Covert Action*, writes that 'Palmer had urged the CIA to expand its ongoing intelligence operations in Poland, such as support to *Kultura*.' Others in the Directorate of Operations believed a new covert programme would have little or no impact.

160. 'It seems to me . . . quite imperative': 'Memorandum from Richard Pipes to William P. Clark, Subject: Statement of U.S. Strategy Toward Soviet Union', 5 March 1982, *Foreign Relations of the United States, 1981–1988*, Vol. III: *Soviet Union, January 1981–January 1983*.

160. Minden's tour in summer 1982 is detailed in his European Trip Reports, GCMP. He first met Chodakowski in May the following year, which is when he remarked on the Anglo-Pole's 'gimmicky ideas'.

160. 'recovering quite quickly': Giedroyc letter to Rudzki, 29 April 1982. For Rudzki's purchases, see e.g. Rudzki letter to Giedroyc, 6 July 1982. In a letter of 26 July, Giedroyc told Rudzki that they must 'put the main

emphasis on miniatures'. Instytut Literacki/Institut Littéraire, Paris.

161. 'to provide modest support': Gates, *From the Shadows*.

161. 'an enhanced covert action for Poland': ibid.

161. done via surrogate cutouts: see Jones, *A Covert Action*.

162. 'Solidarity was the most important development': ibid.

162. The NSC meeting on 4 November: see National Security Planning Group Meeting, Intelligence NSC/ICS 400325, 4 November 1982, available at https://www. reaganlibrary.gov/public/2022-07/ 40-752-81131938-91305-001-2022.pdf, accessed September 2024.

162. QRHELPFUL: Jones, *A Covert Action*.

163. 'The bottom line': CIA Memorandum on Poland, 10 January 1983, available at https://www.cia.gov/ readingroom/docs/CIA-RDP88B00443R001304040163-3.pdf, accessed September 2024.

163. 'printing materials, communications equipment': Gates, *From the Shadows*.

163. QRHELPFUL's budget itemized: Jones, *A Covert Action*.

164. The characterization of the IAD, and of Richard Malzahn, is informed by interviews with Benjamin Fischer.

164. For more on 'active measures' see Fischer, 'Repudiating Yalta'.

164. Cecilia 'Celia' Larkin: author interviews with Fischer, and Jones, *A Covert Action*.

165. $1.5 million in 1983: this, and details of the number of assets and their cryptonyms, are in Jones, *A Covert Action*.

165. Wanda Gawrońska: GCMP and author interviews with Fischer.

166. a landmark op-ed: this was in *Kultura*'s January–February issue, 1983.

167. 'The solutions in this area': Rudzki letter to Giedroyc, 2 February 1983, Instytut Literacki/Institut Littéraire, Paris.

167. QRGUIDE: my identification of Chojecki as the CIA asset QRGUIDE is based on multiple sources. The existence of QRHELPFUL and QRGUIDE was first reported by Seth Jones, a professor at the Center for Strategic and International Studies, in *A Covert Action*. Jones, who told me he did not know QRGUIDE's real identity, gave the asset the pseudonym 'Stanisław Broda' in his book. After publication, a CIA veteran of QRHELPFUL met with Chojecki and told him that he was 'Broda' – aka QRGUIDE. When I ran through the details with Chojecki, he agreed that the pseudonymous asset's description and many of his activities matched his own. A second intelligence source supported the QRGUIDE thesis. That QRGUIDE and Celia Larkin had an 'outstanding' effect on the operation is attested to by Fischer, who told me, 'I have utmost admiration for those people. They really were incredible.'

168. Freedom and Independence Association (WiN): Weiner, *Legacy of Ashes*.

168. 'This is what a person from Eastern Europe knows': author interviews with Fischer.

169. Deniability was key: Gates, *From the Shadows*.

169. Chojecki's meeting with Giedroyc: author interviews with Chojecki.

170. Kaleta's vehicle: Kaleta, *Emigrancka spółka 'Szmugiel'* [The Émigré Smuggling Company].

170. On keeping each other's operations separate: 'There was a rule between us,' Tomasz Łabędź said in interviews, 'even with Giedroyc, that we didn't tell him what we were doing.'

170. 60,000 French francs in 1982 would be worth around $60,000 today.

171. 'I don't believe I ever saw Irving': This was Tom Braden, former head of the CIA's International Organizations Division, cited in Stonor Saunders, *Who Paid the Piper?* According to sources, the CIA did not use American unions or the Brussels office as conduits in this period, although it does appear to have used international labour organizations.

171. anonymous hotel rooms: author interviews with Chojecki. He joked that if his interlocutors had to be either KGB or CIA, he would prefer they were CIA.

171. 'We had this picture here in Poland': author interview with Grzegorz Boguta, February 2022.

172. My account of the fitting out of the Mercedes is based on interviews with Chojecki, Tomasz Łabędź and Jacky Challot. Further details of the vehicle, including some its cargo, are from the SB investigation 'Plan wstępnych czynności do sprawy operacyjnego rozpracowania krypt. Podróżnik' ['Plan of preliminary activities for the case of operational investigation cryptonym Traveller'], published in Radosław Ptaszyński, *Jacky Jean Etienne Challot: Przyjaciel Solidarności* [Jacky Jean Étienne Challot: Friend of Solidarity].

173. 'Jacky for Special Tasks': See e.g. Chojecki's film *Jacky od zadan specjalnych* [Jacky for Special Tasks], dirs: Joanna Jaworska and Catherine Koscielak.

174. 'They said we were crazy': author interviews with Tomasz Łabędź.

174. 'old beds in France were like new beds in Poland': author interviews with Chojecki.

175. 'like entering a drab and disturbing dream': Jan Morris, *Fifty Years of Europe: An Album*.

175. Helmstedt–Marienborn: see Wikipedia, 'Fortifications of the inner German border', https://en.wikipedia.org/wiki/ Fortifications_of_the_inner_ German_border#, accessed September 2024.

176. 'I've come on behalf of Philippe': author interview with Challot.

177. The Chojeckis' life in Paris: author interviews with Chojecki and Jolanta Kessler-Chojecka.

Chapter 13. Oh Sh**! Reactionary Propaganda!

181. Several key opposition figures were released towards the end of 1982, including Lech Wałęsa, in November, but others including Michnik and Kuroń remained in jail. Martial law was suspended on 31 December 1982 and formally rescinded on 22 July 1983, although as Łuczywo points out this made little practical difference.

182. 'sinking underground': author interviews with Helena Łuczywo.

182. 'We had a few very good printers': author interviews with Grzegorz Boguta.

183. My description of the shipment picked up by Władek 'Corduroy' Król is taken from an interview with Król conducted on the author's behalf by Yolanta Łodzińska in December 2021.

186. Details of the kindergarten messaging system: author interviews with Boguta.

187. Weather information from 23 March 1984 is from weatherspark.com.

187. Challot's capture: as well as author interviews with Challot, some of what follows is sourced from Radosław Ptaszyński, *Jacky Jean Etienne Challot: Przyjaciel Solidarności* [Jacky Jean Étienne Challot: Friend of Solidarity], from the film *Jacky od zadan specjalnych* [Jacky for Special Tasks] and from the SB arrest document, 'Plan wstępnych czynności do sprawy operacyjnego rozpracowania krypt. Podróżnik' ['Plan of preliminary activities for the case of operational investigation cryptonym Traveller'], reprinted in Ptaszyński, *Jacky Jean Etienne Challot*.

189. $8,000: at the official exchange rate there were roughly 108 złoty per US dollar. At the unofficial rate they would have been worth far less.

190. 'happy communists': author interviews with Chojecki, October 2023.

190. 'Free Jacky': details are from author interviews with Łabędź. Signatories to the campaign are included in e.g. 'Un appel pour la libération de deux Français détenus en Pologne' ['A call for the liberation of two French people detained in Poland'], *Le Monde*, 30 April 1984.

193. 'It is generally known that the funds': Ptaszyński, *Jacky Jean Etienne Challot*.

194. 'To your health': ibid.

Chapter 14. This Turbulent Priest

195. 'My hands are full of holes': Barbara Sadowska's poetry collection *Słodko byc dzieckiem Boga* [How Sweet It Is to Be a Child of God] was published in the underground in 1984.

196. For Popiełuszko's life and influence, including details of his homeland masses, see Michael Kaufman, *Mad Dreams, Saving Graces*.

196. 'O God, who, for so many centuries': the words and tune of 'Boże, coś Polskę' (roughly, 'God save Poland') have changed several times over the centuries. Kaufman, ibid., reports that Cardinal Glemp had ordered that the line 'O Lord, restore a free [homeland]' be replaced with 'O Lord, bless our [homeland]', but the congregation would ignore this.

197. a puppy named 'secret agent': John Fox, 'Do You Hear the Bells, Father Jerzy?', *Reader's Digest*, December 1985.

197. 'I believe I'm next!': Gabor Danyi, 'A Polish Political Assassination's Echoes in Eastern Europe'.

197. 'Today you can see and feel this even more clearly': Kaufman, *Mad Dreams, Saving Graces*.

197. 'overcoming evil with good': 'Porwanie ks. Jerzego Popiełuszki' ['Abduction of Father Jerzy Popiełuszko'], *Tygodnik Mazowsze* [Mazovia Weekly], 25 October 1984.

198. 'Don't drive through': Wojciech Czuchnowski, 'Waldemar Chrostowski: świadek najważniejszy' ['Waldemar Chrostowski: the most important witness'], *Gazeta Wyborcza* [Election Gazette], 13 October 2014.

198. 'This is so that you don't growl during your last trip': ibid.

198. 'Gentlemen, what are you doing?': 'Porwanie ks. Jerzego Popiełuszki'.

199. 'transformed his apartment into a repository for illegal literature': Leonid Toporkov, *Izvestia*, 12 September 1984.

199. 'black masses': Agnieszka Niegowska, *It All Began in Poland*.

199. 'If even one hair falls from Father Jerzy's head': 'Porwanie ks. Jerzego Popiełuszki'.

200. Congregation's response to his death: BBC News, '1984: Pro-Solidarity priest is murdered', *On This Day*, http://news.bbc.co.uk/onthisday/hi/dates/stories/october/30/newsid_4111000/4111722.stm, accessed September 2024; also Kaufman, *Mad Dreams, Saving Graces*.

200. 'extremely sad': author interviews with Helena Łuczywo.

200. The issue of *Tygodnik Mazowsze* that carried reports of the funeral was dated 8 November 1984.

203. 'Save me, save me!': this and other details from the trial, including Poles' fascination with Piotrowski, are from Kaufman, *Mad Dreams, Saving Graces*. Antoni Dudek and Andrzej Paczkowski, in 'Poland', describe it as 'the first such case since the mid-1950s'.

Chapter 15. The Network

205. Kazimierz Stefan Krawczyk, born in 1950 in Olsztyn, would warrant dozens of pages of SB files. According to one of these documents, 'Notatka na temat Kazimierza Krawczyka, sporządzona w Biurze Śledczym MSW' ['Note on Kazimierz Krawczyk, drawn up in the Bureau of Investigation of the Ministry of the Interior, secret'], 3 February 1987, reprinted in Patryk Pleskot (ed.), *Solidarnośc, 'Zachód' i 'Węże'* ['Solidarity, the West and Snakes'], Krawczyk had a degree in medicine and lived in Oslo, but had a consular passport. In 1987, SB spies said, he gave an interview to Norwegian television in which he admitted smuggling into Poland uncensored literature published in the West.

206. 'our ultra-secret Oslo–Kraków project': Minden, European Trip Reports, June 1984, GCMP.

206. 'new routes to reach the country that have opened up': Giedroyc wrote this to Rudzki on 17 September 1984; Rudzki replied on 25 September. Instytut Literacki/Institut Littéraire, Paris.

206. Details of the smuggling network are based on author interviews with Chojecki. Not all these people knew for certain that they were working with the CIA, and if they had suspicions they didn't really care. Zofia Reinbacher, for example, said she didn't think about it (author interview, February 2020), but that 'if . . . the CIA has paid the translator to translate Orwell's book, and it is a very good translation, so what? It was a good job. For me the effect, the result, is the most important thing.'

207. 'one of the most important events in Poland': Central Intelligence Agency Memorandum, 'DCI/NIO Conference—NIO/EUR', 6 November 1984, available at https://www.cia.gov/readingroom/docs/CIA-RDP87R00529R000200170051-9.pdf, accessed September 2024.

207. 'the climate in which such an act could occur': Central Intelligence Agency Memorandum, 'Possible KGB Involvement in Murder of Polish Priest', 10 January 1985, available at https://www.cia.gov/readingroom/docs/CIA-RDP85T01058R000507230002-8.pdf, accessed September 2024.

207. 'Wisner's Wurlitzer': see John M. Crewdson and Joseph B. Treaster, 'Worldwide Propaganda Network Built by the C.I.A.', *New York Times*, 26 December 1977.

208. volumes celebrating the life of the priest: WorldCat, the online public access catalogue, lists 360 titles about Popiełuszko published

in 1984–5, in a wide range of languages including Norwegian, English, Spanish, Danish.

208. 'I think it will be very successful': Giedroyc to Rudzki, 31 October 1984, Instytut Literacki/Institut Littéraire, Paris.

208. 'huge interest in the country': Giedroyc to Rudzki, 3 November 1984, Instytut Literacki/Institut Littéraire, Paris.

209. 'If this poor priest is declared a martyr': Rudzki to Giedroyc, 7 November 1984. He wrote again on 13 November 1984. Instytut Literacki/Institut Littéraire, Paris.

209. 'We treat this . . . address very confidentially': Rudzki to Giedroyc, 27 November 1984, Instytut Literacki/Institut Littéraire, Paris.

209. 'exceptional interest': Minden, European Trip Reports, 18 November 1984, GCMP.

209. 'a deliberate act that strikes at us all': editorial, *Kontakt*, No. 11, November 1984.

210. 'counterbalance to the saccharine panegyrics': Jerzy Popiełuszko, *Zapiski, 1980–1984* [Sermons, 1980–1984].

210. *The Price of Love*: Minden, European Trip Reports, 28 November 1984, GCMP.

210. 'to receive as many copies': ibid.

210. 'What is certain': *Kochany Księże Jurku: Listy do Księdza Jerzego Popiełuszki* [Dear Father Jurek: Letters to Father Jerzy Popiełuszko].

210. 'the heirs of those who did not shut their mouths': Jerzy Popiełuszko, *Cena miłości ojczyzny* [Father Jerzy Popiełuszko: The Price of Loving the Homeland].

211. Popiełuszko's path to sainthood: the priest has been recognized as a martyr by the Catholic church and was beatified in 2010. As of 2024, a miracle, which is required

for his canonization, is under investigation, but the final decision rests with the Vatican.

211. 'Radio Shack revolution': author interviews with Benjamin Fischer. In 'Solidarity, the CIA, and Western Technology', Fischer, citing the Polish journal *Polityka*, states: 'In the case of VCRs, the per capita rate of private ownership was approaching American levels.'

212. 'Chojecki is providing us with all the cassettes he produces': Minden, European Trip Reports, 23 November 1984, GCMP.

212. 'the most promising [medium]': author interviews with Tomasz Łabędź.

212. Bond films: author interviews with Chojecki. Chojecki said they also sent *The Hunt for Red October*, although this must have been very late, because the film adaptation of Tom Clancy's 1984 novel was not released until 1990. Reagan himself was said to be a Clancy fan.

213. 'very, very well sponsored': author interviews with Tomasz Łabędź. Asked who specifically was paying, Łabędź said, 'I don't know, I think Minden, because I met him and he asked me a lot of questions about video productions.' Minden spent the morning of 28 November 1985 with Łabędź at the Kontakt studio (European Trip Reports, GCMP).

213. '[Chojecki] will supply our outlets': Minden, European Trip Reports, 28 November 1985, GCMP.

214. 'a much wiser man': ibid., 23 November 1984, GCMP.

214. The CIA kept a list of the print sites: Jones, *A Covert Action*.

214. *Mazovia Weekly* circulation peak: the 80,000 is in Doucette, *Books Are Weapons*, although Helena Łuczywo thinks this is an exaggeration.

214. Two thousand uncensored books: Agnieszka Niegowska, *It All Began in Poland*.

214. A *Mazovia Weekly* survey: Doucette, *Books Are Weapons*.

214. Three Musketeers caught: for a detailed account of this operation, see Paweł Sowiński, 'Między policją a opozycją. Historia braci Górskich' ['Between the police and the opposition: the story of the Górski brothers'].

215. Hundreds of raids: see Doucette, *Books Are Weapons*, and Gregory Wolk, 'To Limit, to Eradicate, or to Control? The SB and the "Second Circulation", 1981–89/90', in Zlatkes, Sowiński and Frenkel (eds), *Duplicator Underground*.

215. 'I am horrified': Giedroyc to Nowak-Jeziorański, 23 January 1986, in Nowak-Jeziorański and Giedroyc, *Listy, 1952–1998* [Letters, 1952–1998].

Chapter 16. The Regina Affair

219. Józef Lebenbaum: details of the smuggler's life and activities are derived from author interviews conducted in 2020 and 2021. Kaleta's activities are largely from his memoir, *Emigrancka spółka 'Szmugiel'* [The Émigré Smuggling Company].

221. Catching Bujak: see e.g. Grzegorz Majchrzak, 'Na tropie Bujaka' ['On the trail of Bujak'], dzieje.pl, 2 June 2021, https://dzieje.pl/wiadomosci/na-tropie-bujaka, accessed September 2024.

221. 'were directed and inspired by Western special (intelligence) services': according to Gen. Henryk Dankowski, deputy chief of Poland's secret police, in Roman Rollnick, 'A high-level secret police official Monday accused captured underground . .', UPI, 2 June

1986, available at https://www.upi.com/Archives/1986/06/02/A-high-level-secret-police-official-Monday-accused-captured-underground/8557518068800/, accessed September 2024.

222. dummy run: Kaleta, *Emigrancka spółka 'Szmugiel'*. See also Marek Trzebiatowski, 'Największa kontrabanda środkowej Europy' ['Central Europe's largest contraband'].

222. 'gushing with his usual optimism': Kaleta, *Emigrancka spółka 'Szmugiel'*.

223. 'A stone fell from my heart': ibid.

223. 'most difficult . . . of the disputed matters': Giedroyc to Nowak-Jeziorański, 10 September 1986, in Nowak-Jeziorański and Giedroyc, *Listy, 1952–1998* [Letters, 1952–1998].

224. 'United States secret service': Kaleta, *Emigrancka spółka 'Szmugiel'*.

225. 'going to a beheading': ibid.

225. 'the special services of the overseas superpower': Trzebiatowski, 'Największa kontrabanda środkowej Europy'.

225. 'We were crying when we heard': author interviews with Boguta.

226. Bankruptcy: Kaleta, *Emigrancka spółka 'Szmugiel'*.

226. Järn was released: Barbara Törnquist-Plewa and Maria Heino, 'The Swedish Solidarity Support Committee and Independent Polish Agency in Lund'.

227. 'The Americans thought one such loss was OK': author interviews with Lebenbaum. The high-ranking Polish intelligence officer sent to Sweden in the 1980s was Sławomir Petelicki.

227. 'large delivery of books': Minden, European Trip Reports, November 1987, GCMP.

227. '[I] wasn't going to tell him all the details': author interviews with Chojecki.

228. 'Informers were everywhere': author interviews with Lebenbaum, along with visits to his former properties and premises in Lund.

229. 'I smuggled the photos in my ass': cited in Paweł Sowiński, *Tajna dyplomacja* [Secret Diplomacy].

229. Reagan's note of thanks: Minden noted that '[At] Brzezinski's suggestion, Lebenbaum received a thank-you note signed by the President.' Minden, European Trip Reports, 1 November 1983, GCMP.

230. Many details of the career of Jan Ostrzewski, aka Janusz, aka Regina, are from Witold Bagieński, 'Agent "Regina" i afera z lodówkami, czyli wpadka trójmiejskiej "Solidarności Walczącej" we wrześniu 1987 roku' ['Agent "Regina" and the fridge affair, or the Tri-City "Fighting Solidarity" slip-up in September 1987'].

230. 'organizationally fragmented' and 'divided over tactics': CIA Memorandum from Director of European Analysis, 11 June 1986, available at https://www.cia.gov/readingroom/docs/CIA-RDP86T01017R000404060001-6.pdf, accessed September 2024.

231. 'Warsaw revolutionaries who sat on sofas': Kaleta, *Emigrancka spółka 'Szmugiel'*.

231. Fighting Solidarity: see Andrzej Kołodziej and Roman Zwiercan, *Solidarność Walcząca: Oddział Trójmiasto, 1982–1990* [Fighting Solidarity: Tricity Branch, 1982–1990].

231. 'He was very, very clear': author interviews with Lebenbaum.

231. SB agents heard a different message: details of the SB's

intercept of Lebenbaum's communications are in 'Notatka informacyjna na temat kontaktów Solidarności Walczącej w Europie Zachodniej i USA' ['Information note on the contacts of Fighting Solidarity in Western Europe and the USA'], 21 August 1987, published in Kołodziej and Zwiercan, *Solidarność Walcząca: Oddział Trójmiasto, 1982–1990*.

232. silent 'for too long': 'List kierowany do J. Lebenbaum' ['Letter addressed to J Lebenbaum'], ibid.

233. a shipment of audio cassettes: 'Notatka informacyjna na temat treści instrukcji dla podziemnego ruchu oporu nagranej na kasety magnetofonowe przekazane kierownictwu SW przez Andrzeja Wirgę, sporządzona w MSW' ['Information note on the contents of the instruction for the underground resistance movement recorded on cassette tapes handed over to the SW leadership by Andrzej Wirga'], 21 August 1987, ibid.

233. 'obtaining indirect evidence': staff note, 7 July 1987, cited in Bagieński, 'Agent "Regina" i afera z lodówkami'.

234. Lebenbaum's place in Lund: he had moved away from the 'CIA villa' by this time and was living in a more modern suburban house on Sankt Hans gränd.

234. Diodor: the agent's real name was Eugeniusz Jaroszewski, according to Bagieński.

236. 'a bad feeling': Kołodziej and Zwiercan, *Solidarność Walcząca: Oddział Trójmiasto, 1982–1990*.

236. 'Tell them you don't know where I am!': author interviews with Lebenbaum.

237. Milewski and Pilarska response: in Brigadier General Zdzisław Sarewicz,

'Przejęcia przez Wywiad MSW transportu sprzętu dla podziemia' ['Interception by the Ministry of Internal Affairs Intelligence of the transport of equipment for the underground'], 1 December 1987, IPN BU 0 449/4/6, AIPN.

237. a 'massacre': author interviews with Lebenbaum.

238. 'He said that it was on my initiative': Bagieński, 'Agent "Regina" i afera z lodówkami'.

Chapter 17. A General, a Lowly Recruit and All Ranks In Between

241. 'deepening of mutual animosities, resentment': Brigadier General Zdzisław Sarewicz, 'Przejęcia przez Wywiad MSW transportu sprzętu dla podziemia' ['Interception by the Ministry of Internal Affairs Intelligence of the transport of equipment for the underground'], 1 December 1987, IPN BU 0 449/4/6, AIPN.

242. 'a reprehensible lack of precautions': Nowak-Jeziorański to Giedroyc, 26 October 1987, in Nowak-Jeziorański and Giedroyc, *Listy, 1952–1998* [Letters, 1952–1998].

242. 'looks as bad as it can': Giedroyc to Nowak-Jeziorański, 24 January 1988, in ibid.

243. 'a conspirator by nature': this was Piotr Jegliński, sometime owner of the Librairie Polonaise. Minden, European Trip Reports, 17 May 1983, GCMP.

243. 'great confidence' . . . 'very much': letter from Giedroyc to Nowak-Jeziorański, 24 January 1988, in Nowak-Jeziorański and Giedroyc, *Listy, 1952–1998*.

243. 'very self-assured young freedom fighter': Minden, European Trip Reports, 10 June 1985, GCMP.

244. 'What do they care about us?': author interviews with Helena Łuczywo.

245. Price rises: see e.g. Reuters, 'Protests Erupt in Poland over Big Price Increases', *New York Times*, 1 February 1988.

245. 'impoverished and needy': Kaufman, *Mad Dreams, Saving Graces*.

246. 'popular upheaval': National Intelligence Estimate, 'Soviet Policy toward Eastern Europe Under Gorbachev', May 1988, available at https://www.cia.gov/readingroom/docs/CIA-RDP09T00367R000200080001-8.pdf, accessed September 2024.

246. 'Just as in 1980–1981': 'Information Bulletin for Polish Party Leadership on Western Views of Poland', 4 May 1988, History and Public Policy Program Digital Archive, Institute for National Remembrance (IPN), obtained by Lechosław Gawlikowski, translated by A. Ross Johnson, available at http://digitalarchive.wilsoncenter.org/document/121509, accessed September 2024.

247. 'potentially the worst crisis': CIA Memorandum, 'Talking points for DDCI', 22 August 1988, available at https://www.cia.gov/readingroom/docs/CIA-RDP90G01353R001500230070-8.pdf, accessed September 2024.

247. Preparations for Joanna Szczęsna's single-handed issue of *Tygodnik Mazowsze* [Mazovia Weekly] are reconstructed from author interviews with Szczęsna and Łuczywo, and from Joanna Szczęsna, 'How I Broke Into the Entire Printing Infrastructure of the Mazowsze Region in Three Days', in Zlatkes, Sowiński and Frenkel (eds), *Duplicator Underground*. See also Penn, *Solidarity's Secret*.

248. 'a general, a lowly recruit': Szczęsna, 'How I Broke Into the Entire Printing Infrastructure'.

250. 'I thought you meant you needed me for the *next* edition!': author interview with Joanna Szczęsna.

251. Calling off the strikes: Wałęsa and Kiszczak met on 31 August 1988. The strikes ended in early September, as the opposition began to discuss topics for the Round Table Talks. See e.g. memorandum by Lech Wałęsa, 'On Starting the Roundtable Talks', 4 September 1988, available at https://digitalarchive.wilsoncenter.org/document/memorandum-lech-walesa-starting-roundtable-talks, accessed September 2024.

251. The *Mazovia Weekly* raid: see Jan Olaszek, ' "Tygodnik Mazowsze" – prasa w konspiracji' ['*Mazovia Weekly* – press in conspiracy'], *Polityka*, 4 March 2012, https://www.polityka.pl/tygodnikpolityka/historia/1524447,1,tygodnik-mazowsze---prasa-w-konspiracji.read, accessed September 2024, accessed September 2024.

251. 'They thought that *Mazovia Weekly* was being prepared by men': author interview with Joanna Szczęsna.

252. 'We knew that this was the end': author interviews with Helena Łuczywo.

252. 'Mr Boguta': author interviews with Grzegorz Boguta.

252. 'You will see': ibid.

Chapter 18. Television Free Europe

253. 'Intellectual freedom is essential': a translation of Andrei Sakharov's 'Thoughts on Progress, Peaceful Coexistence and Intellectual Freedom' was published as 'Text of Essay by Russian Nuclear Physicist Urging Soviet-American Cooperation' in the *New York Times*, 22 July 1968.

253. For the history of Poland's satellite TV revolution, see Bartłomiej Kluska, 'Antena satelitarna – telewizja z kosmosu. Historia z PRL-u' ['Satellite antenna – television from space: a story from the Polish People's Republic'], *Gazeta Wyborcza* [Election Gazette], 12 September 2016. Also Urszula Jarecka, 'History and TV in Poland', http://www.e-story.eu/observatory/europe-and-media/history-and-tv-in-poland/, accessed September 2024.

256. '[Chojecki] would . . . like to find money for the broadcasting': Minden, European Trip Reports, November 1987, GCMP.

256. the project was close to fruition: details are from author interviews with Chojecki and with Łabędź.

256. 'directed and subsidized by the CIA': Reisch, *Hot Books in the Cold War*.

256. the Universal Declaration of Human Rights: see Richard N. Gardner, 'Eleanor Roosevelt's Legacy, Human Rights', *New York Times*, 10 December 1988.

257. 'Nothing like this has ever happened': 'Le triomphal week-end parisien de Lech Wałęsa' ['Lech Wałęsa's triumphal Paris weekend'], *Le Monde*, 13 December 1988.

257. 'At the beginning, the French didn't want a political programme': author interviews with Łabędź.

258. Henryk Jankowski's video distribution: author interviews with Chojecki.

258. Footage of Wałęsa's visit can be found at https://www.ina.fr/ina-eclaire-actu/video/cab88047990/sakharov-et-walesa-a-paris, accessed September 2024.

258. 'The men slap their thighs': 'Le triomphal week-end parisien de Lech Wałęsa'.

259. 'I could only see him in photos before that': author interviews with Chojecki.

260. 'CIA arranged the first satellite telecast into Poland': Gates, *From the Shadows*. In his book, Gates misidentifies the first broadcast, describing it as 'a ten-minute program covering recent labor unrest in Poland' broadcast in October 1988. He may have done this deliberately, to avoid identification of Chojecki. According to Łabędź, theirs was 'the only satellite project that existed. [Gates] is thinking about that project.'

260. 'It cost a lot': author interviews with Łabędź. He estimated the budget at 100,000 French francs, worth around $20,000 at the time.

Chapter 19. High Noon

261. 'A crack has appeared in the fortress': Irina Alberti, cited in Agnieszka Niegowska, *It All Began in Poland*.

261. Helena Łuczywo's experiences at the Round Table Talks were related in interviews with the author.

261. the great wooden 'O': Timothy Garton Ash described the round table in 'Make your revolution at a round table, but add a truth commission', *Guardian*, 20 May 2009.

262. Resistance to the talks: see Doucette, *Books Are Weapons*.

262. 'a major confrontation': Special Warning Topic Memorandum, 'Poland: New Confrontation Possible', from Charles E. Allen, National Intelligence Officer for Warning, 9 November 1988, available at https://www.cia.gov/readingroom/docs/CIA-RDP91B00776R000400140010-2.pdf, accessed September 2024.

262. 'Take my dog': 'Le triomphal week-end parisien de Lech Wałęsa' [Lech Wałęsa's triumphal Paris weekend], *Le Monde*, 13 December 1988.

262. The main negotiators: Agnieszka Niegowska, *It All Began in Poland*, lists these as being Bronisław Geremek, Jacek Kuroń, Adam Michnik, Tadeusz Mazowiecki, Zbigniew Bujak and Władysław Frasyniuk. All of these individuals appeared in or worked in the underground press.

263. Details of the members of the mass communications subgroup and their discussions are in Doucette, *Books Are Weapons*. Other members included Tadeusz Mazowicki and Kazimierz Dziewanowski, both of whom had worked for the opposition press.

263. the state's own trade unionists threatened the talks: see John Tagliabue, 'Government Unions Put Polish Pact in Doubt', *New York Times*, 5 April 1989.

264. a moment of dizzying triumph: see John Tagliabue, 'Poland Sets Free Vote in June, First Since '45; Solidarity Reinstated', *New York Times*, 6 April 1989.

264. Description of preparations for the launch of *Gazeta Wyborcza* [Election Gazette] are drawn largely from author interviews with Helena Łuczywo.

265. 'a source of strength, a source of hope' and 'a miracle of conspiracy': in Paweł Wierzbicki, ' "Tygodnik Mazowsze" – cudowne dziecko drugiego obiegu' ['*Mazovia Weekly* – Miracle Child of the Second Circulation'].

267. 'more than modestly': Adam Michnik, 'Michnik na urodziny "Wyborczej" ' ['Michnik on the birthday of "Wyborcza" '], *Gazeta Wyborcza*, 8 May 2019.

267. Continuous contact with Henryk Wujec: author interviews with Chojecki.

268. Fifty fax machines; $105,000 of CIA-funded material: ibid., and Jones, *A Covert Action*. Jones writes that 'During the Round Table Talks, CIA assets like ... QRGUIDE sent $105,000 worth of copiers, fax machines, election materials, and cash for paper, posters, and stickers to Solidarity for the six-week campaign.'

268. 'Western-style election campaign complete with brass bands': National Intelligence Directive, Poland Election Implications, 3 June 1989, available at https://www.cia.gov/readingroom/document/06826743, accessed September 2024.

268. Tomasz Sarnecki's *High Noon* poster: see Tomasz Skory, 'Rozbrojony Gary Cooper, czyli historia jednego plakatu' ['Disarmed Gary Cooper, or the Story of One Poster'], 4 June 2018, available at https://www.rmf24.pl/fakty/polska/news-rozbrojony-gary-cooper-czyli-historia-jednego-plakatu,nId,2589554#crp_state=1, accessed September 2024. CIA folklore stated that the poster was commissioned by the CIA, and Agency lawyers had Cooper's pistol removed to reinforce the non-violent message. In fact sources indicate that the posters were wholly Sarnecki's creation, paid for from CIA funds.

269. 'Monolithic uniformity': Miłosz, *The Captive Mind*.

270. Warsaw International Book Fair: see Anna Husarska, 'Up from the Underground in Poland', *New York Times*, 8 October 1989.

270. 'Three years ago I never could have imagined': Jackson Diehl, 'Light from the Underground:

Polish Publishers Revel in Official Tolerance', *Washington Post*, 24 May 1989.

270. Orbis in Warsaw: see Jerzy Kulczycki, *Atakowac książką* [Book Attack]. For his briefing of Minden, see European Trip Reports, 15 June 1989, GCMP.

270. State publishers taking risks: Husarska, 'Up from the Underground in Poland'.

271. 'historical force of a vast and powerful current': Cable from AMEMBASSY WARSAW to SECSTATE WASHDC, 'Subject: Election '89: Solidarity's Coming Victory', 2 June 1989, available at https://worldhistorycommons.org/sites/default/files/upcoming-89-election_020c90fbac.pdf, accessed September 2024.

271. killed many thousands: estimates of the number who died in Tiananmen Square vary. The British ambassador is reported to have given a figure of at least 10,000 ('Tiananmen Square protest death toll "was 10,000"', BBC News, 23 December 2017, available at https://www.bbc.co.uk/news/world-asia-china-42465516, accessed September 2024).

271. 'would never be the same': Łuczywo speaking to *Radcliffe Quarterly*, cited in Penn, *Solidarity's Secret*.

272. 'Tiananmen in the middle of Europe': George H. W. Bush and Brent Scowcroft, *A World Transformed*.

272. 'If Jaruzelski is not elected president': Cable from AMEMBASSY WARSAW to SECSTATE WASHDC, 'Subject: How to elect Jaruzelski without voting for him, and will he run?', 23 June 1989, available at https://worldhistorycommons.

org/sites/default/files/electing-jaruzelski_31b37f32cd.pdf, accessed September 2024.

273. 'here was an American president': Bush and Scowcroft, *A World Transformed*.

273. 'the publishing movement had played a huge role': author interview with Seweryn Blumsztajn.

273. 'just burst open': author interview with Adam Michnik.

Chapter 20. Bloody Feliks

275. Details of the fire were related in interview by Mirek Chojecki, Jolanta Kessler-Chojecka and Tomasz Łabędź. The Chojeckis lived at the time at 2 Rue Arthur Honegger, in social housing (*habitation à loyer modéré*). The new property was in Saint-Rémy-lès-Chevreuse.

277. 'Snakes': Patryk Pleskot (ed.), *Solidarnośc, 'Zachód' i 'Węże'* ['Solidarity, the West and Snakes'].

277. '[Chojecki] feels that he should help foment a feeling of solidarity': Minden, European Trip Reports, June 1989, GCMP.

278. The Hungarian elections were held in March 1990.

279. Otto von Habsburg: evidence of Chojecki coming to him for help with the satellite TV project is in Minden's European Trip Reports, 1987. The Kontakt film about him was called *Otto von Habsburg: A Certain Idea of Europe* (1989). The CIA had been distributing Habsburg's book *Europa – Grossmacht oder Schlachtfeld* [Europe – Great Power or Battlefield] since 1969. (Highlights Report July–August 1969, dated 16 September 1969, cited in Reisch, *Hot Books in the Cold War*.)

279. Václav Havel, Gábor Demszky: Havel had been on the receiving

end of CIA books (see e.g. Book Distribution Reports, 1967, 1970, GCMP), and is described by the programme veteran Reisch as 'one of the book project's most prominent recipients' (*Hot Books in the Cold War*). His work was also published by NOWa, among others. Gábor Demszky was one of a group of Hungarians Chojecki's printers trained in Paris (author interviews).

279. Wałęsa addressed Congress on 15 November 1989. See e.g. Neil A. Lewis, 'Clamor in the East: Gratitude and a Request; In Talk to Congress, Walesa Urges a Marshall Plan to Revive Poland', *New York Times*, 16 November 1989.

280. The story of Chojecki's return, and his experience of watching the fall of Dzerzhinsky, is based on interviews with the author.

282. The date of 17 November is reported in Anne Applebaum, 'Ukraine has finally removed all 1,320 Lenin statues. Our turn', *Washington Post*, 25 August 2017. See also Ewa Ochman, 'Who Cares About Old Statues and Street Names?', in Sarah Gensburger and Jenny Wüstenberg (eds), *De-Commemoration*.

Epilogue: The Best-Kept Secret

285. 'The Terminator': author interviews with Benjamin Fischer and other sources.

286. Mazowiecki's visit to the Polish Library (and other details) in Minden, European Trip Reports, 1990, GCMP.

286. 'ILC: A short description': GCMP.

286. Minden sent files to Washington: John P. C. Matthews, 'The West's Secret Marshall Plan for the Mind'.

286. 'best-kept secret': author interviews with Benjamin Fischer.

286. showed it proudly to his sons: author interviews with John and Paul Minden.

287. 'perhaps the most successful covert action program': William J. Daugherty, *Executive Secrets: Covert Action and the Presidency*.

287. 'something of a personalized book club': Douglas Martin, 'George C. Minden, 85, Dies; Led a Cold War of Words', *New York Times*, 23 April 2006.

287. 'ideological, political, cultural, and psychological warfare': Reisch, *Hot Books in the Cold War*.

287. Operation Cyclone: see Weiner, *Legacy of Ashes*.

287. 'The bottom line': author interviews with Fischer.

288. 'a great deal of personal pride': Reisch, *Hot Books in the Cold War*.

288. 'I sometimes wondered whether those books': ibid.

289. 'among the most important CIA operations': Weiner, *Legacy of Ashes*.

289. 'We didn't want to accept that somebody is going to tell us': author interview with Joanna Szczęsna.

289. 'It allowed you to look at and assess your own country's history': author interview with Adam Michnik.

289. 'The importance of the press cannot be overemphasized': Arch Puddington, *Lane Kirkland: Champion of American Labor*.

290. 'To George Minden with gratitude': author interviews with John and Paul Minden.

Selected Bibliography

Agee, Philip. *Inside the Company: CIA Diary*. New York: Penguin Books, 1975.

Arendt, Hannah. *The Human Condition*. 2nd edn, Chicago: University of Chicago Press, 1998.

Ascherson, Neal. *The Polish August*. Harmondsworth: Penguin, 1981.

Bagieński, Witold. 'Agent "Regina" i afera z lodówkami, czyli wpadka trójmiejskiej "Solidarności Walczącej" we wrześniu 1987 r.' ['Agent "Regina" and the fridge affair, or the Tricity "Fighting Solidarity" slip-up in September 1987'], in Sebastian Ligarski and Michał Siedziako (eds.), *Solidarnośc Walcząca, 1982–1990: Studia i szkice* [Fighting Solidarity, 1982–1990: Studies and Sketches]. Szczecin and Warsaw: Instytut Pamięci Narodowej, 2019, pp. 64–72.

Bikont, Anna. 'Kopalnia Wujek Miners', in Jacek Kołtan and Ewa Konarowska (eds.). *European Solidarity Centre Permanent Exhibition: Anthology*. Gdańsk: European Solidarity Centre, 2014.

Bielecki, Czesław, Sikorska, Urszula and Krzysztof Kelus, Jan.

Boreyko, Roman M., and André YaDeau. (trans.). 'The Little Conspirator'. *Conflict Quarterly*, Vol. 6, No. 4 (Fall 1986), pp. 27–64.

Borowik, Wojciech. (ed.). *N jak Nowa: Od wolnego słowa do wolności, 1977–1989* [N for Nowa: From Free Speech to Freedom, 1977–1989]. Warsaw: Biblioteka Narodowa, 2012.

Brandys, Kazimierz. *A Warsaw Diary, 1978–1981*. Richard Lourie. (trans.). New York: Random House, 1983.

Brandys, Kazimierz. *Nierzeczywistość* [Unreality]. Warsaw: NOWa, 1977.

Brandys, Marian. *Moje przygody z historią* [My Adventures with History]. Warsaw: Iskry, 1970.

Bush, George H. W., and Brent Scowcroft. *A World Transformed*. New York: Alfred A. Knopf, 1998.

Camus, Albert. *The Plague*. Stuart Gilbert. (trans.). London: Hamish Hamilton, 1948.

Central Intelligence Agency. 'The Legend of Wild Bill: How Donovan Got his Nickname', https://www.cia.gov/stories/story/the-legend-of-wild-bill-how-donovan-got-his-nickname/, accessed September 2024.

Chojecki, Mirosław. 'Rękopis więzienny' ['Prison manuscript']. *Zapis*, No. 15 (July 1980), pp. 7–23.

Christie, Agatha. *They Do It with Mirrors*. London: Collins Crime Club, 1952.

Ciupa, Robert, and Sebastian Reńca (eds.). *Wujek '81. Relacje* [Wujek '81: Accounts]. Katowice: Śląskie Centrum Wolności i Solidarności, 2018.

Codogni, Paulina. 'The Polish Round Table: A Bird's-Eye View'. *New Eastern Europe*, 2 May 2019.

Curry, Jane Leftwich. (ed. and trans.). *The Black Book of Polish Censorship*. New York: Vintage Books, 1984.

Czapski, Józef. *Inhuman Land: Searching for the Truth in Soviet Russia, 1941–1942*. Antonia Lloyd-Jones. (trans.). New York: New York Review Books, 2019.

Czapski, Józef. *Lost Time: Lectures on Proust in a Soviet Prison Camp*. Eric Karpeles. (trans.). New York: New York Review Books, 2018.

Danyi, Gábor. ' "I believe I'm next" – A Polish Political Assassination's Echoes in Eastern Europe'. Open Society Archives, 19 October 2021.

Daugherty, William J. *Executive Secrets: Covert Action and the Presidency*. Lexington: University Press of Kentucky, 2004.

Domber, Gregory F. 'The AFL-CIO, the Reagan Administration and Solidarność'. *Polish Review*, Vol. 52, No. 3 (2007), pp. 277–304.

Domber, Gregory F. *Empowering Revolution: America, Poland, and the End of the Cold War*. Chapel Hill: University of North Carolina Press, 2014.

Doucette, Siobhan. *Books Are Weapons: The Polish Opposition Press and the Overthrow of Communism*. Pittsburgh: University of Pittsburgh Press, 2017.

Dudek, Antoni, and Andrzej Paczkowski. 'Poland', in Krzysztof Persak and Łukasz Kamiński (eds.). *A Handbook of the Communist Security Apparatus in East Central Europe, 1944–1989*. Warsaw: Institute of National Remembrance, 2005.

Dylan, Huw, David V. Gioe and Michael S. Goodman. *The CIA and the Pursuit of Security: History, Documents and Contexts*. Edinburgh: Edinburgh University Press, 2020.

Finn, Peter, and Couvée, Petra. *The Zhivago Affair: The Kremlin, the CIA, and the Battle over a Forbidden Book*. London: Harvill Secker, 2014.

Fischer, Benjamin B. 'Repudiating Yalta'. *International Journal of Intelligence and CounterIntelligence*, Vol. 32, No. 1 (2019), pp. 1–25.

Fischer, Benjamin B. 'Solidarity, the CIA, and Western Technology'. *International Journal of Intelligence and CounterIntelligence*, Vol. 25, No. 3 (2012), pp. 427–69.

Fisher, Rod. *A Cultural Dimension to the EU's External Policies*. Amsterdam: Boekmanstudies, 2007.

Friedman, Herbert A. 'Free Europe Press Cold War Leaflets', psywarrior.com. Available at https://www.psywarrior.com/RadioFreeEurope.html, accessed September 2024.

Friszke, Andrzej. (ed.). *Solidarność podziemna, 1981–1989* [Solidarity Underground, 1981–1989]. Warsaw: Instytut Studiów Politycznych PAN, 2006.

Garton Ash, Timothy. *The Polish Revolution: Solidarity*. 3rd edn, New Haven: Yale University Press, 2002.

Gates, Robert M. *From the Shadows: The Ultimate Insider's Story of Five Presidents and How They Won the Cold War*. New York: Simon & Schuster, 1996.

Giedroyc, Jerzy. *Autobiografia na cztery ręce* [An Autobiography in Four Hands]. Warsaw: Czytelnik, 1999.

Glinski, Mikołaj. 'Józef Czapski's Investigation in an "Inhuman Land"'. Culture.pl, (n.d.), https://culture.pl/en/feature/jozef-czapskis-investigation-in-an-inhuman-land, accessed September 2024.

Gombrowicz, Witold. *Diary*, Vol. 2: *1957–1961*. Lillian Vallee. (trans.). Evanston, IL: Northwestern University Press, 1989.

Gopnik, Adam. 'A Tale of Two Cafés', in his *Paris to the Moon*. New York: Random House, 2000, pp. 27–40.

Instytut Literacki/Institut Littéraire. 'Jerzy Giedroyc: Biografia najkrótsza' ['Jerzy Giedroyc: the shortest biography']. *Kultura Paryska*. Available at https://kulturaparyska.com/pl/people/show/jerzy-giedroyc/biography, accessed September 2024.

Jarecka, Urszula. 'History and TV in Poland'. Available at http://www.e-story.eu/observatory/europe-and-media/history-and-tv-in-poland/, accessed September 2024.

Johnson, A. Ross. *Radio Free Europe and Radio Liberty: The CIA Years and Beyond*. Stanford: Stanford University Press, 2010.

Jones, Seth G. *A Covert Action: Reagan, the CIA, and the Cold War Struggle in Poland*. New York: W. W. Norton, 2020.

Kaleta, Marian, *Emigrancka spółka 'Szmugiel': Wspomnienia dostawcy sprzętu poligraficznego przemycanego do Polski dla opozycji antykomunistycznej w latach 1978–1989* [The Émigré Smuggling Company: Memoirs of a Supplier of Printing Equipment Smuggled into Poland for the Anti-Communist Opposition in 1978–1989]. Warsaw: Instytut Pamięci Narodowej, 2015.

Kaufman, Michael T. *Mad Dreams, Saving Graces: Poland: A Nation in Conspiracy*. New York: Random House, 1989.

Kazański, Arkadiusz. *Alina Pienkowska-Borusewicz*. Warsaw: Instytut Pamięci Narodowej, 2020.

Keller, Michael. 'Kukliński: How the CIA's Best-Placed Cold War Spy Escaped the Eastern Bloc'. Culture.pl, 7 December 2018, https://culture.pl/en/article/kuklinski-how-the-cias-best-placed-cold-war-spy-escaped-the-eastern-bloc, accessed September 2024.

Kochany Księże Jurku: Listy do Księdza Jerzego Popiełuszki [Dear Father Jurek: Letters to Father Jerzy Popiełuszko]. Warsaw: NOWa, 1985.

Kołodziej, Andrzej, and Roman Zwiercan. *Solidarnośc Walcząca: Oddział Trójmiasto, 1982–1990* [Fighting Solidarity: Tricity Branch, 1982–1990]. Gdynia: Fundacja Pomorska Inicjatywa Historyczna, 2017.

Kołtan, Jacek, and Ewa Konarowska. (eds.). *European Solidarity Centre Permanent Exhibition: Anthology*. Gdańsk: European Solidarity Centre, 2014.

Kostrzewa, Robert. (ed.). *Between East and West: Writings from Kultura*, New York: Hill & Wang, 1990.

Kramer, Mark. (ed.). *Soviet Deliberations during the Polish Crisis, 1980–1981*. Washington, DC: Woodrow Wilson International Center for Scholars, 1999.

Kulczycki, Jerzy. *Atakować książką* [Book Attack]. Warsaw: Instytut Pamięci Narodowej, 2016.

Kuroń, Jacek. 'Tezy o wyjściu z sytuacji bez wyjścia' ['Ideas for Getting Out of a No-Win Situation']. *Aneks*, No. 27 (1982), pp. 3–8.

Kwitny, Jonathan. *Man of the Century: The Life and Times of Pope John Paul II*. New York: Henry Holt & Company, 1997.

Le Carré, John. *The Spy Who Came in from the Cold*. London: Victor Gollancz, 1963.

Lipski, Jan Józef. *KOR: A History of the Workers' Defense Committee in Poland, 1976–1981*. Olga Amsterdamska and Gene M. Moore. (trans.). Berkeley: University of California Press, 1985.

Majchrzak, Grzegorz. 'Na tropie Bujaka' ['On the trail of Bujak']. Dzieje.pl, 2 June 2021, https://dzieje.pl/wiadomosci/na-tropie-bujaka, accessed September 2024.

Mandelstam, Nadezhda. *Hope Against Hope: A Memoir*. Max Hayward. (trans.). New York: Atheneum, 1970.

Matthews, John P. C. 'The West's Secret Marshall Plan for the Mind'. *International Journal of Intelligence and CounterIntelligence*, Vol. 16, No. 3 (2003), pp. 409–27, https://doi.org/10.1080/713830448, accessed September 2024.

Meretik, Gabriel. *La Nuit du général*. Paris: Grasset, 1981.

Michnik, Adam. *Letters from Prison and Other Essays*. Maya Latynski. (trans.). Berkeley: University of California Press, 1985.

Mickiewicz, Adam. *Forefathers' Eve* [Dziady]. Charles S. Kraszewski. (trans.). London: Glagoslav Publications, 2016.

Miłosz, Czesław. *The Captive Mind*. Jane Zielonko. (trans.). New York: Vintage Books, 1953.

Miłosz, Czesław. *The Collected Poems, 1931–1987*. New York: Ecco Press, 1988.

Miłosz, Czesław. *Native Realm: A Search for Self-Definition*. Catherine S. Leach. (trans.). New York: Farrar, Straus & Giroux, 1968.

Morris, Jan. *Fifty Years of Europe: An Album*. New York: Villard, 1997.

Niegowska, Agnieszka. (ed.). *It All Began in Poland: 1939–1989*. Warsaw: Oficyna Wydawnicza 'Volumen', 2009.

Nowak-Jeziorański, Jan. *Courier from Warsaw*. Detroit: Wayne State University Press, 1982.

Nowak-Jeziorański, Jan, and Jerzy Giedroyc. *Listy, 1952–1998. Wybór, opracowanie i wstęp Dobrosława Platt* [Letters, 1952–1998: Selection, Compilation and Introduction by Dobrosława Platt]. Wrocław: Towarzystwo Przyjaciół Ossolineum, 2001.

Nowakowski, Marek. *The Canary and Other Tales of Martial Law*. Krystyna Bronkowska. (trans.). London: Harvill Press, 1983.

Ochman, Ewa. 'Who Cares About Old Statues and Street Names? Resisting Change and the Protracted Decommunization of Public Space in Poland', in Sarah Gensburger and Jenny Wüstenberg. (eds.). *De-Commemoration: Making Sense of Contemporary Calls for Tearing Down Statues and Renaming Places*. New York: Berghahn Books, 2024, pp. 551–70.

Office of the Historian, Foreign Service Institute, United States Department of State. 'The Soviet Invasion of Afghanistan and the U.S. Response, 1978–1980', https://history.state.gov/milestones/1977-1980/soviet-invasion-afghanistan, accessed September 2024.

Orwell, George. *Animal Farm: A Fairy Story*. London: Penguin Books, 2000.

Orwell, George. *Nineteen Eighty-Four*. London: Penguin Books, 2000.

Orwell, George. 'Writers and Leviathan', in *The Collected Essays, Journalism and Letters of George Orwell*, Vol. 4: *In Front of Your Nose, 1945–1950*. Sonia Orwell and Ian Angus. (eds.). London: Secker & Warburg, 1968, pp. 407–14.

Ossowska, Maria. *O pewnych przemianach etyki walki* [Certain Developments in the Ethics of Combat]. Warsaw: NOWa, 1977.

Paczkowski, Andrzej. 'The Night of the General', in Jacek Kołtan and Ewa Konarowska. (eds.). *European Solidarity Centre Permanent Exhibition: Anthology*. Gdańsk: European Solidarity Centre, 2014.

Pasternak, Boris. *Doctor Zhivago*. Max Hayward and Manya Harari. (trans.). London: Collins and Harvill Press, 1958.

Pelikán, Jiří. *Socialist Opposition in Eastern Europe: The Czechoslovak Example*. Marian Sling and V. and R. Tosek. (trans.). New York: St Martin's Press, 1976.

Penn, Shana. *Solidarity's Secret: The Women Who Defeated Communism in Poland*. Ann Arbor: University of Michigan Press, 2005.

Piecuch, Henryk. *Służby specjalne atakują: Od Jaruzelskiego do Kwaśniewskiego* [Special Services Attack: From Jaruzelski to Kwasniewski]. 2nd edn, Warsaw: Agencja Wydawnicza CB, 1996.

Piotrowski, Tadeusz. *Poland's Holocaust: Ethnic Strife, Collaboration with Occupying Forces and Genocide in the Second Republic, 1918–1947*. Jefferson, NC: McFarland, 1998.

Pipes, Richard. *Vixi: Memoirs of a Non-Belonger*. New Haven: Yale University Press, 2003.

Pleskot, Patryk. *Solidarnośc, 'Zachód' i 'Węże': Służba Bezpieczeństwa wobec emigracyjnych struktur Solidarności, 1981–1989* [Solidarity, the West and Snakes: The Secret Service versus Solidarity's Émigré Structures, 1981–1989]. Warsaw: Instytut Pamięci Narodowej, 2011.

Popiełuszko, Jerzy. *Cena miłości ojczyzny* [Father Jerzy Popieluszko: The Price of Loving the Homeland]. 2nd edn, Rome: (n.p.), 1985.

Popiełuszko, Jerzy. *Kazania patriotyczne* [Patriotic Sermons]. Paris: Libella, 1984.

Popiełuszko, Jerzy. *Zapiski, 1980–1984* [Sermons, 1980–1984]. Paris: Editions Spotkania, 1985.

Ptaszyński, Radosław. *Jacky Jean Etiennne Challot: Przyjaciel Solidarności* [Jacky Jean Étienne Challot: Friend of Solidarity]. Warsaw: Wydawnictwo von borowiecky, 2013.

Puddington, Arch. *Lane Kirkland: Champion of American Labor*. Hoboken, NJ: John Wiley & Sons, 2005.

Reisch, Alfred. *Hot Books in the Cold War: The CIA-Funded Secret Western Book Distribution Program behind the Iron Curtain*. Budapest: Central European University Press, 2013.

Rudzki, Marek. 'Akcja masowych przekazów książek do Polski w latach 1956–1994' ['The campaign of mass book transfers to Poland in 1956–1994']. *Zeszyty Historyczne* [*Historical Notebooks*], Vol. 132 (2000), pp. 217–24.

Schlesinger, Arthur M., Jr. 'On the Inscrutability of History'. *Encounter*, Vol. 27 (November 1966), pp. 10–17.

Solzhenitsyn, Aleksandr I. *The Gulag Archipelago, 1918–1956: An Experiment in Literary Investigation*. Thomas P. Whitney. (trans.). New York: Harper & Row, 1973–4.

Sowiński, Paweł. 'Cold War Books: George Minden and his Field'.
    East European Politics and Societies: and Cultures, Vol. 34, No. 1
    (February 2020), pp. 48–66.

Sowiński, Paweł. 'Między policją a opozycją. Historia braci
    Górskich' ['Between the police and the opposition. The story of
    the Górski brothers']. *Wolność i Solidarność*, No. 6 (2013), pp.
    192–212.

Sowiński, Paweł. 'The Paris "Kultura" in the Light of the Newest
    American Studies'. Academia.edu, (n.d.), https://www.academia.
    edu/39781151/The_Paris_Kultura_in_Light_of_the_Newest_
    American_Studies.

Sowiński, Paweł. *Tajna dyplomacja: Książki emigracyjne w drodze
    do kraju, 1956–1989* [Secret Diplomacy: Exile Books on their
    Way into the Country, 1956–1989]. Warsaw: Towarzystwo
    'Więź', 2016.

Stonor Saunders, Frances. *Who Paid the Piper?: The CIA and the
    Cultural Cold War*. London: Granta Books, 1999.

Strządała, Gaweł. 'Censorship in the People's Republic of Poland',
    Mäetagused, Vol. 53 (2013), pp. 77–90. https://doi.org/10.7592/
    EP.1.strzadala, accessed September 2024.

Szczęsna, Joanna. 'How I Broke Into the Entire Printing
    Infrastructure of the Mazowsze Region in Three Days', in
    Gwido Zlatkes, Paweł Sowiński and Ann M. Frenkel. (eds.).
    *Duplicator Underground: The Independent Publishing Industry in
    Communist Poland, 1976–89*. Bloomington: Slavica Publishers,
    2016, pp. 453–6.

Tarniewski, Marek [Jakub Karpiński]. *Pochodzenie systemu*
    [Origins of the System]. Warsaw: NOWa, 1977.

Törnquist-Plewa, Barbara, and Maria Heino. 'The Swedish
    Solidarity Support Committee and Independent Polish Agency
    in Lund', in Barbara Törnquist-Plewa (ed.). *Skandinavien och
    Polen: Möten, relationer och ömsesidig påverkan* [Scandinavia
    and Poland: Encounters, Relations and Mutual Influence].
    Slavica Lundensia 23. Lund: Lunds Universitet, 2007, pp. 25–59.

Trzebiatowski, Marek. 'Największa kontrabanda środkowej Europy' ['Central Europe's largest contraband']. *30 dni*, No. 5 (May 2000). Available at www.gdansk.pl/historia/najwieksza-kontrabanda-srodkowej-europy,a,153607, accessed September 2024.

US Congress, Commission on Security and Cooperation in Europe. 'The Crisis in Poland and its Effects on the Helsinki Process'. 97th Cong., 1st sess., 28 December 1981. Washington, DC: US Government Printing Office, 1981.

US Department of State. *Foreign Relations of the United States, 1977–1980*, Vol. VI: *Soviet Union*. Washington, DC: US Government Publishing Office, 2013.

US Department of State. *Foreign Relations of the United States, 1977–1980*, Vol. XX: *Eastern Europe*. Washington, DC: US Government Publishing Office, 2015.

US Department of State. *Foreign Relations of the United States, 1981–1988*, Vol. III: *Soviet Union, January 1981–January 1983*. Washington, DC: US Government Publishing Office, 2016.

Vonnegut, Kurt. *Mother Night*. New York: Dial Press, 1966.

'W obronie Mirosława Chojeckiego i Bogdana Grzesiaka' ['In defence of Mirosław Chojecki and Bogdan Grzesiak']. *Zapis* [Record], Vol. 15 (July 1980), pp. 159–62.

Walc, Jan. 'We, the Free Drum'n'Roller Press'. *Biuletyn Informacyjny* [Information Bulletin], No. 4 (June 1980). Reprinted in Gwido Zlatkes, Paweł Sowiński and Ann M. Frenkel (eds.). *Duplicator Underground: The Independent Publishing Industry in Communist Poland, 1976–89*. Bloomington: Slavica Publishers, 2016, pp. 313–34.

Weiner, Tim. *Legacy of Ashes: The History of the CIA*. New York: Doubleday, 2007.

Weiser, Benjamin. *A Secret Life: The Polish Colonel, his Covert Mission, and the Price He Paid to Save his Country*. New York: PublicAffairs, 2004.

Wierzbicki, Paweł. '"Tygodnik Mazowsze" – cudowne dziecko drugiego obiegu' ['*Mazovia Weekly* – Miracle Child of the

Second Circulation']. *Dzieje Najnowsze*, Vol. 44, No. 4 (2012), pp. 57–74.

'Więzienie przy Rakowieckiej – stalinowskie wrota piekieł' ['Prison on Rakowiecka Street – Stalinist gates of hell']. Polskie Radio, 24 November 2014, https://www.polskieradio.pl/39/156/ artykul/1297081,wiezienie-przy-rakowieckiej-%E2%80%93-stalinowskie-wrota-piekiel, accessed September 2024.

Zaremba, Marcin. '1968 in Poland: The Rebellion on the Other Side of the Looking Glass'. *American Historical Review*, Vol. 123, Issue 3 (June 2018), pp. 769–72.

Żebrowski, Marek. *La Maison Kultura – le guide* [The Kultura House – A Guide]. Anna Ciesielska-Ribard. (trans.). Paris: Instytut Literacki, 2018.

Ziółkowska-Boehm, Aleksandra. 'Correspondence: Jerzy Giedroyc and Melchior Wańkowicz'. *Sarmatian Review*, Vol. XIX, No. 3 (September 1999), pp. 641–50.

Zlatkes, Gwido, Paweł Sowiński and Ann M. Frenkel (eds.). *Duplicator Underground: The Independent Publishing Industry in Communist Poland, 1976–1989*. Bloomington: Indiana University Press, 2016.

Index